Education in Sex
and
Personal Relationships

EDUCATION IN SEX
AND
PERSONAL RELATIONSHIPS

Isobel Allen

Research Report No. 665

Policy Studies Institute

PSI Research Report No. 665, February 1987

Sales Representation: Frances Pinter (Publishers Ltd).
Orders to: Marston Book Services
                    P.O. Box 87
                    Oxford OX4 1LB

PSI Reports are available through all good bookshops,
or in case of difficulty from PSI, 100 Park Village East,
London NW1 3SR.

ISBN 0 85374 330 4

Printed by Blackmore Press,
Longmead, Shaftesbury, Dorset

ACKNOWLEDGEMENTS

This study was funded by the Family Planning Association (FPA) and the Health Education Council (HEC) through the FPA/HEC supported Family Planning Information Service (FPIS). Many thanks are due to members of staff of the FPA, the HEC and the FPIS for their continuing support and encouragement in this research.

We wish to acknowledge the great help which was given to us by staff of the Local Education Authorities in the three cities in which we carried out this research. The authorities and staff remain anonymous but the author was most grateful for all the cooperation and interest shown by officers, advisers and teachers in these areas.

Particular thanks are due to Julia Field of Social and Community Planning Research (SCPR) who directed the fieldwork and was closely involved in the development of the questionnaires and methodological design of the study.

Marie-Anne Doggett prepared the comprehensive review of the literature covering the development of sex education in British schools which is published as an Appendix to this report.

We are grateful to Christine Farrell and Leonie Kellaher for their invaluable advice on the study, and to Lesley Campbell and Sally Walker for their help in the development and piloting of the questionnaires.

We should like to thank Sheila Chetham, Claire Nissel and the interviewers from SCPR for their tireless work in collecting the very rich data for this study. Special thanks must be given to Claire Nissel for her work on the post-coding of the questionnaires.

Finally, we owe an enormous amount to the parents and teenagers who were interviewed in the three cities in which we conducted this study. The research was based on their views and experience of what was actually going on in the schools and families in these areas, and the report is illuminated by their honesty and good humour.

CONTENTS

LIST OF TABLES

INTRODUCTION

The question of education in sex and personal relationships arouses a great deal of interest in the press and in Parliament. In spite of the fact that there have been significant changes in thinking about sex education by educationists and others involved in the provision of health education for schoolchildren over the past ten years, it is still possible for sensational claims to be made about the nature of sex education in schools, alleging that it has ill effects on the behaviour of young people.

It is important to look at these claims against the background of what has actually been happening in schools and in the country as a whole. It is clearly necessary to take account of the recommendations of successive government reports on the importance of personal and social education programmes in the school curriculum. There has been considerable development of pastoral care in primary and secondary schools and stress has been laid by educationists on the desirability of encouraging young people to be aware of the needs of others in relation to their own personal and social development.

The review of the literature in Appendix B examines the development of education in sex and personal relationships in this country, and pays special attention to the past ten years. It should be stressed that there has been no systematic study of the views and experience of parents and schoolchildren on this subject since Christine Farrell's report, *My Mother Said. . ..,* published in 1978, but based on research carried out in 1974 among 16-19-year-olds who had been at secondary school in the early 1970s[1]. There can be little doubt that many things have changed a great deal since then, not least in the schools themselves.

However, alongside these changes and developments in schools, there has been continuing pressure from groups and individuals, claiming to speak for parents, calling for the restriction or abolition of 'sex education' in schools and demanding the right for parents to withdraw their children from lessons, with the implication that if such a right were 'allowed', large numbers of parents would do so. The main argument of such groups and individuals is that sex education of young people is the sole responsibility of the parents and that schools should play no part in it.

Successive governments have stressed the need for the fullest consultation and cooperation between parents and schools on all aspects of the curriculum, and the Education (School Information) Regulations 1981[2] require education authorities and school governors to inform parents of the manner and context in which sex education is provided in schools. Consideration was given during the passage of the 1980 Education Act to whether parents should have the right to withdraw their children from sex education classes, as with religious education, but it was decided both in the House of Commons and in the House of Lords that such a decision should not be made because sex education is not compulsory in schools. Some local education authorities and individual schools do give parents the opportunity of withdrawing their children from certain lessons discussing these subjects, but it should be noted that this option appears to be rarely exercised.

It was against this background that we carried out our study in the spring of 1985 on the views and attitudes towards sex education of samples of 14-16-year-olds and their parents in three cities in England, one in the North-East, one in the Midlands, and one in the South-West. The cities were selected to give a broad geographical spread. They were recognised as having developed comprehensive programmes of personal, social and health education. The cities chosen are not named in this report to protect the identity of individuals, schools and local education authorities, all of whom were guaranteed anonymity. Considerable discussion took place within local education authorities with officers and teachers to provide a sound base for the investigation, both in terms of the type of education provided in different schools in the authorities and to ensure a comprehensive coverage of issues. Details of the methodology are covered in the Technical Report on this study already published by Social and Community Planning Research[3] which carried out the fieldwork for the survey and gave valuable technical advice on sampling, questionnaire design and fieldwork. A summary of the methodology and technical information is given in Appendix A.

Our aim was to interview a teenager between the ages of 14 and 16 and one of his or her parents in 200 families in the three areas. It was assumed that by the age of 14 most children would have received some form of sex education at school and would be of an age when their parents would not mind their being interviewed. We decided to restrict the interviewing to 14, 15 and 16-year-olds since many teenagers leave school at 16 and we were particularly interested in the impact of the education received at school.

We had hoped that we would be able to interview equal numbers of boys and girls and equal numbers of mothers and fathers, although other surveys had indicated that fathers might be less willing to be interviewed than mothers. In the end, we interviewed 209 teenagers, 99 boys and 110 girls—and 212 parents—149 mothers and 63 fathers. There were 205 pairs of parents and teenagers where interviews took place in a household with both a teenager and a parent. In seven households we interviewed only a parent and in four households we interviewed only a teenager.

The subject matter of the questionnaire was very wide-ranging, but was fully structured in that questions were asked in predetermined sequence and identical wording was used for each interview. Many questions were asked of both teenagers and their parents. A fairly high proportion of them allowed for an open-ended response, and the interviewers were expected to record the answers of the respondents verbatim.

The main aim of the survey was to look at how far the present provision of education in sex and personal relationships in schools was meeting the needs of the present generation of secondary schoolchildren and their parents, the extent to which this education was thought to be delivered in an acceptable form and how it was thought to affect the behaviour and attitudes of the children. The views and experience of teenagers and their parents concerning other influences and sources of information on sex and personal relationships were sought in order to put into perspective the education on these matters received at school.

It was important to establish exactly what was being taught at school, at what ages, in what subjects, by what methods and in what context. We asked both teenagers and their parents about this. We had to design a fairly complicated questionnaire to ensure that we elicited full information on this since it was quite clear from our piloting that 'sex education' covered a wide variety of topics taught in a wide variety of ways. The report stresses time and again what an oversimplification it is to treat 'sex education' as though it were a subject which could be eradicated from the secondary school curriculum at the stroke of a pen.

We were particularly interested in the views of the teenagers and their parents on the effects of the teaching at school on the variety of topics which made up programmes of education on sex, personal relationships and bodily changes. We asked detailed questions about teaching methods and other methods of presentation and discussion on these topics, and asked for the assessment of both parents and teenagers on the value and helpfulness of the teaching the children had received at both primary and secondary school on these subjects.

We wanted to explore the experience and views of parents and teenagers on the question of whether parents should take the sole responsibility for educating teenagers in these matters. We asked a series of questions about the extent to which parents and their children discussed these matters at home, and how far they found it easy to talk to each other about such topics. We asked the parents about their own sex education when teenagers, both at school and from their own parents.

We were interested in the views of the parents and children on the effects of other influences, such as magazines, television and videos, on the behaviour of teenagers, and we were particularly interested in the extent to which teenagers were thought to be under pressure from any source to have a girlfriend or boyfriend or to have a sexual relationship at an early age.

Earlier studies on sex education suggested that friends were an important source of information—or misinformation—for young people. We wanted to establish to what extent this was still true, and how far young people today were better able to discriminate than young people of earlier generations between the information they received from friends and that received from more authoritative sources.

It has been the stated aim of educationists over the past ten years or so to place 'sex education' firmly in a programme of personal, social and health education. We were interested to see how far this was happening in the schools attended by the teenagers interviewed. We also wanted to assess to what extent teenagers were learning about sex, reproduction, and contraception within the context of loving and lasting relationships as part of a programme of preparation for parenthood and family life.

The report is essentially about the results of the survey of teenagers and their parents. One of the purposes of the study was to identify a sample of schools through the sample of parents and children, and this has been done, although present funding has not allowed any follow-up of the schools to see how far their aims are related to the experience of the teenagers and their parents. The 209 teenagers interviewed reported a total of 50 schools as their present or most recent school. In both the North-East and the South-West areas the four schools most frequently mentioned were attended by 80 per cent of the teenagers, but in the Midlands area only half the teenagers interviewed attended the four schools mentioned most often. Ninety-four per cent of the teenage respondents attended comprehensive schools, most of which were mixed. Further details are given in Appendix A.

There can be no doubt that this report shows what a long way education in sex and personal relationships at school has come in the past ten years or so. It should be stressed from the outset that one of the main findings was the extent to which parents welcomed the involvement of schools in the education of the teenage children on these topics, and, indeed, the extent to which they regarded it as an integral part of the school curriculum. There were many more criticisms of schools providing too little education on these topics than too much, and the majority of parents expressed satisfaction with the way schools were giving this kind of education, although there was still quite a lot of evidence of parents saying that they felt they did not know enough about what was going on to be able to judge it properly.

Certainly, as this report shows, parents themselves did not always feel very well-equipped to offer their children education on these subjects, and over a quarter of them in fact thought that schools should provide *all* education of this kind to their children. There was considerable evidence of a total lack of discussion between parents and their children on these topics, although many parents laid great stress on the need for their children to know more about sex, contraception, puberty and personal relationships than they themselves had known when they were teenagers.

In spite of evidence of loving and 'open' relationships between many parents and their children, it still appears that there are certain topics which are difficult for teenagers and parents to talk about, and that many parents

4

welcome the involvement of schools, not only to ensure that their children receive accurate and unbiased information on a wide variety of topics, but also because they feel that schools are suitable places in which to learn how to live with other people. Throughout this report, it is notable how much stress both parents and their teenage children place on the need to hear the views and opinions of other people, to learn how to understand more about the opposite sex, and to appreciate that others have feelings and emotions which may be different from one's own. One of the main impressions given in this study of teenagers and parents in the 1980s is that of people who are balanced and reasonable and concerned about other people. There are undoubtedly gaps and poor teaching, and some schools are clearly better than others in designing programmes which handle all these topics with sensitivity and care. But it certainly appears that some of the curricular and pastoral development in schools over the past ten years has had a considerable impact in encouraging young people to behave in a responsible, informed and tolerant manner in their personal relationships.

It is notoriously difficult to judge the 'success' or 'failure' of any health education programme, and it is quite clear that imparting information alone, even if it is understood and taken in, is not enough. At the same time it must be recognised that there are many other influences at work in society which may have a much greater impact on the attitudes and behaviour of young people than the most imaginative programme of education at school on any subject. This report gives up-to-date evidence of the views and experience of samples of parents and teenagers in three large cities in England about education in sex and personal relationships in schools. It should help to correct some of the anecdotal evidence put forward by pressure groups who claim to speak for parents and it should reassure those who are concerned about the development of a generation of young people.

This research was carried out and completed just as the widespread discussion began in this country concerning the full implications of the spread of AIDS (Acquired Immune Deficiency Syndrome). It has become clear in recent months that AIDS represents a major health threat to the whole population and that the Government takes this threat, and the need to provide factual information, very seriously. The importance of educating young people about AIDS cannot be overemphasised, and the findings from this research take on an added significance in the light of the determination of the Government to launch a comprehensive campaign of public education and awareness.

1 EDUCATION IN SEX AND PERSONAL RELATIONSHIPS AT PRIMARY SCHOOL

This chapter looks at the education the teenagers had had at primary school about matters such as animal and human reproduction, development in boys' and girls' bodies, family and parenthood and personal relationships.

We wanted to know how much education on these subjects the teenagers remembered having at primary school, when it had been taught and how it had been presented. We were interested in the extent to which parents had been consulted or informed about the handling of these subjects, and finally, we wanted to know what the teenagers and their parents felt about the way in which this kind of education had been put over and whether they thought it was a good idea to cover these topics at primary school.

We were aware that a straightforward question about sex education in primary schools might not give a very full response for a number of reasons, partly because teenagers—and their parents—might not have interpreted what they were being taught as 'sex education', and partly because the teenagers might have forgotten and the parents might not have known what had been covered. We therefore put an initial question in general terms—asking whether the children had had any lessons, films or discussions about how their bodies worked and sex and personal relationships in their primary school, either in the infants or the juniors, and then followed this up by asking about ten specific topics: animal reproduction/animals being born, human reproduction, pregnancy and childbirth, sexual intercourse, changes in a girl's body as she grows up, changes in a boy's body as he grows up, family and parenthood, personal relationships between male and female, contraception/birth control and 'not going with strangers'.

It will be seen in Table 1 that 39 per cent of the teenagers and 31 per cent of the parents said in response to the initial general question that they had had some education at primary school on sex and personal relationships or how their bodies worked. There were, however, big differences in the responses of boys and girls, mothers and fathers and particularly between the different age-groups of teenagers, with the 14-year-olds reporting far more sex education at primary school than the 15-year-olds, who, in turn, reported more than the 16-year-olds. Further analysis showed that there were also big

Table 1 *Proportion of teenagers and parents reporting that teenager had had education in sex, personal relationships or how body works at primary school*

Column percentages

| | Teenagers | | | | | | Parents | | | Proportion agreeing that topics covered |
	Total	Boys	Girls	14	15	16	Total	Mothers	Fathers	
Base	39 (209)	32 (99)	45 (110)	48 (75)	37 (81)	30 (53)	31 (212)	35 (149)	22 (63)	17 (205)

differences between the teenagers and their parents, with only 17 per cent of the matched pairs of teenagers and parents agreeing that the child had had any education on these matters at primary school.

It appeared from Table 1 that girls had either had more education on these topics than boys at primary school or that they had better memories. There can be little doubt that memory played a large part in the responses, as can been seen by the differences between the fourteen-year-olds and the others. It is probable that other experiences of education in these subjects in secondary schools had superseded or had become blurred with what had happened in primary school, and the 15 and 16-year-olds' responses simply reflected this.

The differences in the proportions of mothers and fathers reporting that the teenager had had sex education in the primary school set the pattern for the whole interview. Fathers had very definite views on what went on, but their actual knowledge of what education their children were receiving on these topics at school was consistently much more hazy than that of the mothers interviewed.

It should be stressed that whereas the teenagers generally gave a positive or negative answer to this initial question, with 39 per cent saying 'yes' and 55 per cent saying 'no', and only 4 per cent saying they didn't know or couldn't remember, the parents were much more likely to say that they did not know whether the children had had any sex education at primary school, with as many as 30 per cent saying that they had no idea. Again the fathers knew far less than mothers, with 37 per cent saying initially that they did not know whether their children had had any education at primary school on these matters.

When we asked the teenagers and their parents about the ten specific topics outlined above there were again big differences between parents and their children and marked differences between boys and girls and among areas. Table 3 sets out the information in detail, but a summary of the responses of teenagers and parents, showing the extent to which they both agreed that the teenager had had education in primary school on these topics, is given on the following page in Table 2, with the teenagers' column ranked in terms of frequency.

The teenagers reported more education on the different topics than their parents did. Even the subject which might be regarded as the most important by parents of children of this age—not going with strangers—was only mentioned by 61 per cent of the parents, compared with 82 per cent of the children. It is interesting to note that, on this subject at least, parents and children tended to agree. As Table 3 shows, mothers were much more likely to know whether their children covered this subject at primary school than fathers were, but, although in general mothers were more aware of what was going on in primary school than fathers, nevertheless it was not always so clear-cut, and certainly similar proportions of fathers and mothers reported their children receiving education on animal reproduction or animals being

Table 2   *Proportion of teenagers and parents reporting topic covered at primary school*

			Column percentages
	Teen-agers	Par-ents	Proportion of parents and teen-agers agreeing that topic covered
Not going with strangers	82	61	56
Changes in a girl's body	27	11	5
Animal reproduction	23	33	10
Changes in a boy's body	20	8	3
Human reproduction	19	13	4
Pregnancy and childbirth	18	9	3
Family and parenthood	11	10	0
Sexual intercourse	9	2	0
Personal relationships between male and female	4	2	0
Contraception/birth control	1	0	0
Base	(209)	(212)	(205)

born. Only in this instance did they report more education on a specific topic than their children, since only 23 per cent of the teenagers said that they had had education at primary school about this. It is difficult to explain this discrepancy, but it is possible that parents were more likely to have been aware of the education on animals than on other topics at primary school, and that they under-reported the other topics simply because they did not know about them, while the teenagers might have been responding in a much more specific way, relating their education on animal reproduction at primary school to their much more detailed education on this at secondary school, and discounting the former.

It was very striking how little the parents appeared to know about the education given in primary schools about changes in boys' and girls' bodies. Teachers and educationists have stressed in recent years the need for girls to know about menstruation before they reach secondary school, since it is not uncommon for girls to start their periods while still at primary school. Over a quarter of the teenagers said that they had covered this topic at primary school, although it should be noted that 37 per cent of the girls (compared with 16 per cent of the boys) said that they had specific lessons on the subject. It will, of course, also be noted that girls appeared to have better memories

Table 3 *Topics on which teenager had had lessons, films and discussions at primary school*

Column percentages

	Teenagers									Parents					
	Total	Boys	Girls	14	15	16	SW	Mid-lands	NE	Total	Moth-ers	Fath-ers	Mid-lands	SW	NE
Animal reproduction	23	20	26	21	22	28	27	18	26	33	34	33	45	23	36
Human reproduction	19	18	19	25	14	17	22	21	15	13	12	16	19	8	14
Pregnancy & childbirth	18	19	16	28	12	11	24	16	16	9	11	3	17	5	8
Sexual intercourse	9	9	8	16	2	8	13	9	6	2	3	0	4	1	1
Changes in a girl's body	27	16	37	31	27	23	31	30	23	11	15	2	19	9	9
Changes in a boy's body	19	17	21	23	17	17	24	21	15	8	11	2	15	8	4
Family & parenthood	11	6	15	12	12	8	11	12	10	10	10	10	15	4	12
Personal relationships	3	3	4	7	1	2	9	1	2	2	3	2	2	1	3
Contraception/birth control	1	1	2	3	0	2	4	1	0	0	1	0	2	0	0
Not going with strangers	82	78	86	88	83	74	84	66	95	61	68	44	62	53	67
Had some lessons but didn't know what	—	—	—	—	—	—	—	—	—	6	5	8	6	5	5
Don't know at all whether had any sex education	—	—	—	—	—	—	—	—	—	22	18	32	17	28	20
(Base)	(209)	(99)	(110)	(75)	(81)	(53)	(45)	(76)	(88)	(212)	(149)	(63)	(47)	(74)	(91)

than boys as far as most things were concerned, including lessons on changes in boys' bodies! It is probable that many girls were given information on menstruation in single-sex groups, since this was commonly reported. However, although we asked about teaching in single-sex groups in secondary schools, we did not pursue the question as far as primary school teaching was concerned.

Fourteen-year-olds consistently reported more education on most topics at primary school than the older age-groups. This was particularly striking for the subject of 'not going with strangers', and certainly in the interviews, 14-year-olds described the films on this topic with much greater clarity than the older teenagers. It is possible that there had been an increase in the amount of primary education on all these topics, but it appears more likely that memory and experience since primary school were more important factors.

There was certainly a difference between the three areas, with teenagers in the South-Western area reporting more primary school education on most topics apart from family and parenthood and 'not going with strangers'. This was a subject which was clearly held to be very important in the North-East where 95 per cent of the children recalled learning about it at primary school, compared with only 66 per cent in the Midlands, and 84 per cent in the South-West.

In general, parents in the South-West also reported more coverage of these topics at primary school than parents in the other areas, and it did appear that the South-Western area had more primary education on these subjects in general than the other areas.

Overall, after being asked about specific subjects covered at primary schools, 89 per cent of the teenagers and 78 per cent of the parents said that the children had had some kind of education on these matters at primary school. This underlines not only the problem of definition of 'education in sex and personal relationships' but also the problem of recall and knowledge. And, of course, it was clear that a lot of parents and teenagers did not immediately think of the 'not going with strangers' topic as part of education in sex and personal relationships.

Visual presentation of topics
We were interested to know how primary schools presented education on these subjects, and we asked both parents and teenagers whether the children had watched any films, slides, television programmes or videos about any of the topics we had mentioned, what they were about and how old they were at the time. We also asked the teenagers what they thought of the films or television programmes, and whether the teacher had discussed them with the class and explained things.

Sixty-five per cent of the teenagers said that they had watched a film, video, slideshow or television programme on one or more of these topics at primary school. One third of them said they had seen only one, while the rest said they had seen more than one. Overall, 25 per cent of the teenager sample said that they had seen a film or other visual presentation in their last year in the juniors, when aged 10 or 11, but it was clear that films or television programmes were shown throughout the junior school, and five per cent of the sample said that they remembered having a film on one of these topics in the infants' school.

Parents, on the other hand, were much more hazy about whether and what their children had seen, with only 24 per cent saying that their children had viewed anything on these topics at primary school, half of them saying that this was in the fourth year juniors.

Forty-two per cent of the teenagers said that they had seen a film or video at primary school on 'not going with strangers', and there was no doubt that this had made the greatest impression on them, since most comments on films were about this subject. Thirteen per cent said that they had seen a film on boys' and girls' bodies, nine per cent said that they had seen a film on pregnancy and childbirth and eight per cent on animal reproduction. Parents had very little idea what their children had seen, and only eight per cent reported that their children had seen anything on 'not going with strangers', although such films were obviously shown in many of the primary schools which the teenagers had attended. This was particularly true in the North-Eastern area, where 57 per cent of the teenagers said they had seen a film on this topic, compared with only nine per cent of their parents.

It is difficult to say why the parents appeared so unaware of what their children had been watching, particularly on a subject like this, which had often made such a striking and lasting impression on their children, some of whom had seen more than one film on the subject, like this 16-year-old boy in the South-West:

> One was about this little girl, and a man opened his car door and asked her if she'd like to see some horses. It told you she should have said, 'No thank you'. There was another one where the man offered her sweets. And in another, a man said he was her Uncle Fred and come to fetch her. She said, 'No thank you', wrote the car registration number down and told an adult. . .

The films had clearly made an impact on him:

> They were helpful. It told you not to take things for granted. Things are not what they seem. . .

Another boy in the South-West had also seen more than one film about this at primary school:

> One was where a little girl didn't ask her ma if she could go out. A man said her mother had sent him to pick her up. She got home eventually. It was basic—don't go with strangers. The others were cartoons—'don't be a lemonhead—don't go with strangers'.

He expressed the views of many teenagers when asked what they thought of the films they had seen at primary school:

> At the time I didn't think they were educational—but you take note of them. . .

The context in which the films were presented had made more impression on some of the children than the films themselves, and it is clear that watching a film without explanation may not make the same impact as having a follow-up. Most of the children who said that they had seen a film at primary school said that the teacher had talked to the class afterwards and explained things, although this was much more marked in the South-Western and North-Eastern areas than in the Midlands areas. Similarly, more children in these areas reported class discussion about the films they had seen than those in the Midlands. The vexed question of whether the 'shock-horror' approach makes more impact than other more subtle ways of presenting material was pointed up by the comments of several children, typified by the girl in the North-Eastern area who said:

> The policeman came into the school and showed the 'not going with strangers' film. I don't think I really understood it, but the policeman scared us so we would take notice. . .

And even children, or perhaps especially children, in primary schools are fairly sophisticated television viewers, and expect up-to-the-minute presentation. It was a theme which often came up among secondary school viewers, but had made an impact even at primary school age:

> The films were bad. They were old-fashioned and not brought up-to-date. The people were old-fashioned—in the 1960s. . .

On the whole, the teenagers who had seen films at primary school had found them informative and said they had helped them to understand the subject. Girls in particular stressed that they had learnt a lot from the films. But about a fifth of those watching films or videos at primary school said that the films were all right but had not made much impact, and a further group, comprising nearly 10 per cent of those watching films or videos, said that they had known it all already!

Books and worksheets

We asked the children whether they had been given worksheets or books when they were taught about these subjects. 11 per cent of the total said that they had used worksheets, and 22 per cent said that they had used books. The majority of the children who had been given worksheets said that they were about not going with strangers, and these worksheets often appeared to have been used in conjunction with a film. Nearly half of the children using books on these subjects had referred to books on animal reproduction or animals being born, while about a third had used books while learning about changes

14

in boys' and girls' bodies. Again, children in the South-Western area and the North-Eastern area appeared more likely to have used books and worksheets than the children in the Midlands.

Parents and sex education in primary schools

The relationship between parents and school on all educational matters has undoubtedly become closer over the past few years, and there has been increasing emphasis from educationists, schools and parents themselves on the need for good contact between them. Information for parents on the subjects taught and the way in which they are taught is now required for all schools, and the Education (School Information) Regulations 1981[2] requires education authorities to inform parents of the manner and context in which sex education is provided. Successive government reports have stressed the need for close consultation between parents and schools as far as education in sex and personal relationships is concerned, and in 1981, the Department of Education and Science published *The School Curriculum*[4] as guidance for local education authorities, which, as Dr Rhodes Boyson, then Parliamentary Under Secretary of State for Education and Science, said in the House of Commons on 28 October 1982, 'emphasised the importance of close cooperation and consultation between parents and schools in meeting the need for sound sex education'[5].

We were therefore interested to know to what extent the parents we interviewed had been consulted and informed about the manner and context in which their children had received education in these matters in the primary school. The problem of definition which we have already mentioned is clearly one which is faced by schools as well as parents, and the report by Her Majesty's Inspectorate on 15 primary schools in Avon[6] pointed out that 'in the majority of schools sex education arose incidentally and naturally as a result of other class activities . . . In only two schools . . . was there a firmly declared policy that the subject of sex education was to be included within the curriculum.' This 'incidental' approach was also apparent in most of the primary schools which replied to the survey carried out in 1983 by the National Council of Women[7].

It was therefore perhaps not surprising that so many of the parents we interviewed were rather vague about the extent to which their children had had education in sex and personal relationships and how their bodies worked, and that even when asked about specific topics, they still expressed a considerable lack of knowledge about what had gone on at primary school. We asked them whether they had ever been invited to their child's primary school specially to hear what was being taught in sex education, and, if they had gone, what had happened and what they thought of the occasion. If they had been invited but not gone, we asked them why not, and if they had not been invited, we asked them if they would have liked to be invited, and, if so, what they would have liked to discuss.

We found that 11 per cent of our sample of parents said that they had

15

been invited to attend a meeting or discussion at their child's primary school to hear what they were learning about in sex education. Of these 24 parents, eight parents (one third) went, all of whom were mothers, and a further three parents (all fathers) said that the child's mother went. This meant that in nearly half of the cases where parents were invited to the primary school, one of the parents attended a meeting or discussion at the school. However, this actually represented only 5 per cent of the total sample of parents we interviewed. The numbers were so small that no meaningful differences between areas could be discerned, but it was interesting that single or divorced parents were more likely to accept the invitation than parents where both were living with the child.

The majority of the visits to the school took place in the third or fourth year juniors, and usually consisted of a talk by the head or another teacher, with discussion. In only a quarter of the cases was a film, video or television programme shown. The visit to the school was generally well-received by the parents who went, but the numbers were so small and the comments so few that it is impossible to draw any lessons from their experience.

However, half those who were invited to attend their child's primary school to hear what was going on in sex education did not go, either because they had a previous engagement or simply could not remember why they did not go.

Of the 189 (89 per cent of the sample) parents who had *not* been invited to primary school to hear about sex education, 58 per cent said that they would have liked to be invited, but a third said that they would not and a further 10 per cent were not sure whether they would have wanted to be invited or not.

There were some interesting area differences, however, with 70 per cent of the South-Western parents who had not been invited saying that they would have liked to go, and all but one of the divorced and remarried parents in the total sample saying the same.

On the whole the parents simply wanted to know what was being taught and how, with some stress on their wish to be aware of what was going on so that they could follow it up or prepare the children for it at home. There was interest in the methods used by the teachers, often because the parents wanted to know for themselves how best to put these things over to their children. There was little mention of any moral component in the sex education given to primary school children, and the small number of parents who said that they would like to have checked that too much was not being taught too early was almost equally balanced by the number who said they wanted to check that enough was being taught early enough. In general, the picture was one of parental curiosity at what was being taught, without any particular interest in finding out. There was widespread evidence that the parents felt that they could have found out what was going on if they had really wanted to, and this was confirmed by the fact that only a tiny number of parents told us later in the interview that they were dissatisfied with the lack of consultation they had had with the primary school about sex education.

This general level of satisfaction or indifference to how and what was being taught at primary school on these matters was reinforced by the fact that nearly half the parents who had not been invited to the school had either not wanted to go or were not sure whether they had wanted to be invited.

We asked the parents whether they had ever been sent a letter or had been given any written information on what their child's primary school was doing about sex education. The majority of the children interviewed would have left primary school before the Education (School Information) Regulations mentioned above[2] were introduced, with the requirement for information on sex education to be made known to parents. Eighteen per cent of the parents said that they had received some written information on the matter, while the rest said that they had not or could not remember whether they had or not. The proportions who said that they had received written information were almost exactly the same in all three areas.

Of those who had *not* received any written information, two-thirds said they would have liked to have some, but, again, a third of the parents who had not had any information said that they did not want any or were not bothered at not receiving any.

Some education authorities and many individual schools have made it a matter of policy to send written information to parents about sex education both in primary and secondary schools. The report by a working party on sex education in schools in Nottinghamshire[8] made certain specific recommendations:

> All schools should recognise the principle that parents have a right to know about the sex education programmes which their children are about to undertake and the right to opt out of such programmes if they so desire. Accordingly it is important that schools should provide parents with every possible opportunity for acquainting themselves with the contents of such programmes.

It was interesting that one-third of the parents in our sample who remembered receiving a letter or written information said that it had given them the opportunity to object to their child having sex education or had asked them for their permission, and a further 13 per cent of those who had received a letter said that it gave them the opportunity to object to their child watching a film on childbirth. The proportions were similar in each of the areas. It appeared that either parents remembered this kind of letter more clearly than general information about what was being taught, or there was little information being distributed at that time about how these topics were covered in primary schools, or it made little impact on parents either because they took it as a matter of course or they were not interested.

Although a high proportion of parents who had not received any written information from the primary schools said they would have liked some, the parents who *had* received such information regarded it as quite a good idea on the whole, but without any great enthusiasm, and a substantial proportion could not remember what they had thought about it.

In the light of this generally rather lukewarm interest in what was going on in primary schools, we asked the parents whether or not they thought it was a good idea to have education or discussion in primary school on the specific topics we had asked them about before, and followed this up by asking them why they thought these topics should be covered or not covered at primary school. We concluded our questions to parents on sex education in primary schools by asking them how satisfied they had been with the sex education their own son or daughter had received at primary school.

It can be seen from Table 4 that the overwhelming majority of parents thought that it was a good idea for children to have education or discussion in primary school on 'not going with strangers'. Parents in the Midlands area were less likely than those in the other two areas to stress that it was necessary, but it should be noted that 96 per cent of the parents in the South-Western area and 97 per cent of the parents in the North-Eastern area thought that children in primary schools should be taught not to go with strangers. Mothers and fathers were in agreement, and fathers often gave very graphic reasons for their wish for their children to be warned of the dangers, like this father in the North-East:

> It's either that or them getting strangled, isn't it? It's the protection instinct. It's for their own safety, isn't it?

He was the father of a 15-year-old boy, and it should be stressed that parents were as anxious about their sons as about their daughters, like this father of a 14-year-old boy:

> Yes I do think it's a good idea. You've only got to read in the papers—kids going off with strangers—and even some relatives are dodgy—so they've got to watch out . . .

Nearly 80 per cent of the parents thought that children should learn about animal reproduction in the primary school, although, again, the proportions of parents in the South-Western and North-Eastern area thinking this a good idea were well over 80 per cent compared with less than 70 per cent in the Midlands.

Considering that parents seemed a bit vague about whether their children had received any information or education on changes in their bodies as they grew up, there was considerable enthusiasm for education at primary school about these matters, with around 70 per cent of parents thinking it a good idea. It was thought important for schools to help prepare the children for puberty and body changes and to make them less frightened of these changes than many of the parents had been. It was also stressed that it was better for them to discuss these matters in the open and to be given correct information than to learn from each other. This view expressed by the mother of a 16-year-old boy was repeated time and time again in interviews:

18

Table 4 *Proportion of parents stating whether it was a good idea to have sex education in the following topics at primary school*

Column percentages

	Total	Parents		Area			Religion			
		Mothers	Fathers	SW	Mid-lands	NE	None	RC	C/E	Hindu/ Muslim
Not going with strangers	91	90	92	96	80	97	92	83	95	14
Animal reproduction	79	79	79	83	68	86	83	69	83	14
Changes in a girl's body	71	70	71	83	62	71	67	66	74	14
Changes in a boy's body	67	68	65	81	61	66	67	62	70	14
Human reproduction	60	60	62	68	57	59	67	45	64	14
Family & parenthood	59	60	57	79	47	58	50	48	63	14
Pregnancy & childbirth	47	46	49	55	38	51	42	52	48	14
Personal relationships between male and female	34	32	40	40	30	35	8	34	37	14
Sexual intercourse	24	18	38	26	18	29	17	28	25	0
Contraception/birth control	22	17	32	28	16	23	8	24	23	0
Base	(212)	(149)	(63)	(47)	(74)	(91)	(12)	(29)	(162)	(7)

I think by the time they get to 11 years old their bodies are starting to change, and I would rather they learned about these things properly rather than behind the bicycle sheds like we had to.

The fact that some girls start their periods at primary school was mentioned by a number of parents, and it was clear that many welcomed the information given to both boys and girls about menstruation.

Teaching facts about human reproduction at primary school was also thought to be a good idea by 60 per cent of parents, although Roman Catholics were less inclined to think it a good idea than others. Similarly nearly 60 per cent of parents thought that children in primary schools should learn about family and parenthood.

There was considerable emphasis among parents that learning gradually about these matters in primary school provided a good foundation for the secondary school, as this mother said:

I think it should be a base on which to build later on in school, so eventually when they are sitting down doing their sex lessons it's not a shock and they don't regard it lightly. . .

The theme of children taking the information more seriously if it came from school rather than from their friends or parents recurred throughout the interviews with parents, and there was little doubt that many parents valued the status given to education in these matters by schools. It was certainly felt by many parents that there was a need for children of all ages to be given 'proper' information and guidance, and that they would take more notice of it if it came from school, as this mother said:

This is the world—modern times. It's thrown at you—page three pin-ups and children's programmes—all involved with sex. It's important for children to be told properly. . .

It was also thought important that children at primary school should regard these topics as 'natural', which was another recurrent theme in interviews with parents, and there was a distaste for 'silliness' and giggling. Some parents whose children had had no education in these matters at primary school were concerned that the school had not done more, like this mother of a 16-year-old boy:

He never had any education at all. He was 11 before he realised anything. He just came home with dirty jokes. He came home crying one day because he thought he'd made a girl pregnant by putting his tongue in her mouth. He was 11 then. It just goes to show. . .

Around half the parents thought that it was a good idea for primary school children to have education about pregnancy and childbirth, although some parents whose children had seen films of babies being born felt that they had been too young and that some children had found it upsetting. It was common for parents to agree wholeheartedly with education in primary schools on human and animal reproduction and bodily changes at puberty, but to start to draw the line at information or films about childbirth. Certainly there was considerably less enthusiasm among parents for education or discussion at primary school on personal relationships between male and female, with only one third of parents thinking this a good idea, and less than a quarter of the parents interviewed thought it a good idea to raise the topic of sexual intercourse or contraception at primary school. Nevertheless, nearly a quarter of parents *did* think it a good idea, and it should be noted that fathers were considerably more in favour of these subjects being discussed at primary school than mothers. Nearly 40 per cent of fathers thought sexual intercourse should be mentioned at primary school and nearly one third thought that contraception should be discussed.

On all the topics there was considerably less enthusiasm for teaching them in the primary school from parents in the Midlands than in the other two areas, and there was a marked aversion to education on such matters in primary schools among Hindu and Muslim parents, who were a small but distinct group.

Finally, we asked parents how satisfied they were with the sex education their son or daughter had had at primary school, and Table 5 summarises their views.

Table 5   *Parental satisfaction with sex education teenager received at primary school*

	Total parents	Mothers	Fathers
Very satisfied	9	10	8
Fairly satisfied	34	40	21
Not very satisfied	8	10	5
Not at all satisfied	8	9	6
Don't know anything about it	39	30	60
(Base)	(212)	(149)	(63)

Column percentages

The table highlights the lack of knowledge among fathers about what their children were taught about these matters at primary school. But it also shows that nearly a third of mothers interviewed said that they did not know what was going on. What is perhaps more interesting is that one of the main reasons for dissatisfaction with the sex education their children received at primary school was lack of knowledge of what was happening rather than dissatisfaction with what was being taught, as this father pointed out:

There was very little information and lack of involvement in what was going on. . .

It was very rare for parents to say that they were dissatisfied with the fact that education in sex and personal relationships took place in primary schools at all or that their children had had too much sex education at primary school, and, indeed, only one per cent of parents thought it should not be discussed at primary school and a further one per cent thought their children had had too much sex education at primary school.

Most of the parents expressing dissatisfaction with sex education in primary school thought that there was too little rather than too much, and the biggest single complaint, expressed it must be said by only 5 per cent of the sample, was that the only sex education their children had received at primary school was on 'not going with strangers'. There was a general feeling among parents that primary schools should gradually introduce subjects and 'touch on' topics as preparation for more specific treatment in secondary schools.

And it is here, of course, that some of the problem lies. The HMI Report on 15 primary schools in Avon[6] spoke of sex education arising 'incidentally and naturally as a result of other class activities . . .' This was exactly what many parents were advocating, but, if it was happening in this 'natural' and 'incidental' way, it is not particularly surprising that parents knew so little about it. Any parent knows how difficult it is to find out from a child what is being taught about specific and tangible subjects, so perhaps we should not be surprised that parents were so ill-informed by their children about what they were learning 'incidentally' on these topics.

However, the question arises whether the schools should keep the parents better informed about what is going on. There was clearly room for more involvement of parents, even if many were not particularly interested while others displayed considerable trust in the school and teachers and did not feel it necessary to be more involved. It did appear that schools and teachers were unnecessarily worried about the effect that their teaching on these subjects might have on parents, and this chapter should help to dispel their fears. It was quite clear that only a tiny minority of parents were against education in sex and personal relationships and bodily changes in primary schools, and that the overwhelming majority welcomed the involvement of schools in preparing their children for puberty and growing up.

Views of teenagers on sex education at primary school

But what did the teenagers think? We asked them what they thought now about the education they had had on these subjects at primary school, whether they thought it could have been improved in any way, and whether they thought it was a good idea to have sex education or information and discussion on how the body grows in primary schools.

About a third of the teenagers still maintained that they had not had much education on these topics in primary school, but the main comment of the remainder was that they had not been taught enough facts and detail or that the education on these topics they had received at primary school had been confined to 'not going with strangers'. Forty per cent of the teenagers who had had any sex education at all in primary school thought that it had been inadequate for one of these reasons, a further 15 per cent thought that it had been 'all right' or 'fair', while around a quarter of those having sex education at primary school thought it had been good, informative and useful. Again, the children in the South-Western area and the 14-year-olds were more likely to have found it useful and interesting than the others.

What was it that they found inadequate and did they think it could have been improved in any way? Certainly teenagers stressed that there was a need for preparation for bodily changes, particularly for children whose parents did not tell them, as this 16-year-old boy said:

I don't reckon it was all that good. They should have told the third and fourth years about how their bodies worked and things like that, but they only taught us about not going with strangers and that was it.

Even where schools had taught about changes at puberty, they had not always given enough detail, in the opinion of many teenagers, as this girl in the North-East pointed out:

You never get to know about boys and they didn't know about girls. They didn't tell you how to cope with pains—only that you had periods.

Forty-one per cent of the children who had had sex education in primary schools thought that it could have been improved, mainly by giving more detail on specific subjects. Certainly two-thirds of those thinking it could have been improved would have liked more information on bodily changes and more preparation for the sex education they would receive in secondary school. Some teenagers' interest went further, like this 16-year-old boy:

I think they should have told us about human relationships—things on child battering—things like that. . .

But sometimes the education was remembered as rather mechanistic, and some girls could obviously have done with more stress on human relationships like this 16-year-old from the South-West area:

It seemed very cold and not at all reassuring. You just wake up in the night and wonder, 'My God, is that how I'm going to spend the rest of my life?'

So did the teenagers think it a good idea to have sex education at primary school? Overall, 58 per cent said 'yes', 32 per cent said 'no' and 10 per cent had mixed feelings. There was a uniformity in these percentages across areas, age and sex, although girls were marginally more likely to say that it was a good idea.

Why did they think it a good idea? The main reasons given were similar to those given by parents—to prepare them for body changes and puberty and for the sex education they would receive in secondary school. Certainly the impact of secondary school was uppermost in the minds of a third of those who thought that sex education at primary school was a good idea, as summarised by these two girls from the South-West, for rather different reasons:

> It's a good idea because some people grow up and don't know anything about anything until the secondary school. Then they're made fun of because they don't know nothing.

> (It's a good idea) because we learn things whilst we are young instead of having to wait until we are 14. We didn't start having sex education in the senior school until we were 14.

Boys were inclined to be circumspect and cautious, like this 15-year-old from the North-East:

> It's best to know about it from a young age—then it's not so bad when you get older. It might be too late then. You hear about a lot of girls getting pregnant at young ages. . .

But a third of the teenagers thought it was not a good idea to have sex education in primary school, mainly because they thought that primary school children were too young. About a quarter of all the teenagers thought that children of that age were either too young to understand or were too 'immature'. It often appeared that they were interpreting the question to cover aspects of sex education that they themselves had had in the secondary school but not in primary school, for example on sexual intercourse. There were a number of comments suggesting that children at primary school only joked about these things and were unable to understand them properly. Some children gave glimpses of their own present anxieties and reinforced the need for educationists and teachers to understand how sensitively these matters should be treated both in primary and secondary school. Some girls in particular felt that these matters were very private:

> You want to enjoy your childhood really and not worry about these things. I think mum should teach you really. . .

The caution and good sense of a lot of the teenagers interviewed came through in response to this question, and this 14-year-old girl in the North-East summarised the views of a number of children:

> Yes, it's a good idea—but not everything. A lot of people wouldn't have understood it all if it had been fed in at that age. But it makes you sure, and it stops people spreading things around the playground making some people feel left out.

There was a widespread impression that the teenagers interviewed who had had education in these matters had felt themselves to be 'mature' enough to have education on these topics at primary school, but that they were concerned about the effect on the 'immature'. There was no doubt that they were distinguishing between different topics, and that by the time we interviewed them—at 14, 15 and 16—they were thinking of 'sex education' as being more about sexual intercourse than about the topics more usually covered in primary schools. Like their parents they were more enthusiastic about covering certain topics than others, and it was clear from their responses that the teenagers who felt that there should not be sex education in primary schools were usually thinking of education referring specifically to sexual intercourse.

2   EDUCATION IN SEX AND PERSONAL RELATIONSHIPS AT SECONDARY SCHOOL

This chapter describes the experience and views of teenagers about their education on sex and personal relationships at secondary school. It was quite clear from the pilot study that the way in which education on these subjects has developed over the past ten years or so demanded much more detailed questioning than previous studies had undertaken.

Educationists, local education authorities, schools and individual teachers have become more aware of the importance of the pastoral care of their pupils, and the organisation of many schools reflects this. There has been much more emphasis on the desirability of trying to integrate 'sex education' into a programme of general education about health and personal and social development[9]. There has been a great deal of work on the curriculum, especially in those areas surrounding personal development[10,11,12,13], and much sensitive and informed thought has gone into developing a secondary school curriculum which takes into account the changing society in which we live together with a concerned and individual approach to teenagers which was quite unheard of in their parents' schooldays. The close and trusting relationships with certain teachers described by many of the teenagers we interviewed gave glimpses of a world unknown and undreamt of by their parents' generation.

This chapter looks in detail at what the teenagers were taught, how it was presented and relationships with teachers. The teenagers' more detailed assessment of the education on sex and personal relationships they received at secondary school is covered in later chapters.

We started by asking the teenagers whether they had had any lessons, films or discussions, whether formal or informal, about any of the following topics in any year at secondary school. The table below summarises the responses of the teenagers, but we should stress that, as in the questions about primary schools, there were certain teenagers who appeared to have blocked out everything that happened at school!

The topics we asked the teenagers about were: animal reproduction, human reproduction, sexual intercourse, pregnancy and childbirth, changes in a girl's body as she grows up, changes in a boy's body as he grows up, family and parenthood, personal relationships between male and female, guidelines on sexual behaviour, contraception and birth control, masturbation, venereal disease, abortion and homosexuality and/or lesbianism. This list covered the same topics as those asked about by Christine Farrell[1], but we added the topics of pregnancy and childbirth and guidelines in sexual behaviour.

Table 6 *Teenagers reporting lessons, films or discussions about specified topics in any year at secondary school*

Column percentages

	1st year	2nd year	3rd year	4th year	5th year	6th year
Proportion of teenagers reporting	76	67	85	81	77	58
Base—all those who reached relevant year	(209)	(209)	(209)	(172)	(96)	(12)

Our piloting had shown that education on these topics was no longer restricted to the biology lesson or to a one-off, eagerly awaited—or dreaded—visit by the family planning doctor who would display sheaths and IUDs and caps to the enraptured eyes of thirty 15-year-olds. There has been a very systematic attempt in many areas of trying to integrate 'sex education' firmly into the school curriculum, with an increasing tendency to put it into a programme of education in social and personal development led by teachers within the school rather than by outsiders. In some areas, the use of outsiders has been discouraged, while in most areas, outsiders are used much more circumspectly than they were a few years ago.

There was no doubt that more subject teachers were expected to introduce 'sex education' into their lessons. But, of course, as this study clearly showed, 'sex education' as it was thought of a few years ago was a very narrowly defined concept. We found it necessary to break it down into 14 topics, and it could have been further refined. It is obviously nonsense to talk about 'sex education' today as though it were an easily definable subject which could be removed at a stroke from the secondary school curriculum. It is part of a much wider programme in curricular terms, and, as in primary schools, it arises 'incidentally' and spontaneously in many subjects and in pastoral care.

It should be stressed that there has been an increasing emphasis among educationists that 'sex education' in the curriculum should be placed in the context of personal relationships[14], and there was no doubt that the trend away from a 'biological' approach to sex education towards more stress on personal and social development was reflected in the responses of the teenagers in our sample.

Table 7 shows the proportion of teenagers who said that they had had lessons, films or discussions on the specified topics in any year in secondary school. The table indicates the differences by sex, age and area of the respondents. The order of the topics remains the same throughout the report for consistency.

The table represents a snapshot of the education in these topics the individual teenagers reported they had had at the age they were at the time. Therefore the most reliable indication of the overall extent of education in these topics can be gathered from looking at that reported by the 16-year-olds. But perhaps what is most striking about the table as a whole is the extent to which 14-year-olds report having had education in such a wide variety of topics by the time they are half-way through the third year in the secondary school, which is when the interviewing for this study took place.

Looking at the individual topics more closely, certain patterns emerge. It can be seen from the table that more than 90 per cent of the teenagers had had education on human reproduction and pregnancy and childbirth. As many as 98 per cent of the 15 and 16-year-olds reported that they had covered human reproduction and 96 per cent of them had covered pregnancy and childbirth, while the proportion of 14-year-olds covering these topics was nearly 90 per cent. Christine Farrell's 1974 study of 16–19-year-olds found that 78 per cent said that they had covered human reproduction at secondary school.

The emphasis placed in primary schools on preparation for puberty was clearly developed in secondary schools, and 89 per cent of the teenagers reported learning about changes in a girl's body as she grows up while 83 per cent had covered changes in a boy's body. As might be expected, more girls than boys said they had received education on changes in girls' bodies and more boys than girls said that they had received education on changes in boys' bodies. Again, by the time they reached the age of sixteen, virtually all the teenagers said they had covered these topics, and this compares with Christine Farrell's 1974 findings of 68 per cent of 16–19-year-olds having covered female puberty and 61 per cent having covered male puberty.

As in primary schools there were certain area differences, with the teenagers in the South-Western area consistently reporting more education in these topics than children in the other two areas. But the differences were relatively small, and some of the differences could be accounted for by the differing age structures of those interviewed in the three areas, with a rather lower proportion of 16-year-olds in the North-Eastern area than in the other two areas. Proportions of males and females interviewed in all three areas were almost identical.

Eighty-three per cent of the children said that they had covered animal reproduction and the same proportion said that they had covered sexual

Table 7   *Topics on which teenager had had lessons, films and discussions at secondary school in any year, by sex, age and area*

Column percentages

Topic	Total	Sex		Age			Area		
		Boys	Girls	14	15	16	SW	Mids.	NE
Animal reproduction	83	84	83	83	79	91	87	79	85
Human reproduction	93	92	94	88	94	98	98	91	92
Sexual intercourse	83	87	80	75	88	89	82	87	81
Pregnancy & childbirth	90	86	94	85	90	96	96	86	91
Changes in a girl's body as she grows up	89	83	95	87	86	98	98	89	85
Changes in a boy's body as he grows up	83	86	80	73	84	94	89	84	78
Family and parenthood	67	58	75	57	69	75	73	71	59
Personal relationships between male and female	70	66	74	57	73	83	76	74	64
Guidelines on sexual behaviour	51	51	51	39	57	58	49	50	52
Contraception and birth control	80	80	81	65	85	94	87	82	76
Masturbation	37	37	36	32	37	43	31	43	34
Venereal disease	67	59	75	56	67	85	76	67	64
Abortion	57	53	61	45	57	74	71	53	53
Homosexuality/Lesbianism	28	27	28	19	21	51	29	22	32
(Base)	(209)	(99)	(110)	(75)	(81)	(53)	(45)	(76)	(88)

intercourse. Again, by the time the teenagers had reached 16 they were much more likely to have had some education about these subjects. This was particularly marked with sexual intercourse, with 89 per cent of 16-year-olds reporting education at secondary school on this, compared with 65 per cent of 16-19-year-olds in Christine Farrell's study. Perhaps it is more interesting to note that 75 per cent of the 14-year-olds in our sample said that sexual intercourse had been covered in lessons, films or discussions in secondary school.

There was a difference between the single-sex and mixed schools as far as the subjects outlined above were concerned, but only 13 teenagers attended single-sex schools and this number was too small to give a reliable comparison.

Eighty per cent of the teenagers said that they had had lessons, films or discussions on contraception and birth control, and as many as 94 per cent of the 16-year-olds said that they had learned about this at secondary school. Sixty-five per cent of the 14-year-olds said that they had covered it, but it is quite clear that most schools have a definite policy of introducing or reinforcing education on this subject in the fourth or fifth year. It is a matter for considerable reflection that virtually all the teenagers in our sample in these three areas were going to leave school with some informed and accurate education about contraception and birth control. Whether they would be able to act upon the information they had been given or whether this education would help them to avoid unwanted pregnancies remains a matter for speculation, but at least very few of them would be in the position of total ignorance about contraception and birth control reported by so many of their parents when describing their own teenage.

It is also in this subject that there has been the most significant increase in education in secondary schools since Christine Farrell's study. She found that 42 per cent of her sample of 16-19-year-olds said that they had had lessons about birth control at secondary school. Although she found considerable differences among areas, with only 23 per cent of teenagers in Tyne and Wear and only 25 per cent in both Humberside and Mid-Glamorgan reporting birth control lessons, nevertheless the highest proportion she found was in Shropshire with 66 per cent of the teenagers saying that they had had lessons about birth control at school. The area differences we found were due almost entirely to the slightly different age structures in the three areas, and in all three areas in our study over 90 per cent of the 16-year-olds had had some lessons, films or discussion about contraception and birth control.

The last ten years have seen increased concern about teenage pregnancies, and there can be no doubt that the wish to prevent unwanted pregnancies among teenagers has been a strong motivation for schools to include contraception and birth control in their programme of health education. As we shall see this has the firm backing of most parents, who stress their desire for their teenage children to be given accurate information at school about birth control and contraceptive methods. It can certainly be said that the schools were taking their responsibility very seriously, and, as the teenagers reported, were usually placing education about birth control in a series of lessons on personal and social development and bringing it up in more than one lesson, by relating it to personal relationships, family and parenthood and other topics. The majority of teenagers said that it had been covered in more than one lesson at secondary school, and often in more than one subject.

Education on family and parenthood, personal relationships between male and female, and venereal disease were reported by around 70 per cent of the total sample, with the 16-year-olds reporting far more than the 14-year-olds. Nevertheless a remarkable 57 per cent of 14-year-olds said that they had had some education in each of these subjects. Girls reported far more education on all three topics than boys, and since it is unlikely that they were always taught in single-sex groups for these subjects, there is an interesting discrepancy here. It does appear that some of the differences might be due to the fact that girls are much more likely to opt for child care or child development as a subject in the fourth year, and, as we shall see, this was a subject in which most of the topics we asked the teenagers about came up. This has interesting implications in terms of options within the school curriculum for the fourth and fifth years. It is also possible that some of the boys were simply more resistant to the information they were being given, or that they did not attend the lessons. Although it could be argued that boys might not notice that they were receiving education on family and parenthood or personal relationships between male and female, particularly if it was taught in an 'incidental' way, it is difficult to explain why 75 per cent of the girls compared with only 59 per cent of the boys said that they had received some education about venereal disease. Certainly some of the most graphic comments about the films seen on venereal disease came from the boys!

Fifty-seven per cent of the teenagers said that they had had some lessons, films or discussion on the subject of abortion, and again, the proportion rose sharply with age, with three-quarters of the 16-year-olds having had some education on the subject, compared with 32 per cent of the 16-19-year-olds in Christine Farrell's study. The question of guidelines on sexual behaviour had been discussed by 51 per cent of the sample at secondary school, with the familiar pattern of the proportion rising with the age of the teenager. Thirty-seven per cent of the teenagers said that they had had lessons, films or discussions which included something about masturbation, again with 16-year-olds reporting more discussion than younger teenagers, but not as markedly as with other subjects. The proportion shows an increase on that found in the Farrell study, but not by as a large a margin as some others. It is clearly still a subject which teachers may find difficult to raise with teenagers. It should be noted that this was one of the few topics for which we had to provide a definition for our interviewers to give to the teenagers, since our piloting had found that girls in particular did not understand what the word meant.

And finally, 28 per cent of the sample said that they had some lessons, films or discussion about homosexuality or lesbianism, with a sharp increase to more than half of the 16-year-olds having covered the topic, compared with around a fifth of Farrell's sample. It is clearly a topic which is felt to be less appropriate for younger teenagers, and the majority of the teenagers who had discussed it in lessons said that it had come up in the fourth and fifth years at secondary school, more usually in personal and social education, social studies or general studies.

Christine Farrell pointed out that education at secondary school in certain of the subjects she asked about, like sexual intercourse, abortion, homosexuality, changes in boys' bodies at puberty, family and parenthood and personal relationships were more likely to have been reported by the 16-year-olds in her sample than by the 19-year-olds. Confirmation of her findings was found in the National Children's Bureau 1974 study of 16-year-olds carried out by Fogelman[15], and she suggested that this indicated that secondary schools had become increasingly conscious of the wider nature of sex education in the early 1970s. Table 8 compares the proportion of 16-year-olds in our sample and in hers reporting education in the topics covered in both studies, with the exception of birth control where she did not give relative age proportions.

Table 8   *Topics on which 16-year-olds reported education at secondary school. Comparison of present sample and Christine Farrell's sample(1)*

Column percentages

	Present study	Farrell's sample
Animal reproduction	91	70
Human reproduction	98	82
Sexual intercourse	89	73
Female puberty	98	69
Male puberty	94	66
Family and parenthood	75	44
Personal relationships	83	48
Masturbation	43	25
Venereal disease	85	60
Abortion	74	37
Homosexuality	} 51	26
Lesbianism		22
Base	(53)	(349)

32

Our sample was, or course, considerably smaller than Christine Farrell's, and restricted to three areas whereas hers covered twelve areas. Nevertheless the table shows a considerable increase in education on all the topics covered by 16-year-olds between 1974 and 1985. Perhaps more important, it certainly suggests that schools have become even more aware over the last ten years not only of the 'wider nature of sex education' but also of the importance of ensuring that teenagers can relate bodily function to the world of emotions and feelings and the wider social and family context in which they live.

Which subjects?

Traditionally, sex education has been the responsibility of science teachers, particularly biology teachers, and to a lesser extent physical education and home economics teachers. Greater emphasis in the curriculum on personal and social development among teenagers has encouraged the consideration of topics to do with sex and personal relationships in a broader context. This was certainly reflected in the responses of the teenagers in our sample when asked in which lessons and in which years they had learned about the various topics.

Christine Farrell found in 1974 that biology teachers were still predominantly responsible for 'sex education' in secondary schools, with outside speakers coming second. By the time we were interviewing, 11 years later, we found a much more complicated pattern of secondary school provision of lessons. We differed from Christine Farrell in that we asked separate questions about the different topics, but nevertheless we found clear evidence that although biology was still the subject in which animal and human reproduction, sexual intercourse, pregnancy and childbirth and changes at puberty were most likely to be discussed, general science lessons, which could be taught by any science teacher, ran biology a very close second in these subjects, usually indicating the extent to which these topics were covered in the first year at secondary school in general science lessons. Table 9 shows the spread of subjects in which the various topics were covered, and it can be seen that even on the 'biological' topics mentioned above, apart from animal reproduction which remained more or less strictly in the domain of the biology or science teachers, the coverage in other subject lessons was quite extensive, particularly in personal and social education or its equivalent, which was usually introduced in the fourth and fifth years.

When the topics of family and parenthood, personal relationships and guidelines on sexual behaviour were discussed, it can be seen that the biology and science teachers, although covering them to some extent, were perhaps less involved with these matters than the personal and social education, social studies and religious education teachers, mainly it appeared because they were more likely to be discussed in the fourth and fifth years.

Certainly on the topic of birth control almost the same proportion of teenagers reported learning about this in personal and social education les-

Table 9 *Subjects in which teenagers had lessons, films and discussions at secondary school in any year*

	General science	Biology	Personal & social education	Social studies	Religious education	Health education	Child development/care	General/Liberal studies	Form period/tutor group	Assembly/year group	Physical education	English/drama	Other	Sep talk outsider	DK/CR	Total having any lesson/any year
Animal reproduction	33	60	2	2	2	1	1	1	1	1	1	1	1	1	6	83
Human reproduction	38	49	16	6	8	6	7	1	2	3	1	2	1	1	11	93
Sexual intercourse	26	33	21	10	6	5	7	1	2	2	1	3	—	1	9	83
Pregnancy & childbirth	25	37	17	10	8	4	9	1	1	3	1	1	1		14	90
Changes in a girl's body as she grows up	29	33	17	8	3	4	7	2	3	5	5	1	1	5	12	89
Changes in a boy's body as he grows up	27	33	17	7	4	3	6	2	2	2	1	1	1	1	9	83
Family & parenthood	9	11	20	11	13	2	8	3	2	1	—	3	2	1	5	67

Table 9 *Subjects in which teenagers had lessons, films and discussions at secondary school in any year* (continued)

Column percentages

	General science	Biology	Personal & social education	Social studies	Religious education	Health education	Child development/care	General/Liberal studies	Form period/tutor group	Assembly/year group	Physical education	English/drama	Other	Sep talk outsider	DK/CR	Total having any lesson/any year
Personal relationships between male & female	10	11	22	12	13	2	6	2	1	1	1	3	—	—	6	70
Guide lines on sexual behaviour	6	11	16	5	6	1	3	2	1	1	—	1	—	1	1	51
Contraception & birth control	11	26	25	11	10	5	8	3	2	2	1	2	3	1	4	80
Masturbation	8	8	11	4	1	2	1	2	1	—	—	1	—	—	1	37
V.D.	7	15	22	10	7	2	5	3	1	3	—	2	—	1	3	67
Abortion	5	9	18	7	13	2	5	3	1	1	—	3	1	—	3	57
Homosexuality/lesbianism	1	4	10	6	4	—	1	2	1	1	—	1	—	—	1	28
Base	(209)	(209)	(209)	(209)	(209)	(209)	(209)	(209)	(209)	(209)	(209)	(209)	(209)	(209)	(209)	(209)

sons as in biology lessons, and abortion, homosexuality and venereal disease were more commonly discussed in personal and social education lessons than in biology or general science lessons. Again the main reason was that they were more usually introduced from the third year onwards.

It is important to note that in the breakdown of lessons given, personal and social education, health education and general or liberal studies usually appeared to be the same kind of lesson under different names, and taken as a programme in the fourth and/or fifth years. Social studies and child development or child care were more likely to be subject options taken in the fourth and fifth years. These subjects were rarely mentioned before the third year, and it should be stressed that the proportion of 15 and 16-year-olds covering the topics in these subjects was higher than for the sample as a whole.

The pattern indicated in the interviews reflects three main things: first the increasing tendency for schools to cover certain topics in each year at secondary school, gradually reinforcing the information given and adjusting the teaching, content and method to the maturity of the children; secondly, the fact that most secondary schoolchildren will do general science and/or biology in the first three years of secondary school, after which only a certain proportion will opt for it in the fourth and fifth years, whereas in many schools a programme of personal and social education, under various names, will be introduced for all children in the fourth and fifth years; thirdly the tendency for the more factual, 'biological' topics to be taught earlier in the school than topics which could be said to have a more personal or moral element. For example, very few teenagers reported covering abortion before the third year or homosexuality before the fourth year.

There were two points of particular interest in the subjects in which discussion of these topics took place. One was the extent to which they came up in religious education lessons, mainly in the third and fourth years, and the other was the virtual eclipse of physical education teachers as 'sex educators'. We were also surprised that coverage of these topics in home economics lessons was hardly mentioned by the teenagers, but that contraception and birth control came up in geography lessons, which, of course, often dealt with population issues.

We should also point out that the table clearly understates the extent to which outside speakers were used in schools. Most of the outside speakers took part in an actual lesson rather than coming in as a special event, and we asked about them in separate questions.

And finally, we were interested to know to what extent the teenagers covered the topics in one lesson only in a year or to what extent they returned to the topic more often. Again we were interested in how far there had been movement away from the 'one-off' sex education lesson towards a more integrated approach.

It was quite clear that in most years the teenagers were likely to have had more than one lesson on the various topics. This was particularly true of animal reproduction, human reproduction, sexual intercourse and pregnancy and childbirth. These were evidently topics which teachers felt could not be covered in one lesson, and of course they sometimes came up in more than one subject in any year. Similarly it was more usual for teenagers to have more than one lesson in any one year about changes at puberty, family and parenthood and personal relationships.

We were interested to see to what extent teenagers reported more than one lesson on contraception and birth control, since it had been the practice in many schools in the 1960s and 1970s to have a separate single talk on the topic. We found that it was much more common for teenagers to report a number of lessons in the third, fourth and fifth years, although it was more likely to have been discussed in only one lesson in the first or second years by the small number of teenagers saying that they had covered it in those years. And this pattern was repeated for abortion and venereal disease. If it came up in the first, second or third years it was usually discussed in only one lesson in a year, whereas in the fourth and fifth years it was more likely to have come up in more than one lesson.

The pattern which emerged of 'sex education' in the secondary school curriculum was one of widespread coverage in a number of subjects over the five years in which 11-16-year-olds were at school. The topics could arise in more than one subject in any year and were likely to be discussed in more than one lesson in any year. There was strong evidence that it was integrated into the curriculum as a whole and was not treated as a 'special' subject.

Visual presentation of topics
The use of visual aids in schools has increased enormously in the past twenty years, and in the last ten years there has been what amounts to a revolution in the use of video equipment in teaching. Certainly outside school teenagers are used to sophisticated and professional presentation of information on television, and these teenagers have been brought up in the television age. We were therefore interested to know to what extent they had seen any films, slides, television programmes or videos in lessons on the topics under consideration and what they thought of them.

As Table 10 shows there can be no doubt that visual presentation of these topics is almost universal in secondary schools, and the proportions show an enormous increase on those reported by Christine Farrell in 1974, when she found that only 56 per cent of her sample said that they had seen 'sex education' films at secondary school.

So what had they seen and when did they see it? Table 11 shows the proportion of teenagers who had seen some visual presentation of the various topics, broken down by topic, sex, age and area. The topic on which the teenagers were most likely to have seen a film or video (and these terms are used in the following section to represent any visual presentation of the topics) was pregnancy and childbirth. Over 70 per cent of both boys and girls who had seen a film or video said that they had seen one on this topic. They had not always liked what they had seen, and although most of the respon-

Table 10 *Proportion of teenagers reporting watching any films, slides, TV programmes or videos at secondary school on 'sex education' topics*

Column percentages

	Total	Sex		Age				Area	
		Boys	Girls	14	15	16	SW	Mids.	NE
	86	81	91	81	84	96	87	89	83
(Base)	(209)	(99)	(110)	(75)	(81)	(53)	(45)	(76)	(88)

Table 11   *Topics on which teenagers had seen films, slides, TV programmes on videos at secondary school*

Column percentages

Topic	Total	Sex		Age			Area		
		Boys	Girls	14	15	16	SW	Mids.	NE
Animal reproduction	39	44	35	34	41	41	44	38	37
Human reproduction	62	63	61	59	63	63	62	56	67
Sexual intercourse	49	58	43	44	49	57	44	53	49
Pregnancy & childbirth	71	71	71	64	76	73	79	72	66
Changes in a girl's body as she grows up	65	58	71	66	59	73	56	65	70
Changes in a boy's body as he grows up	52	60	45	51	46	61	51	62	42
Family & parenthood	24	21	26	20	26	25	18	34	18
Personal relationships between male & female	24	21	27	20	26	27	18	31	22
Guidelines on sexual behaviour	12	14	10	10	16	8	5	21	7
Contraception & birth control	47	51	43	31	51	59	49	56	37
Masturbation	10	11	9	7	12	12	8	19	3
Venereal disease	36	39	33	25	38	45	28	50	26
Abortion	22	20	23	13	22	31	21	24	21
Homosexuality/Lesbianism	4	5	4	3	4	6	3	7	3
Base—all those who had seen films etc. at secondary school	(180)	(80)	(100)	(61)	(68)	(51)	(39)	(68)	(73)

dents said that there was nothing they disliked about any of the films or videos they had seen, the film on childbirth roused more comments than any of the others, with eight per cent of those who had seen films or videos at secondary school saying that they had not liked it. Some people were upset, like this 14-year-old girl in the North-East:

> It frightened me. I'd rather not . . . it put me off—put me off having a baby.

It was not only the girls who were upset, although twice as many girls mentioned it as boys. However, some boys were affected by it, as this 16-year-old boy from the North-East showed:

> I didn't like the film on the birth of a baby. I didn't like the way it was coming out—blood everywhere. I didn't like it at all—the mess . . .

However, most teenagers had no complaints about the films or videos they saw, and many of them stated that they really enjoyed seeing 'real' people, like this 15-year-old girl from the North-East:

> They showed you everything that really happens—not just pictures . . . the actual real thing like the human body or animals being born.

And for some the film of a baby being born dispelled their fears, as this 16-year-old girl from the North-East pointed out:

> I liked the human reproduction film and the pregnancy and childbirth one. I was really frightened of having babies until I saw the film. It's dead nice really . . .

Only 27 per cent of Christine Farrell's sample had seen a film on the birth and development of a baby, although in 1974 this was also the subject on which the teenagers were most likely to have seen a film. Sixty-one per cent of our *total* sample had seen a film or video on this topic, and the fact that the proportion had more than doubled in just over ten years shows to what an enormous extent the use of visual presentation of certain topics is valued by schools. Again, it should be noted that our 15 and 16-year-olds were more likely to have seen a film or video on the subject than the 14-year-olds, so that the difference from the Farrell teenagers is even greater in real terms.

Our teenagers were then most likely to have seen a film about human reproduction and female puberty, which follows the pattern found in Christine Farrell's study, where, of course, the proportions were very much lower. Although, as might be expected, more girls than boys in our sample said that they had seen films or videos on changes in a girl's body at puberty, nevertheless, nearly 60 per cent of the boys who had seen films or videos said that they had seen one on this subject, and the increasing tendency to discuss such topics with both boys and girls was welcomed both by the teenagers and by their parents, as we shall see.

Films or videos on sexual intercourse and contraception and birth control had been seen by rather under half the teenagers interviewed, with the usual pattern of older teenagers being more likely to have seen one. Films or videos on venereal disease had been seen by over a third of our sample, although 45 per cent of the 16-year-olds said they had seen one, compared with 19 per cent of Christine Farrell's 16-19-year-old sample. Certainly it had made an impact on some, but not as much as the films on childbirth. The value of visual presentation was continually stressed by teenagers, and this, together with the back-up of discussion after the films was felt to be useful and informative, as this 16-year-old boy in the North-East pointed out:

> The film with VD was good because you saw the symptoms and you'd know if you had it . . . (The discussion was useful) because I didn't know that syphilis seems to disappear and then comes back. It eats into your body.

About a quarter of the teenagers said that they had seen films or videos on family and parenthood, personal relationships or abortion. These generally appeared to have been part of a health or personal and social education programme in the fourth and fifth years, but it was clear that some schools introduced films on these subjects in the third year or earlier.

And finally films covering guidelines on sexual behaviour, masturbation and homosexuality had been seen by 10 per cent or less of the teenagers, usually in the fourth and fifth years.

The teenagers had certainly seen a lot of films or videos on these topics, as Table 12 shows.

Table 12 *Number of films, videos, slides or television programmes on specified topics seen at secondary school*

Column percentages

Number seen	Proportion of teenagers
None	12
One only	7
2-5	29
6-20	40
More than 20	6
Regularly during course/quite a few	5
(Base)	(209)

There were certain area differences. Although overall there was not a great deal of difference in the proportion of teenagers saying that they had seen a film or video at all, nevertheless it appeared that films and videos were used more in the Midlands area than in the other areas, particularly on topics like personal relationships, family and parenthood and guidelines on sexual behaviour.

On the whole, the teenagers responded favourably to the films that they had seen, and many welcomed the fact that films showed them 'the real thing', presented simply and in great detail, as this 14-year-old boy pointed out:

> They went through every little detail, even the simplest things to make sure you understood it, and they used real people, not just diagrams. I preferred real people. It was easier to relate to.

Apart from the film on childbirth, which, as we have seen, a small proportion of teenagers found upsetting, there was little critical comment on the films, apart from the fact that some of them were old-fashioned and out-of-date, with teenagers wearing clothes of another generation. Since 'another generation' to teenagers may relate to teenagers of five years before there is clearly a problem for film and video-makers in presenting people with whom their audience can relate. It is an important issue, and has wider implications when seen in the context of other influences on these teenagers, like the television programmes and videos which they were seeing outside school.

The importance of having discussions with a teacher after a film or video had been seen on these topics cannot be underestimated, and in the vast majority of cases the teenagers reported that the teacher always talked to the class after a film or video. This might not always have taken place in the same lesson, but if not it was usually followed up in the next lesson. Only in four per cent of cases did the teenagers say that the teacher did not always talk to the class after the film or video.

However, the teacher talking to the class was one thing, but class discussion was another, and we found that 14 per cent of those who had seen films or videos at school said that there was no class discussion after them. These tended to be younger teenagers, and it is possible that class discussion was perhaps not felt by teachers to be as necessary when dealing with 'biological' subjects as with other topics. It was by no means uncommon for class discussion after films to be used sparingly, but nearly 60 per cent of the teenagers said that there was *always* class discussion after films or videos.

Teenagers certainly liked these discussions, with 80 per cent of those who had discussions of this kind saying that they found them useful, mainly because they helped them to understand better both the content of the film and the issues raised in it. The discussion appeared to reinforce the message of the film, and teenagers often stressed that they found it useful to learn from other people's reactions and their questions. The films appeared to act as a trigger to discussion, and the sharing of views and experiences was found useful, as this 16-year-old girl from the South-West pointed out:

> I could cope with it better than at primary school. Instead of laughing

people actually were interested in what was said. A few girls said after they'd have to take more care—so it hit them quite a lot . . .

Other methods of presentation
Ninety per cent of the teenagers said that they had done some written work on the topics, with 14-year-olds less likely to have done some than older teenagers. The majority of written work was, as might have been expected, copying of notes about the 'biological' topics of animal and human reproduction, sexual intercourse, pregnancy and childbirth and bodily changes at puberty. These were also the subjects on which the teenagers were most likely to have done worksheets.

We were interested to know to what extent the teenagers were expected to do any other kind of written work on these topics, such as essays or projects. We found that 20 per cent of those who said that they had done any written work at all said that they had written essays or done projects. Again, these tended to be on the 'biological' subjects, and there was little evidence of essay writing or project work on the subjects with a moral or more personal element. This was perhaps not surprising to find among the 14-year-olds, but we did find it surprising that the 15 and 16-year-olds appeared to have written so little. Much seemed to depend on individual teachers, but considering the stress laid on the importance of personal and social development in the curriculum in these areas, very little seemed to have been translated into written work. Some of it appeared to be very mundane to the teenagers:

> We wrote about the sort of things you have to do as parents—mortgages, buying a house, planning a family and budgeting bills . . .

If the aim in that North-Eastern school was to integrate sex education into other subjects, it had certainly succeeded with that boy.

The most common essay subject, written by only five per cent of the sample it should be noted, was abortion, and this seemed to have been covered in Roman Catholic schools rather than in others:

> I wrote my opinions on abortion—the reasons why and if it was right, and what Jesus's views were on abortion. I wrote about why divorce occurs, what Jesus's views were and what I thought about it and how to prevent it. Marriage should only be for love.

It is possible that the teenagers were under-reporting the extent of written work which they did on these topics other than in general science or biology lessons, but it appears that there is a definite tendency for these topics to be treated in secondary schools by means of films or videos and discussion.

The teenagers had certainly used books when learning about the topics on the card. Eighty-four per cent of them said that they had used biology textbooks, with as many as 92 per cent of the 16-year-olds saying that they had used them in connection with the subjects under discussion. Other textbooks were used by 40 per cent of the sample and encyclopaedias by 10 per cent, again with the 16-year-olds reporting most usage of other textbooks and encyclopaedias.

We asked the teenagers if they had used novels or other books when learning about any of the topics, and only three per cent said that they had. Again, we found it surprising that novels were not used as a point of departure for discussing some of the issues involved in these very sensitive topics, and we can only presume that if they were the teenagers had not noticed!

And finally, we asked the teenagers whether they had been given any pamphlets or leaflets about any of the topics at secondary school. Fifty-nine per cent of them said that they had had at least one, and as might be expected this proportion rose to two-thirds of the 16-year-olds. Girls were much more likely to have had them than boys, mainly, it appeared, because the most common subject for leaflets or pamphlets was changes in a girl's body as she grows up. Forty-five per cent of the girls said they had received a pamphlet on this, compared with 10 per cent of the boys.

The next most frequent subject for pamphlets or leaflets was contraception or birth control, with 23 per cent of the teenagers saying that they had had one about this subject, with fairly equal proportions of boys and girls receiving one. Just under a fifth of the teenagers had had pamphlets on human reproduction or pregnancy and childbirth, with girls much more likely to receive one on pregnancy and childbirth. Just under 15 per cent of the teenagers said that they had received pamphlets on sexual intercourse, venereal disease or changes in a boy's body at puberty. Boys were much more likely than girls to say that they had received a pamphlet on venereal disease, and indeed, 20 per cent of boys, compared with only 7 per cent of girls, said that they had had one. Less than 10 per cent of the teenagers had received pamphlets or leaflets on the other subjects.

There had certainly been a huge increase from Christine Farrell's sample in the proportion of teenagers receiving pamphlets or leaflets, or, indeed, using books, in connection with education on these topics. She found only around 5 per cent of her sample reporting that they had had pamphlets on any of these topics, and only 25 per cent of the boys and 34 per cent of the girls said that they had used books on the subjects. She found a problem of recall, but that her 16-year-olds were more likely to report using books than older teenagers in her sample. She thought this might reflect the increase in interest in sex education in recent years. Certainly our study indicates an enormous upsurge in the use of books and pamphlets or leaflets in secondary schools in the last ten years or so. This, combined with the great increase in the reported use of films, videos or television programmes in lessons about these topics, suggests that teenagers in our sample were being given a much more widely-based programme of education in sex and personal relationships than those who had been at secondary school in the early 1970s, not only in the extent to which topics were covered but also in the way in which they were presented.

Words and pictures

Having established the broadly-based nature of the education in sex and personal relationships the teenagers were receiving at secondary school, we turned to other aspects of how they were learning about these topics. Communication with teenagers can be difficult, and communication with teenagers about sensitive subjects can be especially difficult. We were interested in a number of aspects of communication and learning, so we asked a series of questions about how teenagers thought they should be taught about these subjects. First of all, we wanted to know if they always understood the words that teachers used and how they felt about the use of diagrams and pictures.

There has been some controversy about the extent to which 'scientific' or 'proper' words should be used in discussing these topics. The Plowden Committee, reporting in 1967, suggested that the words used by children would probably be considered as unacceptable for use in schools, and concluded that to avoid 'circumlocution', 'the scientific terms are really the only ones available'[16]. The National Council of Women's 1984 report, *Sex Education—Whose Responsibility*?[7] states, 'We think that this point is as valid today as it was then'. But can this statement be made quite so baldly? Other commentators are not sure, and some suggest that an unwillingness to countenance the use of the vernacular in discussing topics connected with sex and personal relationships may mean that some young people may simply not understand what is being discussed[17].

We therefore asked the teenagers not only whether they always understood the words that teachers used in sex education, but also whether they thought that teachers should always use 'proper' words or whether they thought it would help if they sometimes used the words young people used.

Table 13 *Proportion of teenagers reporting whether they always understood the words teachers used in sex education*

Column percentages

	Total	Boys	Girls	14	15	16
Yes (unqualified)	56	59	54	53	49	70
Most of them/ most of the time	20	19	20	17	25	15
Not really/some of them	13	13	14	17	15	6
No	8	5	11	8	7	9
No sex education yet	2	4	1	4	2	0
Base	(209)	(99)	(110)	(75)	(81)	(53)

The most striking finding in Table 13 is the difference between the 16-year-olds and the younger teenagers, with 70 per cent of the 16-year-olds saying that they always understood the words used by teachers, compared with around half of the 14 and 15-year-olds. Although 25 per cent of 15-year-olds said that they understood *most* of the words used by teachers discussing these topics, only 17 per cent of the 14-year-olds did, and it must be a cause for concern that a further 25 per cent of 14-year-olds in our study either did not understand the words used by teachers or only understood some of them. The proportion was almost as high for 15-year-olds, and even among 16-year-olds, 15 per cent either did not understand the words used or had only a very limited understanding.

It must be asked whether it is right to assert that words used by children should not be used in schools and that the scientific terms are really the only ones available. If the result of this is a lack of communication with children who may well be among the most vulnerable to other influences, perhaps a less rigid approach to words might be more appropriate. We asked the teenagers what they felt about this.

Table 14 *Proportion of teenagers reporting whether teachers should always use 'proper' words or whether young people's words sometimes acceptable in sex education*

Column percentages

	Total	Boys	Girls	14	15	16
'Proper' words	43	49	37	43	41	45
Young people's words	30	28	32	38	27	26
Both 'proper' words and young people's words	26	21	31	18	33	28
Base (all those who have had sex education)	(204)	(95)	(109)	(72)	(79)	(53)

It can be seen from Table 14 that there is a marked desire among the 14-year-olds for teachers to use young people's words when describing things in sex education. The 15 and 16-year-olds tended to take a more balanced view, which was reflected in their comments indicating that they had more experience of teachers using both types of words. It is possible that this was because they were more likely to have had a series of lessons in personal and social education or its equivalent, whereas the 14-year-olds were more likely to have learned about these matters only in biology or general science lessons. A great deal clearly depended on the teachers and the extent to which they felt at ease in using the words that young people used, and it appeared that the teachers taking the personal and social education courses were more aware of the problem and more capable of solving it, like this teacher in the Midlands:

> Our teacher did use words we use. She was young, like us, and then she gave us the scientific words.

Clearly some of the teenagers felt that the words teachers used created a barrier in relationships between pupils and staff, and there were many references to the 'different languages' spoken by teachers and teenagers. It has important implications, not only in whether the children understand the actual subject matter of the lesson, but also in how they feel they can relate to the teacher, as this boy in the Midlands pointed out:

> You have to know slang as well, so you can understand everybody. We might take teachers more into our confidence if they used our language.

Some teenagers thought that if teachers used the same language as teenagers they might lose authority—'The teachers would be coming down to your level if they used the type of words you used'—but this view was fairly uncommon. Those advocating the use of 'proper' words usually had much more prosaic reasons for their view. The necessity for knowing the 'proper' words was quite simple in the view of many:

> Because for a start if you don't use proper words it's going to lead you into using wrong words in exams. Basically that's all there is to it!

Preparation for later life was also uppermost in the minds of some of the teenagers, like this girl in the South-West:

> They should use proper words but explain them using the other words. Proper words are more useful if you have to do anything about it later on—like talk to a doctor or nurse . . .

But a third of the sample thought that teachers should use young people's words, and although some of them thought it would help other people—'Use young people's words so that everyone could understand. I think some of them didn't know what it was all about . . .'—nevertheless most of them were thinking of their own lack of understanding—'Because you might not understand, but if they say it the way you know it is you'd understand better . . .'

The question of whether it might be confusing to have two words for one thing was raised by very few children, and most seemed to be quite able to cope as long as they had a 'translation'—'Most teachers use proper words and explain them in words we know, in case they come in exams'.

It was quite clear that a rigid adherence to the 'proper' words by teachers might lead to greater confusion rather than less:

It's better to use our words. You remember it easier. You can't always remember how to spell the big words because usually they're in Latin.

But the main reason the teenagers felt that teachers should use young people's words was to ensure understanding. There were many references to people losing interest or not paying attention if they did not understand the words used. Teachers were not always as sensitive to the problem as they should have been, it appeared—'You don't like to keep saying, "What's that?", do you? You'll look stupid'.

And even when teachers were clearly aware of the difficulties, it was not always easy to get through to teenagers, as this girl in the Midlands pointed out:

She told us to tell her—hands up if we didn't understand. She'd shorten it down, but sometimes we didn't like to ask her. It's better if we can understand. We don't use long words in conversation—none of us do. . .

And one boy in the Midlands tersely summarised his views on the subject of words:

Put it at our level, I suppose. No good blinding us with science.

If the teenagers did not always understand the words teachers used, did they understand the diagrams or pictures? There can be little doubt that visual presentation of these topics was considered much more successful than words or books alone.

We asked the teenagers whether they always understood the diagrams and pictures the teachers used in sex education, and 80 per cent of them gave an unqualified 'yes' to this question. Again the 16-year-olds were more likely to understand, but nevertheless three-quarters of the 14-year-olds said they did.

However, 90 per cent of teenagers who had had any sex education thought that diagrams and pictures were useful ways of teaching topics like this, with enthusiasm for this method of teaching fairly uniform across the age groups.

Some of the teenagers were quite graphic in their explanation of what they found useful about diagrams, like this 15-year-old boy in the North-East:

It shows you what's really happening inside like and not just pictures in your mind. I couldn't have imagined some of the things they showed pictures of—the insides of people like . . .

Listening to teenagers can help teachers and educationists to identify how best to teach. Sometimes it appears that teenagers could write a handbook on teaching methods themselves:

It's easier to explain with a diagram than just with words. You'd have to write loads of words just to explain a diagram—it's quicker. . .

This stress on speed of learning through diagrams was quite marked among the teenagers. There certainly appeared to be teenagers who found it difficult to relate to the written word—'The words are just a blurb and sometimes don't mean anything whereas a diagram might be more helpful . . .' and obviously some children were much better able to take in things presented visually than in words—'When you see it written it is always complicated. A diagram, you can relate to better. . .'

Some teenagers were sympathetic to others—'For people who can't read that well, it's better to show them . . .'—while others were really enthusiastic about diagrams for themselves—'They show you exactly what's inside you instead of using all the big words and not really knowing what it is. Also you recognise yourself . . .'

Perhaps it is difficult to recognise yourself among the Latin words.

Discussions

It was quite clear from our interviews with teenagers in this study that the traditional picture of sex education being given in one or two lessons by the biology teacher, which was still prevalent in Christine Farrell's study in 1974, was almost totally inaccurate in 1985. We have seen the extent to which teenagers covered a wide variety of topics in more than one subject over a number of lessons and the extent to which 'sex education' was spread over a number of years. We have seen that they used far more books and pamphlets, saw many more films, videos or television programmes than the 1974 sample, and were clearly accustomed to being taught with extensive use of diagrams and pictures.

Perhaps the most striking feature of the way in which teenagers described the education in sex and personal relationships they had at secondary school was their overwhelming enthusiasm for discussion in class about these matters. Ninety-two per cent of the teenagers who had had any sex education said that it was a good idea to have class discussion about things like sex and personal relationships, and this proportion was similar for boys and girls, among age-groups and in each area.

What did the children find so compelling about class discussion on these topics? We asked them about the advantages and the disadvantages.

The main reason given by nearly 40 per cent of the sample was that discussion gave them the opportunity of hearing a variety of views which gave them a wider, less biased understanding of the problems and issues which faced them all in growing up. Discussing it in class at school was felt to give greater structure than that found in discussions which took place informally among friends. It also gave the discussions more authority if a teacher was present to correct any inaccurate information, and it was clearly a forum in which some felt that ignorance could be expressed more freely than among friends, as this 15-year-old boy from the South-West pointed out—'If you talk all together you don't feel so ashamed. . .'

Some people were more circumspect about admitting their ignorance, and there was considerable stress among some teenagers about learning from other people's questions that they themselves were too embarrassed or nervous to ask, as this 16-year-old boy from the North-East said:

You learn and pick up things you don't know. You don't need to let anyone know you don't understand. . .

The sharing of views and opinions was very important for many teenagers—'It helps you to form your own opinions, and it matters to hear the opinions of other people. . .'—while it was certainly reassuring to many teenagers to realise that other people shared their problems—'You know everyone has some sort of problems and questions and it's not just you if you hear other people discussing it. . .'

And for other teenagers the most important aspect of discussions was that they brought matters which might be embarrassing out into the open. There were many comments about the fact that discussions made these topics seem more 'natural' and less embarrassing, and it was clearly felt that it helped people who might not have many social contacts or who found it difficult to learn in a lesson.

Very few teenagers pointed out many disadvantages, although class discussion was thought to be potentially embarrassing for some people, for a variety of reasons. One 16-year-old girl expressed the need for privacy which was sometimes overlooked:

It depends how it's handled. If it's handled badly it can be very embarrassing. You can be forced sometimes to express your opinions when you don't want to. . .

Not everyone wants to be an active member of a group and for some people of all ages, group discussion is total anathema. Sensitive teachers are well aware of this, but clearly some teenagers had suffered. Other members of the class are not always sympathetic and teenagers can be very cruel, as this 15-year-old girl pointed out:

If you try to say something and you don't know the proper word for it, the other people laugh at you. You feel terrible then. It makes you keep quiet next time. . .

It is common for classes to be broken up into smaller groups in some schools, so that individuals get more opportunity to express themselves and to create a rather more relaxed and intimate setting in which to discuss very personal matters. We asked the teenagers whether they had always had their lessons on these topics with the whole class or set, or whether they ever divided up into smaller groups.

Overall, 66 per cent of the sample said that they always had their lessons on these matters with the whole class, but just over a fifth said that they sometimes divided up into smaller groups. Only 4 per cent said that they *usually* had these lessons in smaller groups.

The younger the teenagers the more likely they were to have all their lessons with the whole class, while around a third of the 15 and 16-year-olds reported breaking up into smaller groups. There was quite a marked difference between boys and girls, with 73 per cent of the boys but only 61 per cent of the girls saying that they always had their lessons on these topics in the whole class. This was probably due to the fact that more girls than boys reported that they had had some of their education on these topics in a single-sex group, as we shall see.

The main advantage of small groups was thought to be that it was less embarrassing and easier to talk in a smaller group than in the whole class, as this 16-year-old girl from the South-West put it:

It is less embarrassing to say what you think. Everyone is involved in a smaller group. Shy people are more inclined to say something rather than just sitting there. . .

And boys too found it easier, as this fourteen-year-old said:

You get more chance to air your views. There is more time with fewer people. . .

It was certainly important for some teenagers to be able to get a word in edgeways, and there was a strong impression that some bigger groups tended to be dominated by strong personalities. It was also thought that it was easier to concentrate and take the topics more seriously in smaller groups.

Although two-thirds of the teenagers thought that there were no disadvantages in discussing these topics in smaller groups, it was interesting that the main disadvantage perceived by the others was the possibility that they might miss something, either from not hearing as many different views or from the possibility that the teacher might discuss different things with different groups. This was a rather unexpected finding, and reflects the great emphasis these teenagers put on learning from each other's questions and points of view.

We were interested in the extent to which boys and girls learned about the different topics in mixed groups or classes. The overwhelming majority of our sample attended mixed schools, and there has been an increasing tendency for teenagers to attend mixed secondary schools. About one third of Christine Farrell's sample of teenagers had attended single-sex schools, compared with only 6 per cent of our sample. However, there was some evidence in the piloting that teenagers had some discussions in single-sex groups. Table 15 on the following page shows the extent to which this was true of our sample.

Only 6 per cent of those attending mixed schools said that they always had lessons on these topics in single-sex groups. However, we checked with the teenagers attending mixed schools whether they had *ever* been taught or discussed anything to do with sex or personal relationships or how their

Table 15 *Proportion of teenagers having education on specified topics in single-sex and mixed groups*

Column percentages

	Total	Boys	Girls	14	15	16	SW	Midl.	NE
Always single-sex	11	7	15	11	14	8	18	10	9
Always mixed	52	75	32	58	47	51	53	61	44
Usually single-sex	5	0	10	6	4	8	7	7	3
Usually mixed	27	18	36	19	30	34	18	21	38
Both about equally	4	0	8	6	5	2	4	1	7
Base—all those who had had sex education	(204)	(95)	(109)	(72)	(79)	(53)	(45)	(72)	(87)

Table 16 *Proportion of teenagers attending mixed schools reporting ever having lessons or discussions on these topics in single-sex groups*

Column percentages

	Total	Boys	Girls	14	15	16	SW	Midl.	NE
	42	22	61	34	49	42	38	31	53
Base all those who had had sex education attending mixed schools	(190)	(91)	(99)	(67)	(73)	(50)	(42)	(65)	(83)

bodies worked in single-sex groups (Table 16).

It appeared that the big difference between boys and girls was due to the fact that girls were more likely to have been given specific talks on menstruation, and, to a lesser extent, that those who opted for child-care or child development in the fourth year found themselves in single-sex groups, which would account for the rather higher proportions of 15 and 16-year-olds having had single-sex group discussions. The higher proportion of single-sex group discussions in the North-East must have been due to differences in policy in individual schools.

Nearly half the teenagers thought there were no advantages in discussing sex and personal relationships or how their bodies worked in single-sex groups, but there was a marked difference between boys and girls, with the boys much more likely to say that there were no advantages. Indeed, half the girls interviewed thought that single-sex groups were less embarrassing or offered a more comfortable atmosphere in which it was easier to talk. This 15-year-old girl from the Midlands summarised the views of a number of girls:

> It's better with just girls because most of the things they tell you are about girls anyway, and it makes you embarrassed as you see all the lads looking at you and laughing.

Some boys thought that there were certain advantages in single-sex groups, but far fewer boys than girls thought so. Some boys were concerned about the girls' feelings, like this 14-year-old from the North-East:

> If you want to talk about girls they might not like it. If you ask the teachers questions about periods and girls' figures, that sort of things makes girls mad. . .

It was noteworthy that a much higher proportion of teenagers in the North-East than in the other two areas thought that single-sex groups were less embarrassing.

But over half the teenagers pointed out disadvantages in learning about these matters in single-sex groups. The main disadvantage they perceived was that they did not hear the views of the opposite sex in single-sex groups, and equal proportions of boys and girls made this point. Boys in particular said that there was the problem of not learning about how the opposite sex's body worked, and some boys felt left out, like this 14-year-old in the North-East:

> The girls were told about their body changes on their own whilst we boys did revision. I think that's stupid. We need to know too. You never find out about what the other sex feels about different things. Sex is for two people and everyone needs to know about it. . .

His view was reinforced by a boy attending a single-sex school, whose plaintive comment reflected those of many a lonely teenager:

> The fact is that from my point of view I've no contact with girls except

nipping over to the Girls' High School in the dinner hour. I've no understanding how girls feel, so it might help if we had discussions with girls. . .

Throughout the interviews there was emphasis on learning from others in discussions, and in spite of the fact that girls tended to like discussing certain things in single-sex groups, nevertheless there was intense awareness of the fact that boys and girls appeared to have different views on certain things. Time and again in the interviews teenagers pointed out how important they felt it was to hear the point of view of the opposite sex, and we shall return to this theme again in reporting how teenagers assessed the education in sex and personal relationships they had at secondary school.

Speakers from outside
Although there has been an increasing trend for sex education to be fully integrated into the curriculum, often in a programme of health and personal and social development, with teachers responsible for the lessons, nevertheless some schools find it useful to bring in outsiders to talk to teenagers, show visual material and lead discussions. There is undoubtedly much to be said for calling upon the expertise of specialists, particularly if they are able to communicate with teenagers. But there has been some debate about the usefulness or appropriateness of using outsiders, particular on sensitive matters involved with sex and personal relationships.

Concern has been expressed that the use of outsiders can 'isolate' sex education and there can be no doubt that, in the past, the use of outsiders, particularly to talk about contraceptive methods, has not always been welcomed in schools. If the wish is to integrate education on these matters into a general programme of personal and social development, there is a need for teachers to be able to deal with all aspects of the programme, with expertise and sensitivity. But there is evidence that not all teachers feel secure enough to handle all the topics they are expected to teach, and a number of reports and writers have drawn attention to the necessity for more training for teachers at all levels[7].

The problem is, of course, not only one of expertise, but also in coping with differing values and expectations. The use of outside speakers is obviously potentially contentious for a number of reasons. They may have the expertise, but may present their material in a way which teachers, parents and teenagers may find unpalatable for various reasons. They may introduce a particular view of a subject which may be regarded as biased by their audience. They may represent opinions which some people might find morally objectionable. The use of outsiders has clearly to be treated with great care and with considerable supervision by schools.

We asked the teenagers whether they had ever had anyone in from outside to give talks or show films about anything to do with health or sex education since they had been at secondary school. Our preliminary research in schools had shown that outsiders were often used to talk about drugs, smok-

54

ing, alcohol and other health topics, and we did not wish to isolate 'sex education' from the general programme of health education. However, since the question came half way through the interview, most teenagers now interpreted it only to refer to the topics we had been covering, and there was little mention of outsiders coming in to talk about other health-related topics.

We were fairly surprised at the relatively low level of outside involvement reported by the teenagers. As Table 17 shows, girls were much more likely than boys to have had a talk from an outsider, mainly, it appears, because they had talks from sanitary towel or Tampax representatives about menstruation and were more likely to have had talks from nurses or health visitors about menstruation, changes in the female body at puberty and pregnancy and childbirth.

There were interesting differences in the years in which boys and girls had had outside speakers. As might be expected, given that girls were most likely to have been given a talk about menstruation, they tended to report outsiders coming in the first three years at secondary school, whereas those boys who had had outside speakers were more likely to report them in the fourth and fifth years. In the South-West area those children who had had outside speakers reported that they had come in most years whereas in the Midlands area they appeared to have been used more in the fourth and fifth years. However, it was quite clear that individual schools had different attitudes to outside speakers and it was apparent that there was little area policy on the use of outsiders.

So who came in from outside? By far the most frequent visitor was a nurse, health visitor or midwife, reported by nearly 60 per cent of those who had outside speakers. The most striking finding was that other outsiders hardly figured at all in any numbers, with the next most frequent visitor being a nurse from a sanitary towel firm, mentioned by 7 per cent of those who had outside visitors. Family planning clinic doctors or nurses were only mentioned by 6 per cent, other doctors by 6 per cent, social or community workers by 5 per cent and health education 'experts' by 5 per cent. A mixed bag of other people, including dentists and clergy were mentioned by teenagers, but usually by only two or three, but, perhaps most significant, 15 per cent of the teenagers who had heard outsiders speak did not know who they were or what they represented. This is a cause for some concern, since it is surely important that children know the status and qualification of the person who is giving them information or leading discussions on these issues. Even those teenagers who said that they had received a talk from a 'nurse' were sometimes extremely vague about where she had come from.

What did they talk about? By far the most common topic was menstruation and changes in boys' and girls' bodies at puberty, with nearly 60 per cent of the sample reporting that an outsider had spoken about this. However, the overwhelming majority of these were girls, and three-quarters of the girls who had talks from outsiders said it was about these topics.

The next most frequent topic was contraception or birth control, and 23

Table 17   *Proportion of teenagers reporting talks or films on health or sex education given by outsiders at secondary school*

Column percentages

	Total	Boys	Girls	14	15	16	SW	Mids.	NE
	52	27	75	39	57	64	56	45	57
Base	(209)	(99)	(110)	(75)	(81)	(53)	(45)	(76)	(88)

per cent of those who had had talks from outsiders said that this had been the subject of the talk. However, this only represented 12 per cent of the total sample, and it appeared that talks on birth control and contraception from outsiders were given in only a limited number of the schools attended by our teenagers. The proportion was higher for those in the fourth and fifth years, but, even so, only 20 per cent of the 16-year-olds in the total sample said that they had had a talk on birth control by an outsider.

Just over 10 per cent of the total sample had heard a talk or had been shown a film by an outsider about venereal disease, but otherwise fewer than 10 per cent had heard outsiders speak on the other topics under discussion, although 13 per cent of the girls had heard an outsider speak about pregnancy and childbirth.

It appears that there are certain topics which are considered suitable, and perhaps non-controversial, on which outside speakers are acceptable. These are mainly to do with changes at puberty and pregnancy, and are mainly attended only by girls. Some schools also have outside speakers on birth control and venereal disease, partly it appears for their expertise, and partly because of the visual aids they bring. It is impossible to say from our data whether the outside experts replaced or reinforced the teachers on these subjects, but the possibility must remain that in some schools teachers felt less than confident in teaching certain topics.

Those who had had talks from outsiders found them useful on the whole, and nearly 70 per cent said that they were interesting and informative or that they appreciated the expertise and knowledge of the outsider. However, girls were more inclined than boys to say that they found the talk repeated what they already knew, and there was a lack of enthusiasm among some teenagers for the outsiders. Only four respondents said that they found the talks or films embarrassing or shocking, and it appeared that the teenagers in our sample took outsiders in their stride.

There was some stress on the fact that the outsiders were dealing with these matters all the time in their everyday work, and took them as a matter of course. However, some teenagers pointed out that it depended very much on the outsider, like this 15-year-old in the North-East:

Throughout the interviews, teenagers expressed their concern for confidentiality and privacy, and this was one of the reasons why outsiders were sometimes preferred:

> With the vicar it was a bit rushed and what he was saying was in a different language, We didn't understand half of it quoting from the bible and not explaining it sufficiently. The nurse was straightforward. She wasn't embarrassed so you weren't.

> I learned more because they were outsiders. There's no embarrassment. It's awful asking the teachers. They might go in the staffroom and tell the other teachers. . .

Considering that only just over half of the teenagers had had people from outside to talk to them about any of these subjects, there was a great deal of enthusiasm for outsiders when we asked the teenagers about the advantages and disadvantages of having people in from outside to give talks or discuss sex, contraception or personal relationships. Sixty per cent of the sample said that outsiders had greater experience, knowledge, information and expertise than teachers, and boys, who had had far less experience of outside talks, were more in favour of outsiders than girls. Thirteen per cent of the sample thought that outsiders had the advantage of not being known to the teenagers, which made it easier for the children to ask questions without embarrassment, and it was interesting that 20 per cent of the girls mentioned this.

Some of the teenagers clearly thought that it was a question of horses for courses:

They know more about it than the teachers and it's their job to know about these things. Teachers just know about biology. . .

And there was certainly a suspicion that some teachers did not always feel comfortable talking about these matters:

Teachers get embarrassed. They can't face you every day in class if they have had to talk to you about sex. It makes some of them go red. . .

But the main reason for liking the idea of outsiders was that the information they gave was likely to be more reliable and based on more expertise, summarised by this 15-year-old girl:

They tend to go into more detail than a teacher would. I think they are better qualified to talk about these things. It's their special thing, isn't it?

Girls in particular were concerned about confidentiality and this comment from a 15-year-old in the Midlands summarised the views of an important minority when talking about the advantages of outsiders:

You feel better talking to strangers. . .

But the disadvantages of outsiders were most commonly seen to be that they *were* strangers, and although nearly 60 per cent of the teenagers thought there were no disadvantages in having outsiders to talk about these topics, nevertheless the most common objection to them, expressed by nearly a quarter of the sample, was that the children did not know them or might be shy or afraid to ask them questions. This view was expressed by nearly a third of the North-Eastern teenagers, compared with only just over 10 per cent of those in the Midlands, and there did appear to be a marked area difference here.

The question of confidentiality came up as far as outsiders were concerned and we saw that some teenagers were worried that they could not trust them. Some expressed much greater trust in people they knew, as this 15-year-old boy from the Midlands said:

> You have known the teacher for five years so you don't feel stupid talking to them and they know the facts. If it was an outsider you wouldn't let out all your problems as they might go back and tell someone about them.

The possibility that they might be misunderstood by outsiders who did not know them was also thought to be a disadvantage by some teenagers:

> They don't understand you. You can't express your feelings as much as you can with a teacher. If you say something, and you think it's right but it's wrong, you feel daft, but you wouldn't if it was the teacher. . .

And the credibility of outsiders was brought into question by some teenagers, who acknowledged that they might have expertise, but wanted to make sure that they practised what they preached. This 14-year-old girl preferred the devil she knew:

> You don't know what outsiders are like. You don't know—they might be telling you not to do things like they're doing—like smoking. They might tell you not to smoke while they're doing it. . .

Teenagers' preferences for ways of teaching about sex and personal relationships

It was quite clear that topics concerned with sex and personal relationships and puberty were presented in a variety of ways in the schools attended by the teenagers. Different teachers presented topics in different ways in different years, and it was impossible to generalise. However, it appeared that most of the teenagers had had some experience of most methods of presentation, and we were interested to know what their preference was. We therefore asked them whether they thought it was better to have a teacher giving them the facts, or to have a general discussion with a teacher, to have a film or television programme, to have people in from outside or to have a mixture of methods.

There was a clear preference among the 14-year-olds for a visual presentation of the topics, and boys on the whole were more likely than girls to prefer specific ways of presentation rather than a mixture of methods, but basically there was not a lot of difference between the sexes and the age-groups.

Those who preferred having teachers giving them facts usually stressed that they knew the teachers and trusted the facts that they were giving them, as summarised by this 15-year-old girl:

> Because it's more likely that you would know the teacher so you'd be able to speak to her freely. As long as she's telling you the facts that's all you want to know really.

The stress on 'reality' which many teenagers cited when talking about films was not shared by everyone. This 15-year-old boy preferred his facts from familiar faces:

They can tell you what you want to know. You can ask them questions. The general discussions and the facts are real. TV and people you don't know aren't real. . .

Table 18 *Teenagers' preferences for ways of teaching about sex and personal relationships*

Column percentages

	Total	Boys	Girls	14	15	16
Teacher giving facts	9	10	8	11	9	8
General discussion with teacher	8	9	6	4	9	11
Film or TV pro-gramme	20	21	18	27	15	17
People from out-side	17	17	16	15	19	17
Mixture of ways	46	40	51	43	48	47
Base	(209)	(99)	(110)	(75)	(81)	(53)

The older teenagers were rather more likely to prefer discussions for the reasons frequently cited before—learning from other people in the class and hearing other people's point of view, as this 16-year-old boy from the South-West said:

You can get more out of discussions. You can find out what you want to know. When you have a discussion you concentrate more on what your friends are saying. . .

Films and television programmes were very popular among some teenagers, again for the reasons given before—seeing the 'real thing', and the fact that some people have much better memories for the visual rather than the written word or listening to a talk or a teacher. Some people preferred the rather more passive way of learning that they felt a film provided—'Then I don't have to say anything—I can just watch. . .'—while others felt that films were more authoritative and informative than teachers—'Because they are often more likely to give you the facts clearly and understandably. Often they show you—they illustrate it as well, whereas a teacher just sits and talks. . .'

Nearly a fifth of the teenagers preferred learning about these things from outsiders. We have seen why they liked outsiders because of their expertise, experience and knowledge, and in some cases, because they were strangers. It appeared that familiarity could breed contempt, as this 15-year-old girl from the South-West pointed out:

> Outsiders are best because they are more experienced with those kinds of things. The teachers tend to take everything from books, but outsiders are qualified and people are more interested. The teachers say the same things over and over again and we've had them for years. . .

But around half the teenagers thought that it was better to have a mixture of methods, and there were many thoughtful comments on the best ways of presenting topics of this kind so that the coverage was comprehensive. There was a strong feeling that there was a need for a variety of ways in teaching about things like sex and personal relationships at school so that everything was covered for everybody. There was the constant fear among some teenagers that they might miss something, which we had noticed before when the question of teaching in smaller groups or single-sex groups was raised. Boys in particular were anxious about this, like this 15-year-old in the North-East:

> If you only use one way there could be things they were missing out. By using all the ways you wouldn't miss anything at all. . .

The teenagers were keen to have their information from more than one source as well as presented in different ways. There was plenty of evidence of discriminating schoolchildren—'You can get it from all angles then. . .'—as well as the constant stress that class discussion after seeing a film and talking to the teacher or hearing from outsiders was the best way of making sure that the information was taken in and understood.

But one 15-year-old girl from the North-East summed up the views of many of the teenagers when advocating a mixture of methods:

> Well, the people learn in different ways, and then everyone gets to learn from the way that suits them best.

Topics making greatest impact on teenagers

In looking at the impact of the education on sex and personal relationships and development that these teenagers had had at secondary school, we asked them what stuck in their minds most about the education they had had on these topics. We were most interested in the subject-matter, but mode of presentation and the teenagers' comments were also recorded if they gave them.

Table 19 reflects the extent of education in these matters that the teenagers had had, with the 14-year-olds much more likely than the older teenagers to say that animal and human reproduction and changes at puberty stuck in their minds most. And nearly a third of the 14-year-olds said that

Table 19   *Topic which made greatest impression on teenagers at secondary school*

Column percentages

	Total	Boys	Girls	14	15	16
Contraception/ birth control	16	13	19	9	17	25
Pregnancy/ childbirth	14	8	19	9	12	23
Venereal disease	11	15	7	9	14	9
Changes at puberty	11	4	16	12	9	11
Animal/human reproduction	9	12	5	12	9	4
Sexual intercourse	4	6	2	0	5	8
Personal relationships	2	1	4	1	2	4
Abortion	2	1	3	0	2	4
Family and parenthood	1	1	2	1	2	0
Guidelines on sexual behaviour	1	0	2	1	0	2
Nothing	22	26	18	31	20	11
Everything	4	5	4	8	4	0
Not taught much	2	4	1	0	5	2
Base	(209)	(99)	(110)	(75)	(81)	(53)

nothing had made the greatest impression on them. They were, of course, much more likely to have received education only in the more 'biological' subjects, and repetition of the message was clearly what had stuck in their minds most—like this 14-year-old girl—'I think it's about periods. That's what we've done most about. That's what you remember most. . .'

The older teenagers were much more likely to say that education about contraception or pregnancy and childbirth had made the greatest impression on them, and, indeed, these two topics were mentioned by nearly half the sample of 16-year-olds. These teenagers were certainly concerned about preventing unwanted pregnancies, especially the girls—'They are the things you really need to know when you are older, so you can look after yourself. . .'

But boys too remembered the lessons and films about contraception, and it was clear that they were often put into the context of a loving and equal relationship as recommended by educationists, as this 15-year-old boy from the Midlands pointed out:

Marriage and pregnancy—and if you get a girl into trouble and things like that—what she feels like when she's in trouble and how it really doesn't matter so much for a boy, so it's important to make sure she doesn't get pregnant if she doesn't want to. . .

Girls were more likely than boys to say that films or lessons on pregnancy and childbirth had made an impression on them. In some cases schools appeared to have been anxious that no-one missed anything, as this 15-year-old girl from the Midlands reported:

Mainly films. We remember them. We've had no end of films on childbirth and the different ways—one a woman standing up, one in a bath and one about the three stages of labour. . .

Although not all of them were so capable of taking it all in their stride, nevertheless the general consensus was not unfavourable, even if it was a subject which gave a lot of teenagers something to think about, like this 16-year-old girl:

The childbirth (stuck most in my mind)—all the blood. It was a good film apart from all the girls in the back cringing. It was great to see the little baby's head pop through. . .

Boys were much more likely than girls to recall learning about venereal disease as having made most impact on them, and the films certainly made them remember, like this 15-year-old boy in the Midlands:

The more advanced stuff, like VD. When we saw those spots and rashes they looked horrible. That's why I remember them because I saw them. If I had just read about it I should have forgotten straightaway. . .

There has been some criticism of the 'shock-horror' approach to health education, but it certainly seemed to get through to some teenagers. It must be questioned whether it was always appropriately used, and there was a clear need for careful supervision of some of the material. Very few teenagers had seen anything about abortion, but when they had, they found the experience horrific, like this 15-year-old girl in the North-East:

The abortion—just terrible I think. Because on the film it showed the baby being aborted. It was all broken up and that. I felt disgusted. . .

There was some evidence throughout the interviews that in some schools, education on these topics was concentrated more on girls than on boys. We have already mentioned some of the anxiety that boys felt about 'missing' things. Their anxiety was well-founded in many cases, it appeared, and among those who said that nothing had stuck in their minds, there were many complaints that they had not had enough education in these topics for anything to stick, like this 16-year-old from the North-East:

There wasn't enough. The boys didn't get much but the girls got a lot more films and talks from nurses. Some bits were never explained—VD, abortion, menstruation, homosexuality were never explained to the boys—only the girls got to know. . .

And in some schools there was clearly not enough emphasis on feelings and emotions and too much on facts for some people. In some cases the facts did not go far enough either, as this 15-year-old girl from the North-East pointed out:

There wasn't *any*, basically. With all these things, it's the boy grows up and the girls grows up and then ZING!—the girl is pregnant. No information about why or how you feel about it. They just seem to skip over that bit. . .

Girls in particular were critical of being taught in too 'factual' a way. Many of the teenagers who said that nothing had stuck in their minds demanded far more from their lessons than they had got, and there was certainly food for thought for teachers in their comments, like this from a 16-year-old in the South-West:

Only the fact that it's been on the scientific side, rather than discussing relationships. All the subjects have been done mostly in biology so we have done it as facts and when you do it, it doesn't seem that you are talking about people—it's just, 'This is what happens'. . .

Informal contacts with teachers and other members of staff at school

The development of pastoral care in secondary schools has been considerable over the past ten to fifteen years or so, coinciding with the increased stress in the curriculum on aspects of personal and social development. We were interested to see to what extent teenagers felt able to discuss sex, contraception and personal relationships on an informal basis with teachers or other members of staff at their school. Our piloting had indicated that there was quite a lot of 'incidental' education on sex and personal relationships, sometimes contrived by teenagers who preferred to ask teachers questions on a one-to-one basis rather than discuss things in class.

We therefore asked the teenagers whether there was a teacher or anyone else on the staff at their school whom they felt they could ask a question about sex or contraception, and we followed this up by asking them whether there was any member of staff they felt they could turn to if they had a problem with personal relationships.

Fifty-five per cent of the teenagers said that there was a particular member of staff they felt they could ask a question about sex or contraception. Slightly more boys than girls cited someone, and rather more 16-year-olds—64 per cent—said they could than 14-year-olds—56 per cent. Over two-thirds in the South-West said they could ask someone, compared with less than half in the North-East.

There was a marked preference among girls for asking someone of their own sex, and although this preference was not quite so striking among boys, nevertheless it was obviously an important factor, which has implications when assessing pastoral care. Table 20 gives the details.

Table 20   *Sex of member of staff teenagers felt they could ask a question about sex or contraception*

Column percentages

	Total	Teenagers Boys	Girls
Teacher's sex			
Man	36	56	16
Woman	57	35	79
One woman/one man	3	4	2
Two men	1	2	0
Two women	3	2	3
Base—all those who could ask a teacher a question regarding sex or contraception	(115)	(57)	(58)

The sex of the teacher or member of staff was clearly more important than the subject they taught, although only two per cent of the teenagers said specifically they would ask that person because they were the same sex as themselves. The teacher cited most frequently, as might perhaps be expected, was a biology or other science teacher. But nevertheless, considering their presumed expertise, it was interesting that only 35 per cent of those who felt they could ask a teacher a question about sex or contraception actually cited a biology or science teacher. Nearly a fifth of the teenagers said they would ask a social studies or personal and social education teacher, and this was true as much of the 14-year-olds who had usually not been taught personal and social education as of the older teenagers. The importance of pastoral care was underlined by the fact that nearly a fifth of the teenagers who felt they could ask a member of staff about sex or contraception cited a form tutor, head of year, head or deputy head of school, with the older teenagers more likely to cite the latter, mainly, it appeared, because they had more contact with them or because they taught the personal and social education programme.

The rest of the teachers mentioned represented a wide variety of staff, but it should be noted that 8 per cent said they would ask the school nurse, and 7 per cent said that they would ask the religious education teacher.

Why did teenagers feel that they could ask that person in particular? Although just under a quarter said it was because they were subject teachers and had special expertise or knowledge, and therefore seemed the obvious person to ask, nevertheless the overwhelming stress of the teenagers was on the personal qualities of the teacher or member of staff. And often when expertise was mentioned, it was mentioned in the same breath as the approachability or caring qualities of the particular member of staff, as this 15-year-old girl from the Midlands explained when talking about her deputy head:

> He takes our social education group and has for two years. We have a lot of trust in him. He brings it out in class.

It was interesting to note the special qualities that deputy heads and other pastoral staff brought to their role. Teenagers in all areas had something to say about them, like this 16-year-old boy in the North-East, talking about two women deputy heads—'They always listen to you—others say they have no time'—or a 16-year-old boy in the South-West talking about a male deputy head—'I feel I could go and ask him without him feeling that I'm stupid. . .'

Certainly teenagers felt more at ease with people who took their questions seriously and did not make them feel foolish, like this 14-year-old boy talking about his social education woman teacher:

> She makes you feel comfy and she doesn't make you feel embarrassed and uncomfortable. She joins in with the laughs and sometimes she cracks a joke as well. She's about 27 I would say. . .

The relationship with the teacher was often much more important than their apparent suitability in terms of the subject they taught, as illustrated by this 14-year-old boy who said that he would ask his maths teacher:

> He's open. He isn't like a normal teacher—straight-faced and expects the kids to be good and that—he jokes in the way kids joke —and that's about it. . .

But expertise and approachability together were clearly a very important combination for a lot of teenagers, as this 14-year-old girl pointed out about a female science teacher—'She's nice, she's friendly and she explains and doesn't mind what she's asked. . .'—and this 16-year-old girl talking about her biology teacher—'He's taught us all we know. Nothing shocks him. He's a down-to-earth person. . .'

Nevertheless 43 per cent of teenagers felt there was no member of staff they could ask a question about sex or contraception, and girls were more likely than boys to say it was because they would be too shy or embarrassed, even if they got on well with staff, like this 16-year-old in the Midlands—'I can talk to them but not about them sort of things. I just feel funny. . .'

The question of confidentiality was important to the teenagers, and teenagers of both sexes and all ages did not always trust their teachers, like this 14-year-old in the North-East—'You say to Miss X something about sex and she'd tell all the other teachers what you'd said. . .'—and this 16-year-old boy in the Midlands—'I don't trust them. All false. One moment they're nice—then they talk behind your back. When you're little you like them. In the fifth year you've sussed them. . .'

But several teenagers had very functional views of teachers and simply did not see them as people to be asked about sex or contraception, as this 15-year-old girl pointed out:

They all seem too formal. You think of them as teachers and not as anything else. It's just their job to teach you things. . .

And her view was reinforced by a 16-year-old boy who thought teachers should know their place:

They just do their job. They are not like real friends—or doctors. . .

Rather fewer teenagers felt that there was anyone on the staff of their school to whom they could turn with a problem about personal relationships, but nevertheless as many as 40 per cent said there was someone, again rather more boys than girls, but fairly evenly spread among the age-groups. Again, teenagers in the North-East were less likely to feel able to turn to a member of staff than those in other areas.

Although girls were still much more likely to prefer to turn to a woman for help rather than a male teacher, the boys were also more likely to turn to a woman for help about personal relationships. Whereas 56 per cent of the boys had said they would ask a male teacher about sex or contraception, only 38 per cent of those with a problem on personal relationships said they would turn to a man.

It was interesting that there were quite a few teenagers who felt they could ask a teacher a question about sex or contraception but could not turn to a teacher with a problem about personal relationships, while some could talk about personal relationships but not sex or contraception. Teenagers who felt they could turn to teachers about both matters often cited different members of staff.

The relationship with pastoral staff and familiarity with teachers were emphasised by the fact that nearly a quarter of the teenagers who could talk to a member of staff about personal relationships said they would turn to their form tutor. In many comprehensive schools, the form tutor stays with the class throughout the school, and when the relationship is good, this clearly has advantages for teenagers, as this 16-year-old boy in the Midlands pointed out—'Because if you have any problems, she told us in the first year we could go to her. . .'

There was evidence of very close and trusting relationships with form tutors and other pastoral staff, as this 16-year-old girl in the Midlands said when talking about her deputy head—'I just get on with her. She's like a friend of the family, and she talks to my mum very well when she comes to the school'.

Some of the pastoral staff certainly seemed to have very special qualities, like this form tutor of a 16-year-old boy—'He's trustworthy and reliable and conversations will be strictly confidential. He gives good advice. . .'—and even if they were not particularly well-known or liked, there was something about some people which inspired confidence, as this 15-year-old boy pointed out about his deputy head—'She's the sort that sympathises. I don't like her but she will listen to you and help you. . .'

Again the personality of the teacher was often more important than the subject they taught, as this 15-year-old girl from the north-east pointed out about her English teacher—'She's more interested in *you* and not getting you through exams, and she *does* care. . .'—and the importance that teenagers attached to being made to feel individuals in their own right was stressed frequently. They were much more likely to turn to someone who appeared to care about them, as this 14-year-old in the South-West illustrated when talking about her head of year—'Because he can tell if there's something wrong with you and he'll ask if everything's all right. . .'

It was this fear that they would not be treated as individuals that made some teenagers reluctant to talk to teachers about personal relationships, as this 15-year-old boy in the Midlands pointed out—'There's too many pupils at the school for them to deal with just one. . .'—supported by another 15-year-old boy from the North-East—'I don't think there are any teachers that would pay any attention to *me*. . .'

Teenagers were less likely to say that they would be too shy or too embarrassed to talk to a teacher about personal relationships than about sex or contraception, but they were more likely to say that they would not trust a teacher or did not feel close enough to them to talk about personal relationships. There were some examples of very poor relationships with teachers, and it should be stressed that there were clearly some teachers who gossiped and were really not worthy of the trust put in them by some teenagers. Some teenagers were very bitter, like this 16-year-old boy in the Midlands:

> They'd just listen and get the juicy details and say, 'Sorry, I can't help'. Someone I know talked to a teacher and me and him went to the staffroom for something and heard him talking and laughing about what he'd been told.

Again some teenagers could not see teachers in the role of confidant, and some stressed that they could not get close to teachers even if they wanted to, while others stressed that teachers tended to keep their distance as this 14-year-old girl in the South-West said:

> They've all got their own lives to live and they make sure that everyone knows they've got their own lives to live. . .

But nothing is going to help some teenagers who do not get along with teachers, and there is certainly an important group of teenagers who miss out on the close and trusting relationships that others appear able to build up with teachers. The reasons were succinctly summarised by a 16-year-old boy who explained why he would never turn to a member of staff about personal problems:

> I don't like them and they don't like me. . .'

We asked the teenagers if they had ever had an informal or personal conversation on a one-to-one basis with any member of staff about anything to do with sex or personal relationships in any year. Our piloting had indicated that such conversations were fairly common, and certainly the answers to the questions about whether they felt they could turn to anyone with questions or problems on these subjects suggested that our teenagers in the main study would report quite widespread personal conversations. We were surprised to find that only 5 per cent said that they actually had had such a personal conversation, and we can only assume that many teenagers interpreted the question to mean a much more prolonged conversation than we had intended to cover, since so many of them had already referred to conversations they had had. Perhaps it was also possible that conversations after a lesson were not interpreted in this way, and, of course, it is quite possible that many teenagers, while in theory happy to talk to a teacher about sex or personal relationships, had never felt the need to do so in practice.

It appeared to be totally individual whether the teenagers reported an informal one-to-one conversation with a teacher about sex or personal relationships. Equal numbers of boys and girls reported one; 16-year-olds were rather more likely than younger ones to have had such a conversation, but they were found in all areas. The teachers to whom they talked were a very mixed bag, with a couple of biology teachers, a PE teacher, an English teacher, an 'anatomy and physiology' teacher, an RE teacher and a science teacher.

The conversations arose for a wide variety of reasons, and sometimes it was clearly a matter of interpretation of the question, with certain teenagers reporting conversations which many others had had but did not report in answer to this question. Sometimes it was rather more personal, however, as this 16-year-old girl said about her PE teacher, with whom, in fact, she appeared to have shared problems:

> When I play hockey she always takes me in her car and chats to me and that was when my parents split up and she was getting divorced. It helped to talk to her. . . Talking in the car about how she felt about her divorce helped me understand when mum and dad split up. . .

Teenagers are sometimes in desperate need of help with no-one they feel they can turn to, and teachers perhaps underestimate the help that they can give on a personal level. Certainly all the teenagers who had reported this kind of conversation found it useful.

In the 1970s there was a movement towards school counsellors, since it was felt that teenagers did not feel comfortable talking to teachers about personal problems, and there was considered to be a need to have someone with a counselling role who was not necessarily on the teaching staff. The integration of such counselling into the pastoral care of schoolchildren has been the aim of many schools and education authorities. The advantages and disadvantages of school counsellors are not the subject of this study, but nevertheless we asked teenagers whether they thought it would help if there were someone in every secondary school to whom they could go and ask about problems or questions concerning sex or personal relationships.

Just under 80 per cent thought that it would help if there were a particular person at school who could be asked about such problems or questions. About half thought this should be a teacher, with a form tutor cited most frequently, and about half thought it should not be a teacher. Boys were much more likely than girls to say than it should be a teacher of some sort, whereas girls were much more likely to say that it should be a school nurse. Under a quarter of the total sample of boys thought that it should be a school nurse, compared with 42 per cent of the girls.

Why were nurses so popular among the girls? There was a clear indication that girls often felt inhibited about talking about 'medical' problems with teachers, and simply felt that nurses were more appropriate. They also often felt that nurses had more expertise in these subjects:

A nurse knows more. Say if you had trouble with your periods or wanted to ask about the pill or anything. She's more of an expert. . .

And in some cases a nurse was thought to understand more about personal relationships—'The nurse knows what's going on. She would know how you feel. . .'

The often expressed fear that teachers would not respect the confidence of pupils was repeated many times among those who preferred a non-teaching person to fulfil this role, as this 14-year-old girl in the North-East said—'I don't think I could trust them not to say about it to another teacher. I wouldn't want to be talked about. . .'—and her fear was reiterated by a 14-year-old boy from the same area—'People would be afraid to ask them in case it was discussed in the staffroom. . .'

And again one of the main reasons for not wanting a teacher as the special person to deal with problems or questions about sex or personal relationships was that some teenagers could simply not envisage them in that role:

You see a teacher in your lessons and you might be embarrassed. You might worry about getting on the wrong side of the teacher. . .

And certainly many children had a very limited view of the role of teachers, like this 14-year-old girl—'Teachers don't learn to know the problems of children. They just learn to teach people. . .'

Just over 10 per cent of teenagers, with equal proportions of boys and girls, thought it might be useful to have a special non-teaching counsellor to help, but the response appeared to be more related to the desirability of not having a teacher in the role rather than having someone as a counsellor. It was clearly very difficult for teenagers to envisage someone as a special counsellor when they had never had one.

There certainly appeared to be a need for teenagers to be able to identify a specific person as someone whom they could approach if they had a particular problem. Although many children felt able to approach teachers, some could not, while others appreciated that not everyone felt able to do so. There was a substantial minority who felt uneasy about confidentiality and the trustworthiness of teachers on such personal matters, others were doubtful about the expertise of teachers in such matters, while others found it difficult to see teachers out of their 'instructing' role or not as people 'in authority'. Not all children had been able to strike up the close relationships with teachers that some had, and not every school had the excellent system of pastoral care that others had. Nevertheless, even in schools with apparently good pastoral care there were children who had not experienced it, while in schools which appeared to have little emphasis on pastoral care there were teenagers who had found a particular teacher in whom they could confide.

3   EDUCATION IN SEX AND PERSONAL RELATIONSHIPS AT SECONDARY SCHOOL— THE PARENTS' VIEWS

Parents were much more aware of whether their teenage children had had any sex education of any kind at secondary school than they had been as far as primary school was concerned. Eighty per cent of parents said that their children had received some kind of sex education at secondary school, compared with well over 90 per cent of their children who reported some kind of sex education at secondary school. Fathers were less likely to know whether their children had had any sex education than mothers, but nevertheless 75 per cent of them said that they had. Roman Catholic parents (who represented 14 per cent of the respondents) were also less aware of what their children had been taught, with 69 per cent saying that their children had had any sex education at secondary school, while nearly a quarter of them said they did not know. Again, parents in the South-West were more likely than those in other areas to say that their children had received some sex education at secondary school.

But how much did they know about it? We have already seen that parents were fairly hazy about what went on at primary school. Did they know more about what was going on at secondary school? After all, the majority of the children were still at school, and most of them were receiving some kind of education on these topics. Table 21 indicates that parents were very vague about the extent to which their children received any education other than on the more 'biological' topics, and even with these, well over a third of parents had no idea whether their children had covered them or not.

Mothers consistently displayed greater knowledge than fathers on all these topics, although the differences were not quite as great as they had been with regard to primary school. The most striking finding was the fact that fathers had much less idea of what education sons had received than daughters. We interviewed 33 father/son pairs and 26 father/daughter pairs, and there was a consistent pattern of the fathers of an interviewed son displaying much more ignorance of what he was being taught than the fathers of interviewed daughters. The pattern between mothers and sons and mothers and daughters was much more variable, with mothers knowing more about whether certain subjects had been covered by daughters, like changes in a girl's body at puberty and pregnancy and childbirth, than those with sons. But mothers with sons were more likely to know whether they had covered animal or human reproduction than those with daughters.

Table 21 *Parents reporting whether teenagers had had lessons, films or discussions at secondary school on specified topics*

Column percentages

	Yes	No	Don't know
Animal reproduction	58	6	36
Human reproduction	63	2	35
Sexual intercourse	45	7	48
Pregnancy and childbirth	57	4	39
Changes in a girl's body	57	4	39
Changes in a boy's body	53	5	42
Family and parenthood	37	8	55
Personal relationships	36	9	55
Guidelines on sexual behaviour	30	10	60
Contraception and birth control	44	8	48
Masturbation	15	13	71
Venereal disease	32	11	56
Abortion	22	11	66
Homosexuality/lesbianism	13	15	71
Has had sex education but don't know on what topic	13		
Don't know at all whether had any sex education	14		
(Base all parents)	(212)		

However, as far as all topics were concerned, parents displayed considerable ignorance of what was being taught, as Table 22 shows. It summarises the responses of teenagers and parents on whether the topics had been covered at secondary school, and shows the extent of congruence between the responses of the pairs of parents and their children, with the teenagers' column ranked in order of frequency.

To a large extent the responses of the parents follow the same ranking as those of the teenagers, but the congruence drops off with the less 'biological' subjects, suggesting either that parents were not told by their children that they were covering topics like personal relationships or family and parenthood, or that parents were assuming that such things were not covered. With

73

Table 22 *Proportion of teenagers and parents reporting topic covered at secondary school*

Column percentages

	Teenagers	Parents	Proportion of parents & teenagers agreeing that topic covered
Human reproduction	93	63	61
Pregnancy and childbirth	90	57	56
Changes in a girl's body	89	57	53
Animal reproduction	83	58	48
Changes in a boy's body	83	53	47
Sexual intercourse	83	45	40
Contraception and birth control	80	44	40
Personal relationships	70	36	32
Family and parenthood	67	37	30
Venereal disease	67	32	28
Abortion	57	22	17
Guidelines on sexual behaviour	51	30	19
Masturbation	37	15	9
Homosexuality/lesbianism	28	13	7
Base	(209)	(212)	(205)

venereal disease and abortion there was an even greater lack of congruence, mainly it appeared because many parents simply did not know whether these subjects had been covered or not.

The lack of knowledge on the part of parents was very striking as far as some subjects were concerned. For example, 90 per cent of teenagers had covered pregnancy and childbirth, often more than once and often with a film which had made a big impression on some of them. And yet nearly 40 per cent of the parents said that they did not know whether their teenage children had covered this topic. Mothers were more likely to know than fathers, but nevertheless 37 per cent of the mothers did not know whether their children had covered these subjects at secondary school.

Even with the subject of changes in a girl's body as she grows up, where it might be expected that mothers would be aware of whether their daughters had received any education on this at school, nevertheless less than 70 per cent of mothers and daughters agreed that they had covered this at secondary school and it must be remembered that 95 per cent of the girls said that they had learned about this topic at secondary school.

We wanted to know whether parents were aware of the extent to which these topics were covered in lessons other than biology or science lessons, so we asked a general question to see whether parents knew in what lessons or subjects any of these topics were covered. As we had expected, two-thirds of the parents whose children had had sex education at secondary school said that the topics had been covered in biology lessons, with just over a fifth saying they had been covered in general science.

But we were interested to find that some parents did know that topics like these were covered in other subjects, and a fifth mentioned health education lessons, 15 per cent mentioned personal and social education, 11 per cent spoke of social studies and another 11 per cent mentioned child care or child development. Thirteen per cent mentioned religious education, and this proportion reached 22 per cent in the North-East where we knew that there was a rather higher proportion of Roman Catholics than elsewhere. Little mention was made of form periods or tutor groups, but 6 per cent mentioned home economics and 4 per cent physical education lessons, which, as we have seen, were hardly mentioned by teenagers at all. Perhaps parents were remembering their own schooldays.

Although it was clear that a substantial proportion of parents were totally ignorant of what was being covered at secondary school in these topics, and many of them were fairly hazy about it, nevertheless those who knew that their children were receiving some kind of education on these topics were more aware of the fact that it was being covered in a variety of subjects than we had expected.

We were interested to know whether parents knew *how* the topics were put over to the teenagers and we asked those who said that their children had had some sex education if their children had ever seen a film, video, slides or a television programme about any of the topics. Fifty-seven per cent of the parents said their children had, compared with 86 per cent of the total sample of teenagers. Again, it was the parents' lack of knowledge which was more striking than anything else, since only 3 per cent said categorically that their children had *not* seen a film or other visual presentation. There was very little difference between mothers and fathers or among areas.

However, there was a big difference among these groups when we asked what the film was about. More than half the parents who said their child had seen a film said it was about childbirth, 17 per cent said it was about venereal disease and 16 per cent said it was about contraception or birth control. But mothers were much more likely to mention the film on childbirth than fathers were, and parents in the South-West were considerably more likely to mention it than those in other areas. Mothers were also more likely to mention the film on venereal disease than fathers. Parents were very vague about other films seen by their children, with less than 10 per cent mentioning all the other topics put together. And yet, as we have seen, over 70 per cent of the teenagers who had seen a film had seen one on childbirth, nearly two-thirds had seen a film on changes in girls' bodies at puberty and human reproduction, and around half had seen one on changes in boys' bodies and contraception. Only just over a third of those who had seen a film had seen one on venereal disease, and yet this is what parents tended to remember.

The question of outsiders coming into schools to speak about these topics has been the subject of some controversy, and we wanted to know how much the parents knew about the extent to which outsiders came into the schools and what they felt about it. We had been fairly surprised at the relatively low level of outside speakers reported by the teenagers. Only 52 per cent said that they had had a talk from an outsider at secondary school, and girls were much more likely to have had experience of this, with three-quarters of the girls, compared with only a quarter of the boys, saying that they had had a talk from someone from outside the school—usually a nurse or health visitor.

So what did the parents know about this? Not much, it appeared. Twenty-eight per cent of parents said that their child had had a talk from an outsider at secondary school, 23 per cent said they had not, and 50 per cent did not know whether they had or not. Even mothers were not too sure about their daughters, with only a third of them agreeing with their daughters that they had had an outsider talk about something.

Parents were even more vague about *who* had come in from outside, with well over a third of those who said their children had heard an outside speaker saying that they did not know who it was. Just under a third said it was a nurse or health visitor, while the rest cited doctors or health education experts or sanitary towel representatives. Mothers appeared to know as little as fathers on the identity of the visitor. The parents were even less knowledgeable about what the speakers were speaking about, and the single subject mentioned most often—by less than a fifth of those who said their children had heard an outside speaker—was periods or changes in a girl's body at puberty. As might be expected, parents had very few comments on the outside speakers since they knew so little about them, and one of the few comments was critical:

> A nurse spoke about the use of tampons. I was annoyed about it. It was more like a sales promotion. . .

Given that they knew so little about outside speakers in schools, we were interested to find considerable enthusiasm among parents for the use of outsiders to talk to their children. We asked them what they considered to be the advantages of having people in from outside the school to discuss sex, contraception and personal relationships.

Fifty-three per cent of parents thought that outsiders had the advantage of greater expertise, information, knowledge and experience than teachers, thus reflecting the views of their children. Again it was interesting to note that fathers, like the boys interviewed, were much more likely to stress these attributes than the mothers—and the girls. Some teachers would have been horrified at how parents saw them, like this father in the North-East:

It's like any subject. If you get an expert in the field then they can always put it over better. Teachers are good at the subject they are trained in but the human anatomy needs an expert in that field. . .

It is difficult to say what he thought biology teachers were experts in.

But it was not only their expertise which was called into question. Some fathers in particular were not too certain that teachers were always in full command of their classes, and overall 30 per cent of parents thought that outsiders had an advantage in putting over subjects of this kind because children would take more notice of an outsider and would behave better. Again, fathers were much more likely to stress this than mothers, and often combined it with their view of an outsider's superior expertise, like another father from the North-East:

I think as far as these specific issues are concerned there would be sense in having a medical person or someone associated with health education. Instruction needs to be carefully phrased because the subject is open to abuse. Kids must be at ease with the subject. It could get out of control with the wrong tutors. . .

Parents in the North-East put much greater stress on expertise than those in other areas, and seemed sceptical of the extent to which their children behaved 'properly' with teachers, like this mother:

I think it's a good idea because they take more notice of people outside the school. Well, I think that half the time they take the teachers as a laugh, but if professional people went they would take more notice. . .

It did appear that teachers were perhaps not always very good at getting over to parents the close and trusting relationships they had with teenagers, and the high regard in which some teachers were held because they could have a joke with children was not always appreciated by parents, particularly fathers. There was little doubt that many parents, although very keen that their children should have sex education at school, tended to judge teachers by their own memories of what teachers had been like in their day. They tended to show a certain ambivalence in their answers at times, both criticising the lack of their own sex education at school, and attributing it partly to the 'old-fashioned' attitudes of staff, while at the same time they were unable to see that a more relaxed attitude among staff might not necessarily detract either from their expertise or from their ability to get the subject over to the teenagers. As we have seen, teenagers certainly seemed to have learned a great deal from teachers.

Sometimes parents thought that outside experts were a good idea to reinforce their own efforts, as this mother in the Midlands pointed out:

Having a stranger telling her the same things as I have already told her she knows that I am not just saying it for the sake of it, but will listen more.

Certainly some parents thought that it was a good thing for the teenagers to be taught by strangers so that they would feel more at ease and more able to ask questions, and, like the girls, their mothers laid more stress on the question of confidentiality than the boys—and the fathers—did.

But again, like the teenagers, the fact that outsiders *were* strangers was thought to be their main disadvantage, although, as we found with the teenagers, around 60 per cent of the parents thought there were no disadvantages in having outside speakers. Some parents put a lot of stress on the fact that some children prefer to talk about these matters to people they know, as this mother in the North-East said:

> Outsiders wouldn't have any intimate knowledge of the children. They wouldn't know their emotional lives and it would be difficult for an outsider to judge that. . .

Several parents referred to the possibility that outsiders might not be able to 'pitch it right' for teenagers, either because they had no teaching skills or because they might not be sensitive to children's feelings.

And parents thought that outsiders might be too impersonal or technical for their children—'They might make it sound too clinical—perhaps no mention of love. . .'—and one father in the North-East summarised the views of a number of parents with anxieties about outsiders:

> Good relationships within the school situation are more likely to develop awareness of these things. It's the people they meet day by day from whom they learn about these matters. They can be seen to be a separate subject. . .

And it was this anxiety of making these subjects too 'special' or too 'specialised' that led to other worries among parents, like this mother in the Midlands who was afraid that outside speakers might be more biased than teachers—'Some speakers don't give both points of view on specific subjects and they can indoctrinate sometimes. . .'—and like this mother in the South-West who saw other disadvantages—'If afterwards they wanted to ask questions or anything, they wouldn't be there to follow it through. . .'

But, on the whole, the parents felt the advantages of outsiders outweighed any disadvantages they might have, and it was perhaps surprising that they had not made their views known within the schools.

But, of course, this was not really surprising considering the limited amount of contact that they had with schools about these matters. We have seen that 11 per cent of the parents said that they had been invited to their child's primary school specially to hear what they were teaching in sex education, of whom one third went and 13 per cent sent the other parent. We found that 14 per cent (30 parents) said that they had been invited to their child's secondary school, of whom again one third went and 7 per cent said the other parent went.

This meant that in 5 per cent of the total sample of parents one or the other parent attended a primary school meeting and in 6 per cent of cases one or the other parent attended a secondary school meeting. There was not much evidence of parents being invited to schools for a special meeting about sex education, but there was even less evidence that if they were invited they were prepared to go. Again, as we found when we asked them why they had not gone to the special meeting at primary school, most parents said that they could not remember or that they had had a prior engagement. A meeting on sex education did not appear to have been high on their list of priorities in terms of contact with the school.

Half the parents who had attended a secondary school meeting had seen a film or video and had had a talk from the head or another teacher. They were usually very appreciative of the opportunity:

> Very good—to let us know what they were teaching so we would know and could discuss it with him when he came home. . .

but with such a small band of enthusiasts it would have been surprising if they had not felt strongly motivated towards it.

Of those who had not been invited to a secondary school meeting on the topic, 56 per cent said that they would like to have been invited—almost exactly the same proportion who would like to have been invited to a primary school meeting—but again a third said they would not and a further 10 per cent were not sure whether they wanted to be invited or not.

Again, as in primary school, those parents who would have liked an opportunity to go to a meeting on sex education said that they would like to have known what was being taught and how. On the whole the parents were generally interested in the methods used by teachers in putting over such topics, but some were concerned that it was not being taught in sufficient detail, like this mother of a 14-year-old girl in the South-West:

> I'd like to know how deeply they were taught. Sometimes they tend to skim over the surface of it when I think they need to go into detail—especially about VD and contraception. . .

Other parents were concerned about the extent to which the sex education was related to emotions and feelings about other people, like this mother of a 15-year-old girl in the North-East:

> I think the way they taught it was very clinical. They were taught the mechanics but not the feelings—and not enough of 'thou shalt not' and too much 'go ahead and have a go'. . .

But a lot of parents felt that they wanted to know what was happening at school to help them talk to their children themselves, as this father of a 16-year-old boy in the Midlands said—'It would have been a good idea. If I'd known what they taught we could have gone over it together afterwards. . .'—and this father of a 14-year-old boy in the South-West—'I could know what sort of format it took and I would be able to use the same sort of language that they were putting it across in. My education is not as great as theirs. . .'

As we found in primary schools there were as many parents who wanted to check whether their children were being taught too little as there were parents who wanted to check whether they were being taught too much, and only a handful of parents came into either category. There was little mention of a moral component being either desirable or necessary in sex education at school, although a tiny number of parents expressed concern that sex should be related to marriage. But at the same time, there were parents who were worried that their children might not be learning enough because of the type of school they attended, like this mother in the South-West:

> I would like to have known just what advice they were giving them, because it is a Catholic School. I would like them—all the children—to know all these things on the card (the list of topics). . .

We found that parents were more likely to have been sent a letter from the secondary school their children attended than from the primary school, and over a third of parents said they had received one. The proportions were quite different in the different areas, with 43 per cent of the North-Eastern parents having had a letter, compared with under a fifth of the South-Western parents. The letter usually sought the parents' permission for their child to receive sex education or to see a specific film, but without giving any further information. This was particular true of the North-East, whereas in other areas if permission was sought the letter usually gave some information as well. It was therefore not particularly surprising that parents in the North-East did not feel able to make many comments on the letter other than that it did not say much or that they had had no objection to their child receiving the sex education or seeing a film.

Two-thirds of the parents who had not received any written information said that they would have liked some, mainly to know what was going on at school and how it was being taught. But there were few indications that parents felt in any way upset or worried about the fact that so many of them knew so little, and as we found when they talked about primary schools, there was a general feeling that if they had really wanted to know what was going on they would have felt able to go and ask.

And finally, since the Education (School Information) Regulations 1981[2] now require education authorities to inform parents of the manner and context in which sex education is provided, we asked the parents whether they had received a brochure or booklet when their child went to secondary school about the school's aims and how things were taught. Nearly three-quarters of the parents remembered receiving such a booklet or brochure, but only 13 per cent of them remembered anything about sex education in it. Since it was possible that some of the children had entered secondary school before it was made a requirement for the brochure to contain information, we made further enquiries about whether parents knew whether there was any information on sex education in the brochure now, but the vast majority said that they did not know.

4 PARENTS AND TEENAGERS AND SEX EDUCATION

The idea of the typical family comprising a mother, father and two children, as portrayed in television advertising, does not represent a true picture of family life in the 1980s. We were very struck in our piloting by the extent to which we were finding teenagers living with only one parent, either with this parent *alone* or with a step-parent as well. Our informal research in secondary schools indicated that a substantial proportion of teenagers were living with only one of their parents.

We wanted to know with whom the teenagers were living for a variety of reasons. We wanted to ask parents and children a number of questions about the extent to which they talked to each other about the specific topics we had already asked them about; we wanted to know whether they found it easy to talk to each other about most things, about personal problems and about sex; we wanted to ask the teenagers what they thought their parents felt about their having sex education at school and we wanted to ask the parents whether there were particular topics which they preferred to discuss with their children themselves and whether there were topics they preferred to be covered at school.

It was clearly necessary for our interviewers to establish with whom the teenagers were living and the extent to which they had contact with the other parent if they were only living with one. It was simply not appropriate to ask teenagers some questions about a parent they never or rarely saw. We had established household composition at the beginning of the interview, but we felt it necessary to establish the extent of contact between parents and teenagers before we started asking the teenagers what could be uncomfortable or irrelevant questions. In any case we needed to check on the household composition, since, in some cases, it was very complicated.

Only 70 per cent (146) of the teenagers interviewed lived with both their natural parents, and indeed only two-thirds of the girls lived with both parents. The proportion living with both parents was much higher in the North-East (81 per cent) than in the Midlands (59 per cent) or in the South-West (67 per cent).

A quarter (50) of the teenagers lived with their mother but not their natural father. In a third of these cases their mother had remarried so they

Table 23 *Proportion of teenagers living with 'natural' parents*

Column percentages

Teenager lives with:	Total	Boys	Girls	14	15	16	SW	Mids.	NE
Both natural parents	70	74	66	65	70	75	67	59	81
Mother only	24	18	29	29	22	19	29	32	15
Father only	4	5	4	5	4	4	2	8	2
Neither	2	3	1	0	4	2	2	1	2
Base	(209)	(99)	(110)	(75)	(81)	(53)	(45)	(76)	(88)

lived with mother and step-father, but in two-thirds of the cases they were living with their mother only.

Four per cent (9) of the teenagers were living with their father and not their mother, and in seven of these cases they were just living with father while in two cases they were living with father and step-mother (Table 23).

In the five other cases, two were living with grandparents, one was living with a sister and a step-sister, one was living with a stepmother, while another was living with a step-mother and a step-father.

There are certainly some complicated family patterns around, and we reproduce them in some detail because there are implications for the giving and receiving of sex education from parents or family. Even where step-fathers or step-mothers are not reported, the mother or father often had a live-in partner, and many of the teenagers interviewed had experience of family life quite different from the cosy scene presented in the television advertisements.

We asked the teenagers who lived with only one of their natural parents whether they saw the other parent quite often or not, and 62 per cent said that they rarely or never saw the other parent. This was more marked among those living with a single parent who had not remarried, and over two-thirds of those living with their mother or father only either did not see their other parent at all or only saw them rarely. There was also a marked difference with age, although the numbers were small, but as many as 73 per cent of the 14-year-olds living with one parent (whether re-married or not) said they rarely or never saw the other parent.

We therefore did not ask these children whether they talked to the parent they did not see about the topics we discuss below. The tables are based on the responses of teenagers who were either living with the parent in question or saw them frequently. This means that 95 per cent of the sample were asked whether they discussed these topics with their mothers—94 per cent were living with their mothers and 1 per cent saw them frequently; and 83 per cent were asked about their fathers—74 per cent lived with their father and a further 9 per cent saw them frequently.

It was quite clear from these tables that teenagers were very much more likely to have spoken to mothers rather than fathers about these topics, and that girls were much more likely than boys to have spoken to their mothers, and indeed, were more likely than boys to have spoken to their fathers about more than half the topics.

But what is really very striking is that, according to the teenagers, 43 per cent had never spoken to their mothers about *any* of these topics—58 per cent of the boys and 31 per cent of the girls—and 72 per cent said they had never spoken to their fathers about any of these topics—with equal proportions of boys and girls. The parents reported a different picture as we shall see, but nevertheless this finding cannot be ignored. The question of whether it is better or more appropriate or desirable that children receive sex education from their parents must be seen against the background of the finding

Table 24 *Proportion of teenagers reporting having learned anything or talked to parent(s) about topic*

Column percentages

| | *Mothers* | | | *Fathers* | | |
	Total	Boys	Girls	Total	Boys	Girls
Animal reproduction	10	3	15	3	0	7
Human reproduction	28	14	39	7	6	8
Sexual intercourse	28	19	36	9	12	6
Pregnancy & childbirth	37	20	51	6	5	8
Changes in a girl's body	35	9	57	5	1	8
Changes in a boy's body	18	19	17	6	9	2
Family and parenthood	25	15	34	10	8	13
Personal relationships	27	18	35	11	12	10
Guidelines on sexual behaviour	10	4	14	4	2	6
Contraception/birth control	26	15	35	10	8	13
Masturbation	6	4	7	1	1	1
Venereal disease	12	5	17	6	8	3
Abortion	18	4	30	3	1	6
Homosexuality/Lesbianism	10	7	12	6	6	6
None of these topics	43	58	31	72	72	72
Base—teenagers living with parent or seeing frequently	(198)	(91)	(107)	(173)	(86)	(87)

that over 40 per cent of teenagers said that they had *never* talked to their mother and nearly three-quarters said that they had *never* talked to their father about *any* of the topics in Table 24. And these were teenagers living with their mothers or fathers or seeing them frequently.

Looking in more detail at the individual topics, the reported lack of communication between parents and their children is perhaps even more striking. Pregnancy and childbirth was the topic said to be discussed most often with mothers, but even so, only 37 per cent of the teenagers mentioned it, and it must be thought fairly surprising that only half the girls said that they had talked about it to their mothers. The topic discussed next most often was changes in a girl's body as she grows up, discussed by nearly 60 per cent of the girls with their mothers, but by only 9 per cent of the boys.

Then there comes a little set of topics which might be said to cover similar ground—human reproduction, sexual intercourse, family and parenthood, personal relationships and contraception. But even so only around a quarter of the teenagers said that they had discussed these topics with their mothers, with girls far more likely to have done so than boys. Eighteen per cent of the teenagers said they had discussed abortion with their mothers, and it is interesting that nearly a third of the girls said they had, while 18 per cent of teenagers said they had discussed changes in a boy's body with their mothers—nearly equal proportions of boys and girls.

Around 10 per cent of the teenagers said they had discussed venereal disease, animal reproduction, homosexuality and guidelines on sexual behaviour with their mothers, again with girls reporting more contact than boys on these subjects. And finally only 6 per cent of the teenagers said that they had ever discussed masturbation with their mothers. There are some subjects which are clearly felt to be taboo by teenagers.

The proportions reporting conversations with fathers about these topics follow roughly the same pattern but at a very much lower level, and the fact remains that *no more than* 11 per cent of the teenagers said they had discussed any individual topic with their fathers—and that was personal relationships.

It is perhaps not surprising that the teenagers tended to report more often conversations with parents about matters like pregnancy and childbirth and changes in girls' bodies at puberty, which could be argued to be non-controversial and fairly factual. But what is surprising is that so few reported any conversations on guidelines on sexual behaviour. There was no evidence that the teenagers did not know what we meant, particularly since we had taken them through this list of topics several times before in the interview. It was followed by a question on contraception and birth control and preceded by a question on personal relationships, and in both cases nearly three times as many teenagers reported conversations with both mother and father. It simply appeared that very few teenagers remembered any conversations with parents giving them guidance about sexual behaviour.

We asked the parents whether they had ever discussed any of the topics with the teenage son or daughter we interviewed, and then we asked them whether the other parent had discussed these topics. Table 25 shows that parents reported far more discussion than their children, but even so, there was little indication that the majority of parents discussed these topics, and, indeed, over a quarter of our sample of parents said that they had never discussed *any* of the topics with the teenager—over a fifth of the mothers and nearly 40 per cent of the fathers.

Even though a much higher proportion of parents said they had discussed these topics with their children than was reported by the teenagers, nevertheless the table is striking in that only two topics were said even by mothers to have been discussed by more than 50 per cent of them—and these were pregnancy and childbirth and changes in a girl's body. This pattern reflects the evidence of the teenagers, who also said that these two topics were the most likely to have been discussed with mothers. Nevertheless, although it seems almost inconceivable that more mothers had not discussed

Table 25 *Proportion of parents reporting discussing topics with teenager son or daughter*

Column percentages

	Total	Mothers	Fathers
Animal reproduction	37	38	37
Human reproduction	44	48	35
Sexual intercourse	38	44	24
Pregnancy and childbirth	54	61	38
Changes in a girl's body	46	54	25
Changes in a boy's body	33	35	29
Family and parenthood	45	46	41
Personal relationships	39	42	33
Guidelines on sexual behaviour	42	44	38
Contraception/birth control	36	40	25
Masturbation	9	9	10
Venereal disease	37	40	30
Abortion	32	36	24
Homosexuality/Lesbianism	30	30	30
None of these	26	21	37
(Base—all parents)	(212)	(149)	(63)

these particular topics, less than half the mothers said they had discussed any of the other topics. Between 40 and 50 per cent said they had discussed the group of topics of human reproduction, sexual intercourse, family and parenthood, personal relationships and contraception which their teenage children also reported as the next most frequently discussed topics. However, mothers were more likely than their children to say that they had discussed venereal disease and guidelines on sexual behaviour. Even if their children had not noticed it, the mothers felt that they had discussed it. The one thing they were in more or less total agreement with their children about was that very few of them had discussed masturbation.

Considering how little teenagers reported conversation with their fathers about any of these topics, fathers reported a great deal, although less than mothers. Some of the discrepancies between their accounts and those of the teenagers were very marked, with 38 per cent of the fathers saying that they had talked about guidelines on sexual behaviour, compared with 4 per cent of the teenagers who recalled any such conversation with their fathers, and 38 per cent of fathers saying they had discussed pregnancy and childbirth, compared with 6 per cent of the teenagers. When we looked at the congruence between the answers of the teenagers and their parents in the 205 cases where we interviewed both parents and teenagers, we found confirmation that parents were much more likely to recall conversations on these topics than their children were. We found more agreement between mothers and teenagers than between fathers and teenagers. Fathers, it appeared, were more likely than mothers to recall conversations on these topics which the teenagers did not recall.

But the main message from these tables concerned with discussion of topics which might come under the broad umbrella of 'sex education', is that, in the majority of cases, both parents and teenagers say that no conversation or discussion on particular topics took place between them. Parents are not often seen by their teenage children as people with whom to discuss these topics, and parents often do not see themselves as the people to educate their children in these matters.

We asked the parents specifically whether they preferred to discuss these things with their teenage children themselves or whether they preferred the school to teach them or whether they preferred their child to learn from both. Eleven per cent of the parents said that they preferred to discuss these things with their children themselves, 27 per cent said they preferred the school to teach them, and 60 per cent said that they thought the teenagers should learn from *both home and school*. We asked those who said they preferred teenagers to learn either from home or school whether they thought this should be about *all* the topics on the card, since our piloting had indicated that parents found some topics, like masturbation, very difficult to discuss with their children. The vast majority who preferred *either* school *or* home said that they meant everything, but a few parents said that, on second thoughts, some topics were perhaps better taught either at school or by themselves.

We asked the parents who said that children should learn about these matters from both home and school whether there were any particular topics they would prefer the school to deal with and any that they would prefer to cover themselves. Over half said that there was nothing in particular that they wished the school to cover rather than themselves, but 20 per cent preferred the school to cover venereal disease and homosexuality and 17 per cent preferred the school to cover masturbation. Around 10 per cent of those who wanted their children to be taught about these matters both at home and at school preferred the school to teach about animal and human reproduction, sexual intercourse, changes at puberty, contraception and abortion. Only a very few preferred the school to cover family and parenthood, personal relationships or guidelines on sexual behaviour rather than themselves, although they were in favour of the school covering these subjects as well as themselves.

If it is remembered that 27 per cent preferred the school to teach *everything*, it is clear that there are certain topics where about half the parents interviewed expressed a preference for the school to educate their children rather than themselves—like masturbation, venereal disease and homosexuality. Nearly 40 per cent preferred the school to cover other topics like reproduction, sexual intercourse, puberty, contraception and abortion. And even topics as close to home as family and parenthood, personal relationships and guidelines on sexual behaviour were thought by about a third of the parents we interviewed to be better taught by the school rather than by themselves.

We asked the parents who thought both home and school should cover sex education whether there were any topics they preferred to teach themselves. Nearly 80 per cent said that there were no particular topics they preferred to cover themselves, but 7 per cent preferred to cover family and parenthood, personal relationships, sexual intercourse and guidelines on sexual behaviour.

It appeared that some parents are more at ease covering topics with which they feel 'at home', rather than topics which might be thought to require more expertise, like reproduction or contraception, or subjects on which they feel they do not know enough, like venereal disease or homosexuality, or subjects on which they feel uncomfortable talking to their own children, like masturbation.

Finally, it should be remembered that only 11 per cent of parents said that they preferred to cover the topics under discussion with their children themselves, and even among these there were some who thought that perhaps there were certain topics which should be covered by the school.

The picture given by the parents was overwhelmingly one of a preference for the school to be involved in the sex education of their teenage children, and in over a quarter of the cases, parents preferred the school to teach their children about *everything* on these topics rather than themselves. This was true of both mothers and fathers and in most areas. It was perhaps particularly striking that a third of the single parents preferred the school to take full responsibility for the sex education of their children, and this was reinforced by further evidence that single parents reported more difficulty in talking to their children about sex than other parents in the sample.

We were interested to see what the teenagers thought of their parents' views on their having sex education at school. We asked about each parent separately, as long as the child had contact with them, and then asked whether they thought their mother had different views from their father.

Seventy-one per cent of teenagers thought their mother approved of their having sex education at school and 63 per cent thought their father did. Only a tiny proportion thought that either parent disapproved, but nearly a fifth did not know what their mothers thought and nearly a quarter did not know what their fathers thought. There was little difference between boys and girls, except that boys were rather more likely to think that their fathers approved than girls were, mainly because more girls said they did not know what their fathers thought.

Why did they think they approved? There were two main reasons. The most important reason, given by nearly 40 per cent of the teenagers who thought they knew the views of their parents, was that their parents wanted them to learn as much as possible on these topics so that they were well-informed and did not make mistakes. The teenagers were often quite explicit

Table 26   *Teenagers' views of what parents thought about their having sex education at school*

Teenager's view	Re Mother	Re Father
Approves strongly	14	15
Approves	57	48
Neither approves nor disapproves	8	10
Disapproves	1	2
Disapproves strongly	1	2
Don't know	17	24
Base: teenagers living with parents or seeing frequently	(202)	(177)

in what they interpreted to be their parents' desire for the school to teach them about risks and to stress the preventive role of sex education, as this 14-year-old boy from the North-East summarised:

> Well it like protects me. . . the diseases and making a lass pregnant and that. They don't want me to make a mess of anyone's life and that. . .

Certainly the teenagers were aware that some parents felt either embarrassed or inadequate in talking to them about these topics and this was the other main reason cited by the teenagers for their parents' approval of their having sex education at school. Both boys and girls recognised their parents' embarrassment, but knew they wanted them to have sex education at school—'. . . so that they know you know the right things without them explaining. . .' was the view of a 15-year-old boy in the North-East, echoed by a 15-year-old Midlands girl—'. . . because they don't like talking about it themselves. . .'—and a 15-year-old girl from the South-West—'because it learns me more about it, and she prefers them to learn me at school than her telling me herself as she gets embarrassed. . .' Some teenagers stressed that their parents preferred them to learn at school than from friends or in the playground, while others said that their parents thought they would take in more if they were taught at school—'. . .because they get it in your head like a lesson and the parents would have to do it if the teacher didn't. . .'

There was certainly a feeling among teenagers that their parents thought that it was the school's proper function to teach these matters, as this 15-year-old boy in the South-West pointed out:

> It's just something we learn at school now, like Maths or English. Well, we've got to learn sometime and I suppose they think it might as well be at school.

And a 16-year-old girl in the North-East summarised the views of a number of teenagers talking about their parents' feelings:

> They just take it for granted that these things are taught at secondary
> school and accept it and that's all. . .

The majority of children thought that their parents shared the same views on
their having sex education at school, but 8 per cent thought they had different views, usually saying that their father was more 'strict' or 'old-
fashioned' than their mother. Teenagers who thought their parents held
different views often found it very difficult to talk to their fathers, like this
15-year-old girl from the South-West:

> I couldn't speak to my dad, but I think my mum would want me to learn
> as much as I can from everywhere. I think my dad would think it was my
> mum's job to tell me and not the school. . .

**Teenagers talking to their parents about things in general, personal problems
and sex**
It was quite clear that many parents did not feel comfortable talking to their
children about sex or contraception or bodily functions with a sexual
connotation, although most of them thought it necessary for their children to
have education on these topics. There was evidence in our interviews of many
close and trusting relationships between parents and their children, and yet
there were obviously topics which both parents and their children found
difficult to discuss. This clearly has far-reaching implications and must affect the extent to which parents feel able to give education on sex and personal relationships and the extent to which teenagers feel comfortable in
receiving such education from their parents. The ecology of a parent-child
relationship is very subtle and complicated, and there was evidence that both
parents and their teenage children felt that discussion of some topics was too
disturbing to be attempted. Relationships between parents and teenagers can
be stormy enough without introducing even more potential points of
embarrassment or disagreement, and it was quite clear from this study that
both parents and teenagers in many cases preferred to avoid the issue.

We therefore asked both parents and teenagers whether the teenager
found it easy to talk to their mother and their father about most things,
about personal problems and about sex.

The first thing to be said about Tables 27 and 28 is that teenagers find it
much easier on the whole to communicate with their mothers than with their
fathers. Girls in particular are more likely to find their mothers easier to
communicate with than their fathers. Looking at the figures in more detail, it
can be seen that the majority of both boys and girls find it easy to talk to their
mothers about most things, but that girls find it easier to talk to their mothers
about personal problems than boys do, and considerably easier to talk to
their mothers about sex than boys do.

As far as fathers are concerned, there is quite a big difference between
boys and girls, with only just over half the girls saying they found it easy to
talk to their fathers about most things compared with nearly 70 per cent of

Table 27 *Teenagers' views of how easy to talk to mother about most things, personal problems and sex*

Column percentages

	Most things			Personal problems			Sex		
	Total	Boys	Girls	Total	Boys	Girls	Total	Boys	Girls
Easy	78	80	77	61	53	69	42	28	55
Not easy	12	9	16	22	26	19	33	41	27
Varies/depends	5	6	5	10	13	7	5	5	5
Don't talk much to her	4	5	3	6	9	5	19	26	13
Base—all teenagers living with mother or seeing frequently	(201)	(93)	(108)	(201)	(93)	(108)	(201)	(93)	(108)

Table 28 *Teenagers' views of how easy to talk to father about most things, personal problems and sex*

Column percentages

	Most things			Personal problems			Sex		
	Total	Boys	Girls	Total	Boys	Girls	Total	Boys	Girls
Easy	61	69	53	36	39	33	21	26	15
Not easy	28	23	33	43	36	51	51	41	60
Varies/depends	4	2	6	8	13	3	3	5	2
Don't talk much to him	7	6	8	13	13	13	25	28	23
Base—all teenagers living with father or seeing frequently	(175)	(87)	(88)	(175)	(87)	(88)	(175)	(87)	(88)

the boys. However, only 39 per cent of boys found it easy to talk to their fathers about personal problems compared with a third of the girls, and only 15 per cent of the girls found it easy to talk to their father about sex, compared with just over a quarter of the boys.

The boys did not find it easy to talk to either parent about sex, with only 28 per cent finding it easy to talk to their mothers about sex, whereas over half the girls found it easy.

So why did the teenagers find it difficult to talk to their parents about sex? The main reason that they gave was that they were too embarrassed. Nearly a third of those who did not find it easy to talk to their mothers gave this as the main reason, and this was particularly true of boys. They often found it difficult to explain, like this 16-year-old boy in the South-West—'I feel pretty embarrassed about it. Just talking about it to my parents embarrasses me. . .'—and it was striking how often boys used the words 'embarrassing' or 'embarrassed' to describe their reluctance to talk about sex to either parent, like this 16-year-old in the Midlands—'I'd rather talk to friends. I find it embarrassing discussing these things with my mother. . .'

Certainly there were boys who found it difficult to talk to a woman—'She's the opposite sex isn't she?'—while others preferred to talk to their fathers—'. . . because I'd rather talk to a man about it than a woman. . .'—and some thought mothers might not understand—'. . . because she's a woman and it wouldn't be right to talk about *men's* problems. . .'

But there were other boys who did not see it as their parents' role to talk about these things at all—particularly not their mother's, like this 15-year-old from the South-West:

> We get taught at school, so I ask the biology teacher. The biology teacher puts things straight and mum and dad may not know all the answers, and mum tends to go on a bit. . .

Among both the boys and the girls there was a small group who never seemed to find their mother on her own to talk to, like this 15-year-old boy—'I don't see her all that much really. She's usually busy. . .'

But the girls who did not find it easy to talk to their mother about sex were rather more likely to say that it just had not come up or that they did not talk much to their mothers in any case—'I've never talked to her about it so I don't really know. . .'—while there were instances of poor relationships—'She just wouldn't understand, and he wouldn't understand either. . .'

So what about father? The main reason given by the girls was that they preferred to talk to their mother or to a woman. There was considerable evidence of good relationships between mothers and their daughters, which often seemed to exclude father, like this one described by a 15-year-old girl in the North-East:

> I haven't got a close relationship with my dad on that side. I've never had any need to talk to him. I always talk to my mum. . .

There was evidence that girls felt that their fathers would not understand their feelings—'It's the sort of thing you take to your mum. I expect her to know more what I'm talking about. . .'—There was certainly evidence of a female camaraderie to which men were not admitted, which was curious to hear so often from these teenage girls—'I've just always talked to mum about things like that. I think it's because mum is the same sex as me and understands more about me than dad would. . .'

But boys too often found their mothers easier to talk to, like this 16-year-old boy in the Midlands:

It's easier to talk to mother. I just never associate him with talking too much. He's not a gorilla or mean—but we don't talk. . .

Some boys found their fathers talked too much—'He's the one who does the talking usually. . .'—while others found they did not talk enough—'I just don't talk to him. I've never tried and he doesn't talk to me about anything much. . .'

Again there was evidence of some rather strained relationships and evidence of cultural problems from a Muslim girl—'His views are different from mine. It's not thought the girl's place to think like that. I can talk to him about my school and religion but not other personal things. . .'

There was also quite a lot of evidence of fathers being more preoccupied with their work than their family life, as summarised by this daughter of a doctor:

We don't find it easy to talk to each other—full-stop. He doesn't get involved. He's more work than family orientated. He's reached a high position and lost all communication with my brother and me. . .

There was also some evidence of a total lack of contact particularly with girls—'I don't know. He's Scottish and got strong views about things like that and doesn't talk about sex and bodies in front of women. . .'—while a 14-year-old in the South-West summarised the poorness of some relationships between fathers and their daughters—'I don't know. He's just weird. We've got different views on everything. I can't say anything to him. . .'—and another 14-year-old girl in the same area said—'He doesn't want to hear anything about me. . .'

The sensitivity of teenagers was not always recognised, it appeared, and some fathers did not always know how to treat their teenage children's developing sexuality, as this 16-year-old boy said of his father—'Friends are better. He takes the mickey out of me and says have I got a girlfriend?'

And a 15-year-old boy in another area was equally worried about his mother—'I don't know why really—just that she's female, and she's a wee bit daft about it—she would take the piss out of me. . .'—and fathers with a sense of humour were not always appreciated by their sons in particular—'I'm embarrassed. Dad's not really. He can joke on— but I don't know where to look. . .'

Table 29   *Parents' views of how easy teenager found it to talk to them about most things, personal problems and sex*

Column percentages

	Most things			Personal problems			Sex		
	Total	Mothers	Fathers	Total	Mothers	Fathers	Total	Mothers	Fathers
Easy	78	78	79	53	60	37	42	46	33
Not easy	12	11	14	24	16	41	33	31	40
Varies/depends	4	5	3	14	13	14	8	7	10
Doesn't talk much to me	5	6	3	9	9	8	16	15	17
Base—all parents	(212)	(149)	(63)	(212)	(149)	(63)	(212)	(149)	(63)

And there certainly seemed to be a complete breakdown of communication between parents and their children sometimes, as epitomised by this 15-year-old boy—'He doesn't understand me. He talks different from me. I can't understand the way he talks. It's mumbo jumbo. . .'

So what did parents feel about this? How easy did *they* think their teenage children found it to talk to them about things in general, about personal problems and about sex?

Table 29 shows that the proportions of parents saying that their teenage children found it easy to talk to them about most things, personal problems and sex, were, on the face of it, very similar to the proportions of teenagers saying that they found it easy to talk to their parents, with, for example, 78 per cent of teenagers saying that they found it easy to talk to their parents about most things reflected by 78 per cent of parents saying that their children found it easy to talk to them about most things. Fifty-three per cent of the parents said their children found it easy to talk to them about personal problems compared with 61 per cent of the teenagers who said they found it easy. And 42 per cent of the samples of both parents and teenagers said that they found it easy to talk about sex. However, these figures concealed differences between the sexes, with boys and fathers considerably less likely to think it was easy to talk about both sex and personal problems than girls and mothers.

We looked more closely at the relationships of the parent respondents with the teenager we interviewed, and Table 30 shows the differences between mothers and fathers when we asked them how easy they thought their son or daughter found it to talk to them about the various topics.

Table 30   *Parents' views of how easy teenager found it to talk to them by relationship with teenager*

Column percentages

	Most things easy	Personal problems easy	Sex easy
Relationship			
Total parents/teenagers	79	54	43
Mother/son	85	57	42
Mother/daughter	74	65	53
Father/son	79	39	33
Father/daughter	81	31	35
Mother/teenager	79	61	48
Father/teenager	80	36	34
Base—all parents where teenager also interviewed	(205)	(205)	(205)

As the girls had reported, the mother/daughter relationship appeared to be the one in which the teenager found it easiest to talk to a parent. On the whole both parents and teenagers thought that teenagers found it easy to talk to both their mothers and fathers about most things, and our analysis of the congruence of the answers indicates that parents and teenagers in the same family tended to agree on this more than on a number of issues. Nevertheless it was not always so, and in over a quarter of cases, parents and teenagers gave different answers to this question.

Fathers clearly felt that the teenagers found it less easy to talk to them about sex and personal relationships than to their mothers, but they certainly underestimated the extent to which teenagers found it difficult to talk to them about sex. Only just over 20 per cent of the teenagers said that they found it easy to talk to their fathers about sex, compared with just over a third of the fathers who said their children found it easy.

Looking in more detail at the congruence in teenager and parent views on whether they found it easy to talk to their father or mother about sex, mothers clearly overestimated the extent to which their sons found it easy, and fathers definitely overestimated the extent to which their sons and daughters could talk to them about sex, in spite of the fact that a third of the father/teenager pairs agreed that it was not easy.

So why did the parents think that the teenagers found it difficult to talk to them about sex? We have seen that the main reason given by the teenagers was that they were too embarrassed, and this was also the main reason given by their parents. Some teenagers were thought to be too reserved or shy about such matters, as this mother said about her 16-year-old son:

He thinks you'll judge him no matter how open you are—or think you are. They think 'mother will interfere'. . .

Both fathers and mothers thought that teenagers were too embarrassed or reserved about the subject. Some parents tried to talk to them, without much success, like this father of a 14-year-old boy:

He just doesn't talk on the subject of sex and if I pull him up about it he says, 'It's nothing to do with you—that's my business'. If I want to talk about it he always says he's in a hurry or has to go somewhere with a friend.

The lack of congruence between the answers of the parents and those of the teenagers was not always due to the parents saying the teenagers found it easy to talk to them but the teenager disagreeing, as this mother of a 16-year-old girl illustrated. Her daughter said she found it easy to talk to her mother about sex, but her mother thought she did not:

. . . because I don't get any response. Basically she just doesn't talk about these things—anything—not just sex. I think she's one of these people who finds it more difficult to talk to her parents than other people, but I don't know why. . .

Nearly 10 per cent of the parents who thought the teenager found it difficult to talk to them about sex said the child was too young. This was particularly true of mothers of 14-year-old boys, like this one:

> His mind doesn't grasp things like this. I don't know—he's young for his age—a Peter Pan you would call him. . .

And some mothers preferred their sons to remain like that:

> I don't feel that he's old enough. He's a young 14. To me he's still a child. He still goes out to play. I don't want him to grow up. I don't feel people let kids be kids for long enough. Nothing has cropped up yet that he's needed to talk to us about. . .

We asked the interviewers to give an assessment of the teenager's maturity at the end of the interview. In many cases the assessment confirmed the views of parents, but there were clearly some 'Peter Pans' who were considerably more mature than their parents imagined as our interviews with them indicated.

Some parents were worried about their child's maturity for other reasons, like this mother of a 14-year-old girl who said that she thought her daughter had difficulties in talking about sex:

> It's because of the large age gap between her and her boyfriend. It's because she's under age for sex. If she was sleeping with her boyfriend I don't want to know. I disapprove, but as long as they are doing things to avoid getting pregnant I don't want to know. We do discuss personal problems but we never discuss whether she's having sex. . .

Sometimes parents found it embarrassing themselves:

> He doesn't talk much about sex. I would find it very difficult. I'm old-fashioned and can't discuss things like that. I'm lost for words. . .

And parents from the Indian sub-continent had particular difficulties, like this father of a 15-year-old girl:

> I suppose it's maybe because of my mental attitude, being from India. Maybe I'm more restricted on that score than the English gentleman is—particularly with a daughter. It is a delicate point. . .

But some parents were not at all concerned that their teenage children found it difficult to talk about sex to them, like this father of a 14-year-old boy—'It's not taboo in this house but it's not something we talk about much. Life goes along very nicely—we have no pregnant daughters here. . .'—while others felt it was not necessary, like this father—'Partly because we never discuss it with him. We're not a family to discuss such matters. We just leave it to the school. . .'

We asked the parent whether the teenager found it easy to talk to the other parent about most things, personal problems and sex, and as seemed predictable by this time, fathers were much more likely to say that teenagers found it easy to talk to mothers about all these matters than mothers were to say the same about teenagers and fathers. There were a variety of reasons, with the teenager's embarrassment mentioned most often. Certainly there was thought by many of the mothers to be a distinct barrier between daughters and their fathers on the subject of sex:

> The natural barriers are there between father and daughter. I think he would find it harder than her. I don't think she would bother. . .

But there were also thought to be difficulties between fathers and sons on the subject of sex, and another mother in another area also used the word 'barrier' to describe the nature of the relationship between her son and her husband:

> There's a barrier between the two, probably because my husband came from a home where the subject wasn't talked about. It's always 'ask your mum'—unless I specifically ask him to discuss something with him, and then he'll make an effort. . .

Other fathers thought that boys found it difficult to talk to their mothers about certain subjects, like this father of a 15-year-old boy:

> Well, it's not so easy for a boy to talk to his mother about things like masturbation for instance. He can always talk to me. . .

Some mothers reinforced the views of some of the teenagers in talking about their fathers, like this mother of a 16-year-old girl—'Well he is totally wrapped up in his work and just really doesn't give her enough time. . .'— while other parents were faced with a blank wall with their teenage children—'She just doesn't talk to anybody. It's like getting blood out of a stone sometimes. . .'

Parents talking to teenagers about sex, contraception and personal relationships

We asked the parents whether they themselves had ever had any difficulty in talking about sex, contraception or personal relationships to their teenage son or daughter, since this could clearly have influenced whether their child found it easy to talk to them. We were also interested to know to what extent the parents felt comfortable in giving education on these matters to their teenage children.

Twenty-seven per cent of parents interviewed had either had some difficulty or expected some difficulty in talking to their teenage children about sex, with fathers more likely to find or expect some difficulty than mothers. Just under a quarter of parents had either found or expected difficulty in talking to their teenage children about contraception, and 14 per cent had found or expected difficulty in talking about personal relationships.

In this question we were asking the parents about their own particular

Table 31 *Parents' assessment of difficulty in talking to teenager about sex, contraception or personal relationships*

	About sex			About contraception			About personal relationships		
	Total	Mothers	Fathers	Total	Mothers	Fathers	Total	Mothers	Fathers
Had some difficulty	18	18	17	6	7	5	6	5	6
Has no difficulty	63	67	54	43	48	32	69	69	68
Hasn't come up yet:									
Expect difficulty	9	7	13	17	15	19	8	9	5
Expect no difficulty	6	4	10	26	22	37	10	9	13
Don't know how it will be	4	3	6	7	7	8	7	7	8
Base—all parents	(212)	(149)	(63)	(212)	(149)	(63)	(212)	(149)	(63)

experience with the teenager we were interviewing. From Table 31 it can be seen that nearly 70 per cent of parents said that they had no difficulty or expected no difficulty in talking to the teenager about sex, even though only 43 per cent of parents in general thought the teenager found it easy to talk to *them* about sex (see Table 30), and it must be remembered that only a third of fathers thought their teenage children found it easy to talk to them about sex, compared with nearly half the mothers.

What made so many parents so sure that they themselves had no difficulty in talking to the teenage children about sex, contraception or personal relationships? The main reason, given by nearly a quarter of the parents when talking about sex, was that the home atmosphere was open, that the parents themselves were outgoing and that the children had been brought up to regard the subject as 'natural' and acceptable. And this explanation was given by a third of the parents when explaining why they found or expected no difficulty when talking to the teenagers about contraception or personal relationships. Parents often backed up this general assessment of the 'open' and 'natural' family atmosphere with the observation that the relationship between them and the teenager in question was close and trusting and that they found it easy to discuss anything with them, as this mother of a 16-year-old girl explained:

> We've always been able to talk naturally about these things. They aren't considered anything special . . .

And her view was reinforced by the father of a 16-year-old boy:

> We've always been close ever since he was a baby, and he's known that I won't laugh at him . . .

Many parents put a lot of stress on the strength of the 'family group' in creating an atmosphere in which there were no 'taboo' areas and sex was a matter which could be discussed as naturally and openly as any other, as this mother of a 15-year-old boy pointed out:

> I have no difficulty, probably because we're just open about it. If he wants to know anything we just talk about it and tell him. If any bedroom scenes come on television we don't send him off. We just let him sit and watch . . .

The use of the word 'open' in describing their family life was striking among many of the parents who said they found no difficulty in talking to their teenager children about these matters, as pointed out again by this father of a 15-year-old girl:

> We are a very open family and don't hide things from them. They all know the wife and I bath together and that families should be close . . .

Some parents stressed that they made a point of being 'open' with their children because of their own upbringing in which sex had been a taboo subject, like this mother of a 15-year-old girl—'I've always been open with her. My own stepmother would never mention it and I suffered agonies as a teenager . . .'

Some parents felt that it was important to have established a good base in answering their children's questions when they were younger, but acknowledged that teenage children sometimes found it difficult to talk to their parents even if the parents did not find it difficult to talk to them, like this father of a 16-year-old girl:

> She asked a lot of questions when she was very young and got straight answers when my wife was pregnant. Since then we haven't talked much. When they get to the age of puberty they decide which parent they want to ask the questions . . .

So why did parents find it difficult to talk to the teenagers about sex? Sometimes it appeared that their attitude might put the teenager off, like this mother of a 16-year-old boy—'I say if he gets a girl pregnant I'll kill him, but he doesn't tell me much or ask me anything . . .' or like this father of a 15-year-old girl—'I try to explain things to her. I don't want her messing about with boys before she marries, or I'll shoot the lot . . .'

But the main reason that parents found it difficult was related to shyness or embarrassment on the part of the teenager or of the parent or sometimes of both, as this mother of a 15-year-old girl pointed out:

> She's never really asked me anything. I feel she'd rather ask her friends. We can't talk to each other. You see, I'm shy and her dad's shy and she's shy too . . .

Parents were very wary about moving in on their children's private development, however close the relationship, and many parents recognised that the teenager in question was different from brothers and sisters, as this mother of a 14-year-old girl with an older brother and sister observed:

> She just giggles. She won't even talk about her periods and she washes her own knickers and doesn't ever talk to her sister about anything. When she had chicken-pox she wouldn't even let me rub anything on her back. She's a very funny girl. . .

And it was not only girls who were 'funny' as this mother of a 15-year-old boy pointed out:

> He's so shy—a funny type of kid and blushes up straight away—so we can never really talk. I think he wants to talk about it but just can't make himself . . .

It is important to acknowledge individual differences among different children and to recognise that parents may find it easy to talk to one child but not to another, as this mother of a 14-year-old boy pointed out:

> It depends on the child. I find it very easy to talk to my daughter, but I

wait for my son to ask. You know what you're trying to say, but it's difficult to put it into words, especially if it relates to your own personal relationship with your husband . . .

There can be no doubt that many parents find it difficult to talk to their children about sex in a way which does not bring into the open their own sexuality. Some find it particularly difficult with teenagers as they observe the teenagers' own emerging sexuality, but few parents found it easy to put the problem into words. This mother of a 15-year-old girl summarised the views of many:

It's embarrassing when they're older. It's easier to talk when they're younger. Some things are difficult to talk about. You can't go deeply into these things with them . . .

It was quite clear that parents were aware that their teenage children were often embarrassed at the thought that their parents might have a sexual relationship, as this father observed—'The biggest difficulty is the child's own embarrassment. Today's youngsters seem to think they invented sex and parents don't know anything about it . . .'

And there was no doubt that some parents found it easier to talk about certain things rather than others, like this father of a 15-year-old boy:

I think it's embarrassing to talk about sexual intercourse and masturbation. Contraception can be difficult too. You just can't mention these things in passing to a child . . .

It certainly appeared that some teenagers had spotted the fact that their parents found difficulty in talking to them about sex, as their parents observed, like this father of a 15-year-old boy from the North-East—'They get embarrassed and walk out of the room if I start talking about these things . . .' and his view was reinforced by another father of a 15-year-old boy—'The children are always in a hurry to run off and do things with their friends. My son would probably change the subject and say, I know all about that!'.

We were certainly given the picture of some parents absolutely bursting to talk to their children about sex, contraception and personal relationships only to find a disappearing audience, like this mother of a 15-year-old girl—'My problem is she seems to know and doesn't want to be told, and I've got too much to say and no-one to say it to . . .'

But we also had some glimpses of family life which were far from happy, and there can be no doubt that some parents found it very difficult to talk to their teenage children about these matters because of particular circumstances, like this mother of a 14-year-old girl:

Yes I find it difficult because of the experience we had with my first husband who committed incest with my eldest daughter. She tends to speak to one particular sister . . .

Parents were rather less likely to find it difficult or potentially difficult to talk about contraception to their teenage children, although, as can be seen from Table 31, it was less likely to have been discussed with the child than sex. Mothers were often very frank in their reasons for wanting to discuss contraception, particularly with their daughters, and prevention of unwanted teenage pregnancy was uppermost in the minds of many mothers, like this mother of a 15-year-old girl:

> I didn't want her to grow up ignorant like I did. Most of her friends have had sex at an early age and I didn't want it to happen to her . . .

As other studies have shown, mothers are often actively concerned with their daughter's contraceptive practice, as this mother of a 16-year-old girl indicated—'I told her that if she wanted to go on the pill I'd go to the doctor and see about it for her . . .'—and there was evidence of close mother-daughter discussion of contraception and birth control—'She has seen me taking the pill so it will be a lot easier to talk about . . .'

Certainly there was also evidence of some fairly robust parental guidance as far as contraception and teenage pregnancy was concerned. The present author's study of counselling in connection with termination of pregnancy[18] indicated that mothers were often very much involved in putting pressure on teenage girls to have a termination of pregnancy, and this study also showed that some mothers made it quite clear to their daughters that pregnancy would not be acceptable, like this Roman Catholic mother of a 15-year-old girl:

> She doesn't like the idea of abortion, but I've told her the Church isn't going to dictate to me about having children, and if she's pregnant at 15 she will have to have an abortion. I'm not having her life ruined with a baby, when she's only a child herself. It would hurt me, mind—I wouldn't like it, but I'd have it done. If when she is 16 she has a permanent boyfriend I will get her on the pill . . .

But as far as talking about personal relationships was concerned, most parents felt considerably more comfortable, as this mother of a 15-year-old girl explained—'It's a different thing isn't it? It's not to do with sex . . .' Nevertheless, 14 per cent of parents, with rather more mothers than fathers surprisingly, still felt that it was difficult or potentially difficult to talk to their teenage children about personal relationships, and this fact should not be forgotten when it is advocated that parents should take the full responsibility for educating their children about sex and personal relationships.

We were aware that parents might say that they themselves did not find it difficult to talk to the teenager we were interviewing even if in fact they did not find it quite as easy as they said they did. They certainly often seemed to be aware of the difficulties of communication with the teenager about sex in that so many of them admitted that the teenager found it difficult to talk to them. Towards the end of the interview we asked the parents whether they thought that in general parents had any particular difficulty in giving sex education to their children. It can be seen from Table 32 that parents were much more likely to say that parents in general had difficulty in giving sex education to teenagers than that they themselves had difficulty. However, it was quite clear that in answering this question many were talking about their own experiences. It should also be remembered that we asked them in this question about sex *education* rather than 'talking about sex', as we had in the earlier question.

Table 32   *Parents' views on whether parents in general have difficulty in giving sex education to their children*

Column percentages

	Total	Mothers	Fathers
Yes—parents have difficulty	62	64	59
No- parents do not have difficulty	14	14	13
Depends/varies	24	22	28
Base—all parents	(212)	(149)	(63)

The overwhelming reason for difficulty encountered by parents in general in giving sex education to their children was said to be embarrassment on the part of the parents. This was thought to be the case by 43 per cent of the total sample of parents, while 16 per cent thought that parents might not know *how* to give sex education since they did not know enough themselves or did not know how to put it over to teenagers. The two answers often came together.

We have already seen that parents found it difficult to talk to their own children about sex in spite of the fact that so many stressed that they had a good and open relationship with their children. It was quite clear that a lot of parents felt embarrassed because they did not know how to go about it. This mother of a 14-year-old boy spoke for many—'A lot of parents get embarrassed and don't know how to discuss it. They're lost for the right words and don't know what to say or how to say it . . .' Her stress on the 'right words' was echoed time and again in interviews with parents, and some parents did not know how to cope, like this mother of a 16-year-old girl who said what she found difficult—'Well—trying to explain things a nice way without being vulgar and crude . . .' Mothers in particular emphasised the problem of putting over the 'facts' as well as emotions, like this mother of a 15-year-old boy:

> It's difficult just talking to them without making it look dirty or anything. I don't know how to start even, when I never learned it myself. I can't teach my children. I don't know how to put it over, and that's why I prefer it to be done for me. My husband wouldn't even consider it . . .

Some parents were very much aware that their children might know more than they did, and their embarrassment was related to the possibility that they might 'lose face' if they tried to discuss sex with their teenage children, like this mother of a 15-year-old girl:

> Most of the time children learn from each other and can put parents on the spot. It makes it difficult for parents to communicate with a child. It was easier in my day. Kids today would fall over laughing—because they already know the answers—at some of the parents' attempts to explain

Some parents saw that there was a potential danger in assuming that teenager children knew 'the answers', but did not know how to tackle talking to the children themselves. There was little doubt that many parents were very thankful that their children were apparently receiving sex education at school, like this mother of a 15-year-old boy:

> The vast majority of parents would prefer the school to teach it. Parents find it difficut to use the right language. Perhaps they don't know the correct language themselves. People just don't talk about sex. They are embarrassed. We're very inhibited as a race . . .

Certainly many parents acknowledged that parents could have difficulty in talking to their chidren about sex not only because of their own lack of knowledge but also because of the way they were brought up and their own inability to communicate, as this mother of a 14-year-old girl pointed out— 'Some parents can't talk about things like sex even to each other, so they can't help their children when they ask questions . . .'—and it was certainly stressed that the family background of many of the parents and their own lack of sex education from their own parents inhibited them from speaking freely to their children, as this mother of a 15-year-old boy pointed out:

> They feel embarrassed talking to the children. They can't communicate with their children about anything else—let alone sex. It stems back to their parents. It was all hushed up at one time . . .

Sometimes in reading the interviews with these parents it is difficult to realise that they were mainly men and women in their thirties and forties who were therefore at secondary school in the 1950s and 1960s. Their description of their own sex education both from parents and school, as we shall see, sometimes appeared more reminiscent of the nineteenth century than the latter part of the twentieth century, and many felt that it had given them little help or preparation for giving education in sex and personal relationships to their own teenage children, as this mother of a 15-year-old boy in the North-East summarised:

> It's more embarrassment than anything else. I don't know how to talk about it really. I just can't bring myself to discuss it. I was taught to keep quiet about things like that when I was young . . .

Some parents thought that parents who found it difficult just could not communicate with their children or were in some way lacking in good 'parental qualities'. But it was fairly surprising that only five per cent of the respondents thought that it was mainly parents who were 'uncaring' who had difficulties in giving sex education to their children, and comments like the following from the mother of a 16-year-old girl were uncommon—'They must find difficulty. Some parents couldn't care less or there wouldn't be so many unmarried mothers, divorces and abortions and diseases . . .'

But 14 per cent of the sample thought that parents in general did *not* have difficulty in giving sex education to their children and a quarter thought that it depended on the circumstances or varied according to the parents and children. There was considerable stress on the greater 'openness' of society today which, it was felt, gave parents many more opportunities for bringing the subject up in a 'natural' way, as this mother of a 16-year-old pointed out:

> It's easier today than when my mother told me. Television does help if you can watch the programmes with your children. It gives them permission to discuss it with you and you can give your views . . .

Some parents said in answer to this question that it was easier for parents to give sex education to their children today because of the part played by schools and some parents stressed what they saw as a partnership between home and school in ensuring that children received a balanced education in sex and personal relationships, as this father of a 14-year-old girl pointed out:

> Kiddies are well grounded in basics at school. Initial discussion which can be embarrassing is got over quickly because the child already knows a certain amount . . .

As we shall see, this was a theme which was developed considerably when we asked parents what they felt about the relative responsibilities of school and parents in giving sex education.

And a mother of a 14-year-old boy thought that many parents had no difficulty in giving sex education to their children—'If they are young parents they will have had sex lessons at school so they will know what to say . . .'

But, as we have seen, the majority of parents did not feel that it was so easy and there was overwhelming evidence that our respondents thought that parents in general still had considerable difficulty in giving sex education to their children.

The sex education of parents

It was quite clear throughout the interviews with parents that their own experience of sex education, or rather, their own lack of sex education, had made many of them determined that their own children should not grow up with such little knowledge about sex and personal relationships and bodily functions. We asked the parents how they would rate the sex education they themselves had had at school and from their own parents when young.

Table 33   *Parents' rating of own sex education when young*

Column percentages

| | *From school* | | | *From parents* | | |
	Total	Mothers	Fathers	Total	Mothers	Fathers
Very good	2	1	5	6	7	2
Fairly good	7	9	2	9	9	10
Not very good	9	11	5	14	13	16
Very poor	28	29	27	17	18	13
None given	53	50	61	54	52	59
Base all parents	(212)	(149)	(63)	(212)	(149)	(63)

Table 33 indicates the very low esteem in which the vast majority of parents interviewed held the sex education they had been given both at school and by their parents when young. If it is a matter of concern that over 80 per cent of these parents, most of whom had been at secondary schools in the 1950s and 1960s, said that their school sex education had either been non-existent or very poor, it must also be a cause for concern that over 70 per cent said the same about the sex education they had received from their parents. Only 7 per cent of the parents interviewed thought their school sex education was even 'fairly good' with only 2 per cent rating it 'very good'. They felt much the same about the sex education they received from their parents, with only 9 per cent rating it 'fairly good' and only 6 per cent rating it 'very good'.

We asked the parents whether they had ever wished that they had been given more or better sex education when they had been young, and 57 per cent said that they wished that they had. There was an interesting difference between the men and women, however, with 63 per cent of the mothers saying that they would have liked better sex education when young, compared with only 41 per cent of the fathers. We asked the parents whether they would have liked this sex education from parents, school or both. Just over a quarter said they would have liked more from their parents, just over 40 per cent said they would have liked more at school, while 30 per cent said they would have liked more from both home and school. The men were more likely to have wanted more from school, and the women more likely to have wanted more from their parents.

We asked them what they would have liked to have known more about, and in what way. There was astonishing evidence from women of lack of knowledge about the most basic facts of life, including menstruation. Over 10 per cent of the women said that they had known little or nothing about periods, and for some women, the onset of menstruation had been a traumatic experience, as this 34-year-old mother illustrated:

> I remember when I started menstruating, mother said nothing. I was horrified and shocked. I thought I was bleeding to death. No-one ever said anything. I thought I was turning into an ape when I grew hairs and I thought my vagina was deformed . . .

A mother of 42 in the Midlands gave an equally alarming picture of life in the 1950s:

> My generation went into it with their eyes shut. We were never told anything. The first girl to start her periods screamed blue murder. She thought she was dying . . .

If there was very little indication that all parents could be relied upon in the 1950s and 1960s to give their children even the basic minimum of information, there was also evidence of misinformation being given within the family circle, causing distress, as this 35-year-old mother pointed out:

> I'd like to have been taught all the things they are taught now. My periods were late and I had one aunt who said I must be pregnant, so I had to go to the doctor, but I'd never even been with a boy. I didn't know what happened . . .

There was certainly evidence from our respondents that they would have preferred more sex education from school rather than from their parents since they were not confident that their parents were well-equipped for the task, as this mother aged 33 in the North-East illustrated:

> They told us nothing at school. I remember seeing a film about a woman having a baby, but they never told us anything about contraception and nothing about VD. My mother was so naive that she thought that babies breathed through your tummy button even after she'd had two children. She thought that if you plastered a penny over your tummy button you wouldn't get pregnant again as it stopped the baby getting air. . .

Over a fifth of the mothers interviewed said that they knew *nothing at all* about sex in their teenage, and there was considerable evidence that many of them felt that this ignorance had adversely affected their lives. There were bitter comments from some of the mothers, like this 34-year-old mother of a 15-year-old — 'I wish we'd been told about how to stop from having babies until we were more mature . . .'—and this 45-year-old mother from the South-West—'If I'd known more about babies—getting pregnant—more detail—perhaps I wouldn't have got into trouble. I had a baby before I got married . . .'

Some women felt that they had learned the hard way, like this mother of 49—'I couldn't have gone to my parents. I would have liked to have had some education from someone because I was very promiscuous and it was only because I'd been playing about with so many boys I couldn't have counted that I got any sex education . . .'

But it was not only women who appeared to have been totally unaware of the facts of life. Men too gave graphic accounts of their total ignorance, like this father of 41—'It would have been helpful to me. I knew *nothing* about sex and contraception when I got married . . .'—and this man of 38— 'We were married at 18 and just so naive. We had to get tit-bits from friends and then learn very fast . . .'

Men also tended to stress the difficulty they had in developing personal relationships, like this father of 37 from the North-East:

I'd have liked more on things in general. It would have cut out all the standing on the corner asking other boys. It seemed rather smutty then and it was difficult to imagine having a worthwhile relationship with a girl . . .

And another father from the North-East summarised the inadequacy of his own sex education:

At school I think they should have got beyond the rabbit and done some human reproduction. I think we should have had the social study lessons they have now.

Certainly most school sex education, if parents had had any at all, was deemed to have been inadequate if not worse, as this mother of 46 pointed out—'We just had what we picked up. We had a biology lesson on that, and if you were away, that was it. I must have been away . . .'

This lack of sex education made many parents absolutely determined that their own children should not suffer in the way that they had had to, as this mother of 44 said:

I learned from other people as I grew up. I learned a lot from other people and that's why I wanted to be able to tell my own children all about it because I didn't know anything and when I first had my period I thought I'd hurt myself and my mother would be cross . . .

There was evidence of great fear and anguish on the part of some of the women in describing their own teenage years, and it must be remembered that these were people talking about what had happened only 20 years ago in an apparently enlightened country. Sometimes they were talking about events in the early 1970s, it appeared, like this mother of 33—'I'd like to have known about sex and having babies. I never knew anything when I got married. When I had a baby I was terrified . . .'—and another mother who had, in fact, received help from a teacher at school:

When I was 14 I got kissed at school and I thought I was pregnant. I was worried for weeks and weeks. Luckily I had a good relationship with one of the teachers who even had to tell me what to do about periods because my parents didn't even tell me that . . .

Parents often pointed that out that sex education did not cause sexual experimentation and indeed many stressed that it was their own lack of sex education which had made them unaware of the risks they were taking, like this 35-year-old divorced mother:

> In my case I was married at 16 through pregnancy, and if I'd had more sex education I wouldn't have got married at an early age and in trouble. I don't think it's fair on a young girl to be a mother at 15 or 16. I didn't know about birth control or contraception . . .

And a mother of 28 summarised her views very tersely:

> Maybe if I'd known about contraception I wouldn't have had (my son) when I was 13 . . . his father was 17 . . .

But, as we have pointed out before, it was not only the facts of life which parents felt they had needed more information on when they were younger. Many parents were aware of the extent to which their own children were being given a programme covering personal relationships at school, and certainly many fathers in particular had felt that this had been lacking in their own teenage, as this 40-year-old divorced father of two said:

> More sex education would have helped me. I've had to make a lot of mistakes myself and if you know about personal relationships between people it could have helped . . .

We asked the parents if they felt they needed more information now on any of the topics which we had been asking them about throughout the interview that would help them in discussing things with their own children. Twenty-two per cent of the parents said that they thought they did need more information, although this represented 26 per cent of the mothers compared with only 11 per cent of the fathers.

We asked them if there were any particular topics they would like to know more about and two topics stood out among those who needed more information—venereal disease, on which nearly two-thirds wanted to know more, and homosexuality, on which nearly 40 per cent wanted to know more. Nevertheless nearly a fifth wanted more information on contraception and the same proportion wanted more information so that they could discuss guidelines on sexual behavour with their children. And over 10 per cent of mothers who wanted more information wanted to know more about development in boys' and girls' bodies at puberty and sexual intercourse.

The majority of those who wanted more information wanted to get it from literature, books, magazines or pamphlets, often because they said they were too embarrassed to ask anyone or admit their own ignorance. Just under 10 per cent of the total sample of parents said they would like to get information from a doctor, health clinic, nurse or other expert in the field, while 2 per cent of the total mentioned school and only 1 per cent mentioned films or classes. But there was some evidence that some parents felt themselves hopelessly inadequate for the task of helping their own children, like this divorced mother of two teenage boys:

Not from books. Somewhere where it's talked about—in a group. I would like to be taught how to talk to him. I'd like to hear the experts talk about it—in a Health Centre or school or somewhere like that. I'd go anywhere really . . .

5 INFLUENCES ON THE SEXUAL BEHAVIOUR OF TEENAGERS

There can be little doubt that teenagers today are exposed to more open and explicit discussion and display of sex than teenagers of their parents' generation. Pornographic magazines are on open display in every corner newsagent and few teenagers will not have seen the Page Three girl in national newspapers. Sexually explicit videos are readily available and some people would argue that late-night television films show far more sex today than would have been possible twenty years ago.

It is also argued that 'society' itself is far more sexually permissive and that teenagers are more likely to experiment with sex than their parents' generation. Some commentators and pressure groups suggest that sex education in schools encourages such experimentation. But as Donald Reid shows[14], and as Judith Bury reiterates in her review of the literature *Teenage Pregnancy in Britain*[19], there is of course no evidence that school sex education does anything of the kind. Indeed, as Judith Bury points out, 'Young people develop sexual feelings and desires as a natural part of their development; these feelings are not implanted by sex education. If schools offered even less sex education than they do at present, young people would be more likely to rely on their friends for information and, as we have seen, this would be more likely to encourage early sexual experimentation than discourage it.'

The influence of friends and contemporaries

In the next chapter we shall look in more detail at the views of parents and teenagers on whether they felt that sex education at school encouraged or discouraged sexual experimentation. But the question of the influence of friends and peer-group on the sexual behaviour of young people was one which we felt necessary to explore first. Christine Farrell[1] and Michael Schofield[20] had both found that many teenagers got most of their information—or misinformation—on sex from friends and classmates. We explored in some detail what the teenagers and their parents felt about the influence of friends and peer-group on their behaviour. We then went on to ask both parents and teenagers what they perceived to be the influence on young people about sex and personal relationships from magazines, television, videos and other media.

Peer-group pressure on behaviour has always been an important factor in the development of adolescents, and the influence of friends and contemporaries on the behaviour and attitudes of teenagers cannot be underestimated. The importance that our teenage respondents attached to discussion with other people of their own age came through very clearly when they were talking about the ways in which they learned about sex and personal relationships in a formal setting at school. As we shall see, they certainly learned a lot about sex and personal relationships from their informal contacts with friends. But did they feel there was any pressure on them from their peer-group to enter into personal or sexual relationships? And what did they feel about the influences of their peer-group in general?

Our piloting had indicated that some teenage boys and girls felt insecure in their sexual development and that they experienced pressure, whether explicit or implicit, from their peer-group to conform to the 'norms' of the group which sometimes encouraged early sexual experimentation. We asked the teenagers whether they ever felt or had ever felt that people of their own age knew more about sex that they did, and if so, what made them think that and what they felt about it (Table 34).

Table 34 *Teenagers' views on whether people of own age knew more about sex than they did*

Column percentages

	Total	Boys	Girls	14	15	16
Yes	28	28	28	32	31	19
No	69	70	68	63	68	79
Don't know	3	2	4	5	1	2
Base	(209)	(99)	(110)	(75)	(81)	(53)

Nearly 30 per cent of teenagers did think that people of their own age knew more about sex than they did, and it was quite striking that equal proportions of boys and girls felt this. But there was a marked age difference, with nearly a third of both 14 and 15-year-olds thinking that people of their own age knew more about sex than they did, compared with under a fifth of 16-year-olds. Younger teenagers were much more likely to feel insecure about their own knowledge in comparison with their peer-group than older teenagers. There was very little difference between the areas, but children living with only one parent felt much less secure about their sexual knowledge than those living with two parents or step-parents. Most markedly, however, a far higher proportion of those attending single-sex schools

113

thought that other people of their own age knew more about sex than they did, compared with those attending mixed schools, but the number attending single-sex schools was too small[13] to measure the differences reliably.

So what made the teenagers feel that other people knew more than they did? More than half of them said it was the way that other people were 'always on about it', or the way they acted or behaved or talked, as this 15-year-old boy said—'They're always talking about it and you think they must know more than you. . .'

It was clear that some teenagers could make others feel outsiders, as this 14-year-old boy from the South-West pointed out—'They come up to you and say, "Do you understand this word?" and if you say, "No", then they say you don't know enough about it . . . I just don't care what they say. I just don't take any notice . . .'

But of course, many teenagers did take notice, and felt left out, as this 16-year-old girl from the North-East showed:

A few have had sex and when they talk they miss you out and ignore you. . . In a way it's hurtful. Because they actually have had sex doesn't make them better than me. They don't necessarily know more . . .

It was quite obvious that some teenagers were aware that their manner might prevent them from learning as much about sex from their peer-group as others, as this 16-year-old girl from the Midlands said—'They are more forward than what I am. They are not shy. They laugh and joke about it and I don't talk about it. . .'

So what did the teenagers feel about other people of their own age knowing more about sex than they did? Nearly two-thirds of them said that they were not bothered and took no notice, and there were a number of comments doubting whether everyone knew quite as much as they said they did. Nevertheless there were indications that some of the teenagers felt rejected or left out by the group.

We knew that parents were concerned about pressure on teenagers to have early sex, and we asked both teenagers and their parents whether they thought young people today were under pressure to have a boyfriend or girlfriend (Table 35). We wanted to know from whom or what our respondents felt this pressure came.

It is clear that parents were more likely to think that young people were under pressure to have a boyfriend or girlfriend than the teenagers themselves were. However, it should be noted that 16-year-olds were much more likely than 15-year-olds to think they were under pressure, and the 15-year-olds were more likely than the 14-year-olds to think so.

It was quite striking how parents and teenagers alike regarded friends of the teenagers' own age and sex as likely to be the most important source of pressure on young people to have a boyfriend or girlfriend, with pressure from friends of the opposite sex being regarded as much less important. Apart from pressure from class-mates or people at school, who were, of

Table 35 *Whether teenagers and parents felt that young people were under pressure to have a girl friend/boyfriend*

Column percentages

| | Teenagers | | | | | | Parents | | |
	Total	Boys	Girls	14	15	16	Total	Mothers	Fathers
Yes	43	40	45	32	46	53	53	52	54
No	52	53	52	60	48	47	37	37	38
Don't know	5	7	4	8	6	0	10	11	8
Base	(209)	(99)	(110)	(75)	(81)	(53)	(212)	(149)	(63)

Table 36 *Where teenagers and parents felt that pressure to have girlfriend/boyfriend came from*

Column percentages

	Teenagers			Parents		
	Total	Boys	Girls	Total	Mothers	Fathers
Friends own age/sex	76	78	76	81	86	71
Friends opposite sex	16	15	16	14	17	9
Class-mates/ people at school	26	30	22	25	24	26
Parents	4	8	2	4	4	3
Siblings	0	0	0	2	1	3
TV/radio	1	0	2	11	13	6
Films/videos	1	0	2	0	0	0
Magazines	4	0	8	7	8	6
Advertising	0	0	0	3	3	3
Other media	0	0	0	2	2	0
Society/ community	1	0	2	3	1	6
Sex education at school	0	0	0	2	3	0
Boredom/ unemployment	0	0	0	3	1	6
Base—all who thought young people under pressure to have boyfriend/ girlfriend	(89)	(40)	(49)	(112)	(78)	(34)

course, often of the same age and sex as the young people, other influences were thought to be minimal, although it can be seen that parents were much more likely to think that television or radio influenced the young people. We asked in more detail about the influences of the media in further questions, but Table 36 shows the unprompted response of the parents and teenagers.

We asked the parents from what age they thought the pressure started, since our piloting had indicated that parents were worried that it started at too early an age. Ten per cent of parents who thought that young people were under pressure to have a boyfriend or girlfriend said that the pressure started at the age of ten or younger, a quarter of them said that it started at 11 or 12, a third said that it started at 13 and a fifth said that it started at 14, while only

8 per cent said it started at 15 or over. The average age at which parents thought the pressure started was 12.7 years.

What did the parents feel about this pressure to have a girlfriend or boyfriend? The main response was that it came when the teenagers were too young and that they should enjoy their youth and childhood without this kind or pressure, as this mother of a 15-year-old boy summed it up:

> I'm all for encouraging children to have a wide circle of friends but I think 13 is a bit too young to have a relationship. I think you have to accept it as it happens, and always tell them, 'You're much better off with a crowd of friends'. I think at that age they ought to be enjoying themselves and not be too tied. . .

Some parents felt very strongly that too much pressure on teenagers to have a boyfriend or girlfriend could make them feel left out and lonely if they did not have one, as this mother of a 16-year-old girl said:

> It makes me very cross. If they don't conform they feel unattractive and it makes them so unhappy. Some children feel quite worthless before they even start at secondary school because they haven't been 'going out' with anyone of the opposite sex . . .

Certainly mothers sometimes felt that pressure from friends led to unhappiness among girls in particular, like this mother of a 14-year-old girl:

> I think it's a pity they are under pressure, because if a girl is growing up naturally then she will eventually get a boyfriend anyway. I've had this problem with my daughter. She was very concerned that she didn't have a boyfriend and all her friends did. She thought there was something wrong with her. But I was able to console her by telling her there's time enough later. And now she has a boyfriend . . .

Fathers sometimes felt that mothers were occasionally responsible for pressurising girls, like this father of a 14-year-old girl:

> I sometimes think some mothers push girls into being romantic. It's not a good thing. They've got too much else to bother about than a one-to-one relationship at that age. It makes them grow up too fast . . .

And there were indications from some interviews with mothers that his comment was not without foundation, as this mother of a 14-year-old girl said:

> I feel all right about it. It makes them grow up quicker. From my daughter's point of view it brings it out in the open—it makes her feel more grown up. She takes a pride in herself—her looks and her clothes. . .

And another mother with a 16-year-old agreed—'There is something

rather nice about having a boyfriend when you're young. It's a new experience—it's nice to feel needed and wanted . . .'

It must be remembered that more than half the teenagers did *not* feel
that young people were under pressure to have a boyfriend or girlfriend. But
even those who felt under pressure mainly said that they were not particularly
bothered, like this 16-year-old girl:

I think it's a load of rubbish. If you don't want a boyfriend you don't
have to have one. I tell all my friends to take a running jump . . .

There was some evidence, however, that not all teenagers were so san-
guine about it, and it was quite clear that both boys and girls suffered, like
this 14-year-old boy:

If you haven't got a girlfriend they get you down about it and say you're
ugly and a lot of other rubbish, and if you do go out with someone they
say that *she's* ugly . . .

And his view was reflected by a 16-year-old girl—'I think it makes you
desperate because you think everyone has got a boyfriend except me, and you
think, "What's wrong with me? Nobody wants me" . . .'

And so, in spite of the fact that the majority did not feel under pressure
or were not affected by the pressure they felt, nevertheless there was little
doubt that peer-group pressure affected some teenagers very badly, like this
15-year-old girl—'My friends come to school and say they've got a boyfriend
and ask if I have one. It you say, "No", they kind of push you out of the
group. . .'

Table 37 *Teenagers' rating of how important it was to them to have a
boyfriend or girlfriend*

Column percentages

	Total	Boys	Girls	14	15	16
Very important	5	5	5	4	4	8
Important	22	29	15	24	20	21
Not very important	59	54	65	57	56	68
Not at all important	14	12	15	13	21	4
Base—all teenagers	(209)	(99)	(110)	(75)	(81)	(53)

We asked the teenagers how important it was to them to have a boyfriend or girlfriend. It was interesting that it was more important for boys to

have a girlfriend than for the girls to have a boyfriend, in spite of the fact that several parents commented that girls tended to 'do the chasing'. There was not a great deal of difference between the age-groups, although the older teenagers were rather less likely to say that it was 'not at all important'.

Some of the 14-year-old boys were clearly rather frightened of the idea—'If you go with a girl at our age and she gets pregnant you get done for rape. . .'—while others of that age took a rather more functional view—'It gets you used to how girls are and it's useful when you get married later on and it's good to know how girls feel and how they react . . .'—and certainly some 14-year-old boys held views about girlfriends which would have surprised some of the girls we interviewed. It was important to this 14-year-old boy from the North-East to have a girlfriend:

> She can make you feel comfortable and you can get to know her mum and dad and brothers and sisters, and they can do you favours and you can do them favours. . .

The need for companionship and friendship was marked among these teenagers, and nearly half those who felt it important to have a boyfriend or girlfriend said it was nice to have someone to talk to seriously and to turn to with problems. Boys were more likely to say this than girls, like this 16-year-old boy:

> It's someone to share problems and have a close relationship with. It takes the pressure off you at school—off schoolwork. It's nice just to go out and enjoy yourself. . .

But the fact remains that the majority of teenagers said that it was not very important to them to have a boyfriend or girlfriend, and a third of the boys said that they were simply not bothered whether they had a girlfriend or not. Both boys and girls said that they enjoyed the company of friends of their own sex and girls were more likely to say that they were too young or that there would be 'plenty of time later on'. There were many comments among girls which reflected the views of their parents about 'not tying themselves down'. Girls were considerably more likely than boys to say that studying or school work or career came first, while boys were more likely than girls to say that they had hobbies or other interests which came first, summed up succinctly by this 14-year-old boy:

> I've never really bothered. I've got other things that interest me. I'd rather go fishing. . .

If parents were more worried about pressure to have a boyfriend or girlfriend than the teenagers themselves were, they were certainly more worried about pressure on young people to have sex than the teenagers were, as Table 38 shows.

The proportion of parents who thought young people were under pressure to have sex was almost exactly the same as that of those who thought

Table 38   *Whether teenagers and parents felt that young people were under pressure to have sex*

Column percentages

	Teenagers							Parents	
	Total	Boys	Girls	14	15	16	Total	Mothers	Fathers
Yes	31	21	39	31	23	42	51	52	51
No	60	72	49	57	69	49	34	32	41
Don't know	8	6	10	12	5	8	14	17	8
Base	(209)	(99)	(110)	(75)	(81)	(53)	(212)	(149)	(63)

they were under pressure to have a boyfriend or girlfriend. But considerably fewer teenagers thought that young people were under pressure to have sex than to have a boyfriend or girlfriend, and indeed only a fifth of the boys thought that young people were under pressure to have sex. It was quite clear that girls felt more pressure brought on them personally, particularly the older teenagers, and it was quite noticeable that the 16-year-olds were much more likely than the others to say that young people were under pressure to have sex.

So where did they think the pressure came from? There were big differences between the teenagers and their parents, as Table 39 shows.

It was quite clear that if girls thought young people were under pressure

Table 39   *Where teenagers and parents felt that pressure to have sex came from*

Column percentages

	Teenagers			Parents		
	Total	Boys	Girls	Total	Mothers	Fathers
Own boyfriend/ girlfriend	31	10	42	—	—	—
Friends own age/sex	55	76	44	68	71	59
Friends opposite sex	31	19	37	25	26	22
Class-mates/people at school	16	24	12	25	23	28
Parents	2	0	2	0	0	0
TV/radio	5	5	5	36	34	41
Films	0	0	0	6	3	13
Videos	2	0	2	6	8	3
Books	0	0	0	2	1	3
Magazines	3	5	2	15	13	19
Advertising	0	0	0	9	6	16
Sex education at school	0	0	0	3	4	0
Society/ community	0	0	0	2	3	0
Base—all who thought young people under pressure to have sex	(64)	(21)	(43)	(109)	(77)	(32)

to have sex they felt that this pressure came from boyfriends or from friends of the same age and sex, whereas boys were much more likely to think that pressure to have sex came from other boys. The girls were not happy about pressure from boys—'I reckon it's mean of the boys. The boys make it difficult to be just friends. . .'—and another 15-year-old girl had some advice for girls who found themselves under pressure—'I reckon they should pack them up as soon as they say anything. That's all they want you for, isn't it—boys of that age. . .'—while another 15-year-old girl expressed the views of several girls of her age in talking about the dual pressure from friends of both sexes -'Lads say there's something wrong with you and they only want you for one thing. Friends think they're better than you if they've done something you haven't, and they try to make you feel a freak or little. . .'

Pressure from other boys on boys to prove their 'maleness' was thought to be prevalent, and some boys felt very uncomfortable about it, like this 14-year-old from the North-East:

> It's just stupid—the ones who just do it for a dare. If they say, 'Do it with her tonight . . .'—that's really stupid. They should do it because they love them like . . .

But there was little evidence of the teenagers thinking that pressure to have sex came from any source other than their peer-group. As Table 39 shows, hardly any of them cited the media or any pressure other than from friends and class-mates. Parents, on the other hand, although emphasising the importance of the peer-group in putting pressure on young people to have sex, with mothers in particular thinking that the main pressure came from friends of the teenager's own sex, nevertheless put the blame much more firmly on the media, with television programmes being considered particularly influential.

What did the parents think about this pressure which they observed even if the teenagers did not? There was a lot of regret that teenagers might be missing out on 'fun' and their childhood, and having to grow up too quickly, as this mother of a 15-year-old girl summarised:

> I think it's wrong. They're only children. They are emotionally unfit for it. They should just be having fun. . .

And there was considerable concern on the part of some parents that young teenagers were having sex without understanding that it should be part of a 'relationship', as this mother explained—'I think it's awful. They're not ready for it. It's just sex without any proper feelings for each other. . .'—and a mother of a 15-year-old boy reinforced her comment—'I think it's a great shame because I think sex is a lovely experience and children that age can't understand how good it can be, and it can put them off if they have a bad experience. . .'

The feeling of sadness at the thought of having sex too young was expressed more often by mothers than fathers, who tended to be more concerned that it might lead to pregnancy or worse, like this father from the South-West:

> It's not good for a young girl of that age, allowing someone to use her body. It's all right if she goes out with one lad. She won't stand an earthly in later years if she's been with a lot of boys. No-one would want to marry her. . .

It often appeared that the parents were expressing their fears of young people being under pressure to have sex rather than their experience that young people were actually under pressure. They were certainly worried that the age at which young people were exposed to pressure was getting lower, like this mother—'I feel the age is getting younger all the time. Younger children try to be more grown up now. . .'

Parents thought that pressure to have sex started rather later than pressure to have a girlfriend or boyfriend, but nevertheless nearly a fifth of those who thought young people were under pressure to have sex thought it started at 12 or younger, and a further half thought it started at 13 or 14. Only a quarter thought it started at 15 or older. The average age of when they thought pressure started was 13.7 years, and there was clearly considerable anxiety among some parents that it started very young.

Some of the parents went to great lengths to make their children aware of the dangers, like this mother of a 14-year-old boy in the North-East:

> I think it's very hard on them as I don't think it's right to have sex, I talk to him every day about this and warn him about the forward girls who are about who will do anything to get a boy. . .

But mothers were often concerned that girls were under more pressure than boys, and some stressed that the pressure came not only from boys but also from other girls, as this mother of a 16-year-old girl said:

> I think it's hard for a girl who doesn't share the same feelings as other girls who are practising sex. It's a bit like smoking really. They can be really plagued to smoke when they don't really want to. . .

But there were other parents who were not sure that the pressure was really any greater than in their own day, and it must be remembered that only half the parents thought that young people were under pressure to have sex.

We were interested to know how parents and teenagers felt about the age at which sexual activity was acceptable. We did not wish to ask our teenage sample whether they had ever been sexually active, partly because we knew that at least two-thirds of our sample—the 14-and 15-year-olds—would be below the legal age of consent for girls, and partly because we did not consider it to be a necessary question in an interview which was concerned mainly with education in sex and personal relationships. We considered that the potential intrusion into the trust developed by the interviewer with parents and children in the course of these interviews did not justify asking this question. We decided to approach the question of sexual activity more obliquely, since we also felt that this approach might give us greater insight into the attitudes of both teenagers and their parents towards teenage sex. We asked them at what age they considered it all right for a girl to have sex and what age they considered it all right for a boy to have sex. We asked about the two sexes separately, since our piloting had indicated that both teenagers and their parents had rather different attitudes to teenage sex for boys and girls.

Table 40   *Age at which parents and teenagers thought it 'all right' for a girl to have sex*

Column percentages

| | *Teenagers* | | | *Parents* | | |
	Total	Boys	Girls	Total	Mothers	Fathers
15 and under	12	16	7	3	2	5
16	33	31	34	20	17	25
17	10	8	11	11	13	6
18	15	12	18	21	21	19
Over 18	5 }	8	13	3	5	0
If married	4 }			14	14	16
Don't know/ depends	21	25	17	28	28	29

Age at which parents and teenagers thought it 'all right' for a boy to have sex

Column percentages

| | *Teenagers* | | | *Parents* | | |
	Total	Boys	Girls	Total	Mothers	Fathers
15 and under	15	18	12	4	3	5
16	34	33	35	18	16	22
17	9	6	11	11	11	11
18	13	12	14	18	19	16
Over 18	2 }	8	11	4	5	2
If married	5 }			12	13	13
Don't know/ depends	21	23	17	32	33	32
Base	(209)	(99)	(110)	(212)	(149)	(63)

It was quite clear that teenagers thought that sex was acceptable for both boys and girls at an earlier age than their parents, with very few parents thinking that it was 'all right' under the age of 16, compared with well over 10 per cent of the teenagers. Indeed, nearly a fifth of the boys thought that sexual activity was acceptable for boys at fifteen or less. A further third of boys and girls thought that sexual activity was 'all right' at the age of 16. Sometimes it appeared that they were acknowledging that this was the legal age of consent, and there was clearly some variation in their response. About a fifth of the parents thought that sexual activity was acceptable for both boys and girls at the age of 16, with fathers rather more likely than mothers to accept it at that age.

Teenagers almost never stipulated that sex was only acceptable when people were married, but over 10 per cent of the parents did. It was notable that one-fifth of the teenagers and about a third of the parents did not feel able to put a particular age at which sexual activity was acceptable, but stressed that it depended on the individual or the circumstances. Many of the parents, when giving an age, also stressed how much it depended on the individual or the maturity or the nature of the relationship. Teenagers were much more likely to say that it was 'up to the individual', and displayed remarkable tolerance of other people's behaviour, like this 16-year-old girl— 'I have no views. It's up to her. For me when I'm married. . .'—and this boy of 16—'For a girl whenever she wants it—that's whenever she feels mature enough to have it. . . For a boy—when he has found someone he feels a lot for and wants to show his affection deeper to create a bond between him and the girl. . .'

Another 16-year-old girl gave a typical answer—'For both boys and girls—no specific age, but 15-16 if they are mentally mature and responsible. There's no black and white answer. . .'

Parents often stressed the need for an established relationship before sexual activity was considered, and there was a feeling among mothers in particular that it should take place when the person concerned felt it to be 'right', as this mother of a 14-year-old girl said—'My feeling is when she thinks it's right. I tell her, "Wait for the right person. Don't bed around." It's not right for parents to dictate that they must wait till 18 or 19. . .'—and another mother of a 16-year-old thought there was no particular age—'It's a thing that comes naturally when they fall in love. . .'

Fathers too were fairly discriminating in their views of the 'right' age, as this father of a 14-year-old girl said—'When she's mentally mature enough to accept it. It depends on the individual. And boys are the same. . .'

The comments from parents on this question tended to fall into two categories, with the majority stressing that it depended on the individual but a minority stressing the importance of keeping sex within marriage, a comment which was rarely heard from the teenagers. However, even those parents who preferred sex to be within marriage sometimes recognised that this might not always be possible, like this father of a 15-year-old girl:

I must admit to being old-fashioned here. I prefer it when they're married. (For boys)—this seems unkind. It seems to be weighted against a girl. The fair answer is to say when they're married but it's virtually impossible these days. As long as they take precautions—after the age of 18. . .

And fathers often found problems in sorting out their feelings as far as boys and girls were concerned, like this father of a 14-year-old boy:

A girl—after she's married. A boy—after *he's* married. The terrible thing is a boy should be experienced when he's married but then who does he get experience with?

But to summarise the views of the majority of parents, this mother of a 15-year-old boy puts it tersely—'When is it ever right? It's just one of those things that suddenly occurs. It's right when you feel it's right. . .'

The influence of the media on young people
It has been a feature of British society in recent years for assertions to be made on behalf of parents or by pressure groups who claim to speak for parents that young people today are being adversely affected by the media, particularly as far as sexual behaviour is concerned. The fear has been expressed that the presentation of sex and personal relationships in the media encourages promiscuity, early experimentation with sex and 'immoral' behaviour.

We were interested to know what the teenagers and parents we interviewed felt about this, since it is clearly possible for a vociferous minority of any kind to distort or misrepresent the views of the people for whom they claim to be speaking. We therefore asked both teenagers and their parents whether they thought that young people today were influenced about sex and personal relationships by the magazines they saw, by anything they saw on television, by videos or by any other external influence. We followed this up by asking what kind of magazines, television programmes or videos were thought to influence teenagers, and in what way they were influenced by them, since it was quite clear from our piloting that the media might be held to influence young people, but that the influence might be considered beneficial.

Influence of magazines
It had been clear from the answers to our questions on whether teenagers and parents felt that there was any pressure on young people to have a boyfriend or girlfriend or to have sex that parents were more likely to think so than the teenagers, and much more likely to think that this pressure came from magazines. The teenagers hardly mentioned magazines spontaneously as a source of pressure.

So what did our respondents think was the influence of magazines? We started by asking them what sort of magazines girls were influenced by and in what way and followed this up by asking them about boys, since our piloting had suggested that girls and boys were thought to read different types of magazines and to be influenced in different ways.

Table 41 *Whether teenagers and parents thought that young people were influenced about sex and personal relationships by the magazines they saw*

Column percentages

| | *Teenagers* | | | *Parents* | | |
	Total	Boys	Girls	Total	Mothers	Fathers
Yes	58	51	65	76	76	78
No	29	32	26	16	14	17
Don't know	12	16	8	8	8	8
Base	(209)	(99)	(110)	(212)	(149)	(63)

However, when we asked our respondents what kind of magazines girls were influenced by as far as sex and personal relationships were concerned, 20 per cent of the teenagers and 15 per cent of the parents who had asserted that they were influenced could not specify what kind of magazines influenced them. There was obviously a possibility that some of the assertions were based on little evidence. As far as the boys were concerned there was even less evidence, with 39 per cent of the parents and 15 per cent of the teenagers who said that teenagers were influenced by magazines being unable to say what kind of magazines influenced boys.

We found that rather more than half the parents and teenagers who thought that girls were influenced by magazines thought they were mainly influenced by magazines aimed specifically at teenage girls, and around 15 per cent of both teenagers and parents thought they were influenced by 'romantic' or love story magazines. Girls and mothers were more likely than boys and fathers to cite teenage girls' magazines as an influence.

There was a big difference between parents and children in that 14 per cent of parents who thought girls were influenced by magazines cited sex or pornographic magazines, while only 5 per cent of the teenagers mentioned them. Similarly pop magazines were much more likely to be mentioned as an influence on girls by parents rather than the teenagers themselves.

What did our respondents think was the influence of these magazines on girls? The teenagers and their parents were both fairly clear that magazines might make girls want to imitate or copy the stories or people represented in them. But in what way? There was little doubt that teenagers stressed the 'love' element in magazines much more than the parents did. But it was plain that both boys and girls were very much aware that the 'romantic' tales of love were often only fantasy. There was evidence that, although girls thought 'other girls' might be influenced, nevertheless they themselves were often very sceptical about what they read, like this 15-year-old girl from the North-East—'It's just the way they go on about it in the stories. It's all romance. They don't talk about the bad bits. . .'—and this 16-year-old girl from the same area — 'The stories have girls going to bed with boys and it sounds good and those girls never get pregnant so it sounds good. . .'

The boys were even more condemning of 'romantic magazines', like this 15-year-old boy from the Midlands—'They see a girl meeting a boy and having a beautiful relationship. They think it's always going to be like that. . .'—and this 16-year-old from the same area—'It sends them all daft. They think they've got to do what the daft girls in the stories do . . . well going to bed with their boyfriends—things like that. . .'

But some of the girls thought that there was often a message in the romantic stories which could suggest that life was not all roses and honey, as this 16-year-old girl pointed out—'They read the stories and try to copy them to an extent. And they identify with the people, but I think it's as helpful as it's destructive. . .' —and her view was endorsed by a 16-year-old girl from the South-West—'They're influenced by personal stories and problems they read. If they read about true experiences that might put them off doing something. . .'

The parents were much more concerned than the teenagers that girls might be given an unrealistic over-romantic view of life and love. Both mothers and fathers held strong views on this, like this father from the North-East—'They form an image and then suddenly they are in deep water. They think it's all love and romance and then find it's babies and wet nappies and no money. . .' — and this father from the South-West—'It makes it look as if everything is rosy. The magazines show that even if he has a row with her they get back together again and everything is rosy. Life is just not like that. . .'

Parents were also more concerned than teenagers that girls would want to copy what they read, like this mother in the Midlands—'They think they can do as they see in the pictures. It gives them the idea that sex is all lovely but it doesn't show them the responsibilities. . .'—and this father in the South-West—'It's like fashion. If they see things in a book they want to wear them, and it's the same if they read about sex—they want to copy. It's the "in thing"—if it's written down there's nothing wrong with it. . .'

Advice pages, both in women's magazines and teenage magazines, were thought to have an influence on some girls, as this mother pointed out—'The teenage magazines are all full of 15 and 16-year-olds with sex problems. The problems seem to sound exciting to them so they look to experiment themselves. They get so cocksure and feel, "My mum can't stop me". . .'

There was little evidence that parents had observed adverse effects on their own children, but there was a clear concern among some parents that the presentation of love in girls' teenage magazines was too romantic.

But what about boys? What did the teenagers and parents feel about boys and magazines? Although, as we have seen, parents tended not to know much about the influences of magazines on boys, there can be no doubt that boys were thought to be influenced by pornographic or sex magazines. Half the teenagers and parents who thought boys were influenced in sex and personal relationships by magazines cited this kind of magazine, which was hardly mentioned by teenagers in connection with girls. Other types of magazines were hardly mentioned in connection with boys, and it was clear that boys were thought to be less influenced by magazines in general than girls were.

Both teenagers and parents thought that pornographic magazines made boys want to have sex or copy what they saw in the magazines. Girls tended to condemn this more than boys 'They think all girls want is sex. . .'—as one 15-year-old girl said. And girls tended to say that this kind of magazine made boys want to copy what they saw because it was grown-up, as this 16-year-old pointed out—'It's made out that sex is a good thing to do—very macho and big and they want to do it. . .' Boys thought that 'other' boys were influenced by the pictures—'. . .and they think their partner will look like that. . .' as a 14-year-old boy said.

But a comment from a 14-year-old boy should remind us that pornographic magazines are not only bought or acquired by teenage boys—'Boys are influenced by rude books—they get them off their dads and take them to school. . .'

Parents also felt that boys were 'turned on' sexually by the magazines they saw in a way that girls were not. There was considerable anxiety on the part of mothers in particular that this kind of magazine gave boys the wrong 'image' of women or girls, as this mother of a 15-year-old boy in the Midlands said—'I think it cheapens their attitude towards women and just makes them feel that women are fair game. . .'—and mothers also felt that it would affect their attitude towards the girls they met—'It's just exciting them and making them think, "This is how a woman should be". . .'—and this mother of a 14-year-old girl was very concerned for the girls—'It doesn't do the boys any good looking at pictures of naked girls and getting the idea that all girls are the same. . .'

It was this danger that young boys would develop a stereotypical picture of a girl as a sex object or submissive that concerned a lot of parents, and this father of a 14-year-old boy said—'It's pushing sex, and some of the articles are so extreme it's unbelievable. They are biased towards the male being number one. . .'—and his view was reinforced by another father of a 14-year-old boy—'Certain individuals can be influenced in an unnatural way. You can lose sight of the woman for what she is and just see her as a sex object rather than as a partner and a wife. . .' And fathers of daughters were similarly concerned, as this father of a 14-year-old girl said—'It reduces their attitudes to girls to an object of self-gratification rather than to look at them as a person. . .'—and another father of a 15-year-old girl was very critical of 'soft porn' magazines—'The macho image is to have laid a lass early. They see girls as something to be used for their own satisfaction. It's bum and tits on Page Three—that sort of thing. . .'

Parents were often more likely than teenagers to mention the 'warlord' type of magazine or pornographic magazines which included war heroes or encouraged a 'macho' type of behaviour. Fathers again were worried about the effect this might have on boys—'It's nothing to do with sex, but it's male domination. . .' while other fathers thought that this exclusion of women was also an unhealthy influence on boys—'The wartime magazines, the ones with a macho image—the heroes are tough, hard—it probably makes them too macho. . .' And mothers too were concerned about this, like this mother of a 14-year-old boy—'They like the macho image—virile men—usually in uniform dominating everybody, including women. . .'

But some mothers felt differently about boys and magazines like this mother of a 15-year-old boy—'My boys see my magazines — quite serious ones. They just read the articles about contraception and so on. It just gives more knowledge really. . .'

Influence of television

The effects of television programmes on teenagers has also been the subject of much speculation and assertion, but little evidence has been presented which can in any way prove or disprove any connection between the behaviour of young people and the television programmes they see. We asked the parents and teenagers if they thought that young people today were influenced about sex and personal relationships by anything they saw on television.

Table 42   *Whether teenagers and parents thought that young people were influenced about sex and personal relationships by anything they saw on television*

Column percentages

| | *Teenagers* | | | *Parents* | | |
	Total	Boys	Girls	Total	Mothers	Fathers
Yes	56	47	64	77	73	86
No	37	44	30	17	19	11
Don't know	7	8	6	7	8	3
Base	(209)	(99)	(110)	(212)	(149)	(63)

The proportions of teenagers and their parents thinking that young people were influenced by television programmes as far as sex and personal relationships were concerned were very similar to those thinking young people were influenced by magazines, although more teenagers said that young people were not influenced by television. Boys in particular were more likely to say that young people were not influenced by television programmes even if they did not know about magazines.

But fathers were more likely to think that young people were influenced by television than by magazines, and they were much more likely than mothers to think that young people were affected by television.

It should be remembered that teenagers almost never mentioned television spontaneously when asked where they thought pressure to have a boyfriend or girlfriend or sex came from, while a third of those parents who thought young people were under pressure to have sex thought that this came from television.

What kind of programmes were thought to have an influence on young people? Parents were much more likely to say that all television programmes had a potential effect on young people, and as many as 11 per cent of the total sample of parents thought that sex could be found in most programmes, like this father of a 15-year-old boy—'It comes in everywhere. You can't pick out any programme that doesn't have sex in it—even the news. . . They see people rolling about in beds and places and it makes them think they could have a go too. It's under their noses all the time. No wonder they want to try it for themselves. . .'

Both teenagers and their parents thought that the television programmes with the most influence on young people regarding sex and personal relationships were films portraying sex, including 'pornographic' films. However, overall, this only represented 20 per cent of the teenage sample, and under a third of the parents' sample. What did they see as the influence of this kind of film? Again the teenagers tended to show that they were discriminating, and did not believe everything they saw, although they thought others might be affected, as this 15-year-old girl from the North-East pointed out—'Films make relationships look very glamorous. It's not like real life. . .'—while other teenagers were worried about the messages put across by the 'blue' films—'It might be that it makes it look so easy. They might think they can go ahead and do it without using contraceptives. . .'

But the parents again were more concerned that films or programmes of this kind might make the teenagers try to copy what they saw or experiment and 'follow the example' of the stars, as this mother said—'If the stars do it the kids think it's all right for them to do it—like Clint Eastwood—in one film he grabbed a girl and pushed her into a barn. My kids thought it was great. . .' Teenagers too thought that films with sex in them might make young people want to copy what they saw, as one 16-year-old boy put it—'It's a kind of persuasion in a way. If you see someone else doing it and it looks good, you'll want to. . .'

Soap operas and serials were thought by some parents and teenagers to have a more insidious influence, but girls thought they had more influence than boys did. Again the question of copying behaviour arose, and it was suggested that familiarity with the 'stars' or 'idols' might make their behaviour more acceptable, as this girl of 15 pointed out—'They see all these broken relationships and lovers on the side and they might think that is the proper way to behave if they do it on the tele. . .' And parents too were concerned about teenagers modelling their behaviour on that of stars who appeared regularly—'Terry being in bed with someone different every week. They say if he can do it it must be OK. . .'

But not all parents and teenagers who thought television had an influence thought that the influence was necessarily bad, as this mother of a 15-year-old boy said—'It depends on the films and plays. Sometimes it can be good and sometimes bad. It makes them see both sides of men and women. It can help them understand relationships in general between male and female. . .' Some parents thought that there was a danger that teenagers would take what they saw at its face value and that they should be helped to discriminate, like this mother:

> I think it might make them feel they are missing out on something and they want to find out what they are missing out on. That's why I think it should be talked about and discussed more in schools. . .

Influence of videos

But if teenagers were much less inclined than parents to think that magazines or television programmes influenced young people as far as sex and personal relationships were concerned, there was certainly less doubt in their minds as far as videos were concerned. More children than parents thought that videos influenced young people, and teenagers thought they had more influence than magazines and television programmes.

In our pilot study there was evidence that the viewing of videos by teenagers after school or when their parents were not at home was fairly widespread. Although we did not specify any particular type of video in our questioning, there was no doubt in the minds of teenagers what type of video might influence young people about sex and personal relationships, and nearly 70 per cent of the teenagers who thought videos had an influence said that they were pornographic, 'blue' or those showing explicit sex, compared with 50 per cent of parents who thought videos had an influence. Parents, on the other hand, were more likely to cite 'video nasties' with sex, horror and violence in them as having an influence on young people. One third of parents thinking videos had an influence mentioned these, compared with only 15 per cent of the teenagers. Parents rarely mentioned other types of videos apart from 'soft porn', but teenagers mentioned comedy videos with sex.

So what did the teenagers think were the main influences of these types of videos? The girls were worried about the effect on boys and their relationships to girls, as this 16-year-old pointed out — 'Blue movies—they are the lowest of the low. They probably think that's the thing to do—treat each other without thinking of any emotional connections. . .' and sometimes the teenagers were clearly worried about the videos they had seen or heard about —'Blue videos—things like that—even these horror videos. They make the women out to be sex objects. Girls get attacked and raped in these videos. A lot of people will just laugh but some will think they should be going out and doing these things. . .' But some thought that watching these videos might have a cautionary effect, even if of a particularly unpleasant kind, as this 16-year-old girl suggested—'Video nasties. Some girls go right off sex after watching nasties. . .'

Table 43   *Whether teenagers and parents thought that young people were influenced about sex and personal relationships by videos*

Column percentages

| | *Teenagers* | | | *Parents* | | |
	Total	Boys	Girls	Total	Mothers	Fathers
Yes	70	68	72	68	67	70
No	19	20	18	12	12	11
Don't know	11	12	10	20	21	19
Base	(209)	(99)	(110)	(212)	(149)	(63)

The teenagers certainly thought that the main problem of this kind of video was that it might make young people want to copy what they saw, and it was the violence and the rape which upset them more than explicit sex. Parents were even more worried that it might affect young people, and there were many references to the possibility that this kind of video might make violence appear acceptable. Some parents thought, however, that such videos might have the opposite effect, as this mother of a 15-year-old boy pointed out:

It can be good or bad. It can make them think of doing things they wouldn't otherwise think of. But the one our son saw here about the rape he thought was awful. The man was awful. Our son felt sorry for the girl. . .

Parents were more inclined than teenagers to point out that such videos portrayed relationships between men and women in a very brutal way, as this father of a 14-year-old boy said—'I think they seem to think that to be aggressive is the only way to get anywhere in our society. If you are shown to be a compassionate person today it's a sign of weakness. . .'

And there was no doubt that parents were worried that teenagers would develop a cold and violent view of sex and personal relationships which would 'cheapen the value of human dignity', as one father put it. The mother of a 15-year-old boy was especially concerned:

They see the worst aspects of relationships and not the best. I think when they watch them with their parents they get the feeling that the parents condone that kind of behaviour as well. . .

Although it might seem unlikely that teenagers would be watching this kind of video with their parents, it had become apparent in our piloting that even quite young children were used to seeing pornographic and violent videos at home. We asked the teenagers if they themselves had ever seen a video of a sexual kind or of the kind they had been describing.

Table 44 *Proportion of teenagers who had seen a video of an explicitly sexual nature*

Column percentages

	Total	Boys	Girls	14	15	16	SW	Mid-lands	NE
	42	52	33	43	42	40	40	43	41
Base	(209)	(99)	(110)	(75)	(81)	(53)	(45)	(76)	(88)

Athough considerably more boys than girls said that they had seen an explicit sexual video, nevertheless, as can be seen from the table, there was a remarkable uniformity among areas and age-groups, with around 40 per cent of all teenagers having seen a video of this kind. We asked them how many they had seen, since we wanted to establish whether this kind of viewing was a regular habit or a rare occurrence. A quarter of those who had seen such a video said they had only seen one, a further quarter said they had seen two, and a further 15 per cent said they had seen three. Only a fifth of them said they had seen four or more of these videos. The 16-year-olds had seen more than the 14-year-olds, as might have been expected. One rather unexpected finding was that 56 per cent of teenagers living with only one parent had seen a video of this kind.

We were interested to know where and when they had seen these videos and with whom they had watched them, as our piloting had suggested that it was not uncommon for teenagers to get together in 'a friend's house' and watch videos which their parents had hired for their own viewing.

Thirty-eight per cent of the teenagers who had seen a video said they had watched them in their own home and 72 per cent said they had watched them at a friend's home, with 1 per cent saying that they had seen them in a video shop. These proportions indicate that some teenagers had clearly watched them both at home and elsewhere. The 14-year-olds were more likely than the older teenagers to have watched them in their own homes . Seventy per cent of the teenagers who had seen a video of this kind had seen them in the evening, a quarter of them at weekends and over 10 per cent late at night.

Only 6 per cent said they had seen them after school, a further 6 per cent in the school holidays, and 1 per cent in the dinner hour.

The picture which emerges is one of nearly 60 per cent of the boys and a third of the girls watching this kind of video with friends of their own sex, while nearly half the girls but only a quarter of the boys said they had watched them in mixed groups of friends. This pattern had been suggested by our piloting. What we had not expected was that a quarter of those who had seen this type of video would say that they had seen them with their parents. This represented 11 per cent of our total sample of teenagers. It should perhaps be stressed that the wording of the question could have allowed some teenagers to interpret 'videos of a sexual kind' as meaning something rather less explicit than was intended, but the comments did not suggest that they had misinterpreted it.

Table 45   *With whom teenagers had watched sexually explicit videos*

Column percentages

	Total	Boys	Girls
Parents	25	25	25
Brothers/sisters	22	18	28
Friends own sex only	47	59	31
Friends opposite sex only	1	0	3
Friends both sexes	34	25	47
Alone	1	2	0
Base—all those who had watched sexually explicit videos	(87)	(51)	(36)

In view of the fact that so many parents were concerned about the effect of sexually explicit videos on young people, it is of interest that some were apparently prepared to watch videos of this type with their teenage children. It would be misleading to assume that it was only parents who were not concerned about the influence of videos who were watching them with their children. Although it was not usually a regular occurrence, as can be seen from the number of videos the teenagers had seen, nevertheless it was a consistent finding across age-groups and areas, and the effect of watching such a video with parents, or, for that matter, brothers and sisters, can only be a matter for speculation. Sexual abuse of young people more often takes place within a family circle than outside it, and it is becoming increasingly apparent that the incidence of such abuse may have been under-reported. There is the possibility that the watching of sexually explicit videos in the home with parents or step-parents may have a more damaging effect on young people than encouraging the teenagers to copy what they see. Perhaps there should be more attention paid to the motives and attitudes of parents who allow or encourage this viewing in the family. It provides a different perspective to the recommendation by certain pressure groups that all sex education should be given in the home by parents.

Other external influences
And finally we were interested to see whether parents thought there were any other important influences on young people as far as sex and personal relationships were concerned. Nearly a fifth of the parents thought that the home background was an important factor, and that it did not always have a beneficial influence, as this mother of a 15-year-old girl pointed out—'The parents—if they see mum jumping out of bed or dad with another girlfriend they think it must be right as they look up to mum and dad. . .'—and several parents thought that children used their parents as role-models, as this mother said—'Parents and their behaviour. If I decided to go out with another man, my kids would be sure to notice and think, well, that's all right. . .'

Other influences were rarely mentioned and the effect of advertising and other media was brought up by very few parents. Some parents thought that the 'permissive society' had affected the morals of teenagers in an adverse way, but some of the comments of this kind had a certain apocalyptic air which few shared—'The whole breakdown of everything. The whole system is going to pot. . .'

6 TEENAGERS AND THEIR SOURCES OF INFORMATION ON SEX, CONTRACEPTION AND PERSONAL RELATIONSHIPS

One of the greatest concerns of those who wish to prevent teenage pregnancy has been the need to ensure that young people receive the correct information about sex, contraception and personal relationships in a form which they can understand and which encourages them to use this information wisely and responsibly. This concern is shared by all those who simply wish to see the development of young people equipped with knowledge about the workings of their bodies and their emotions which will help them to become happy and responsible adults who can form trusting and equal relationships with other people and who can bring up families in their turn.

Teenagers' attitudes towards seeking information
The agonies experienced through lack of information have been eloquently described by parents we interviewed in talking about their own experience as teenagers and young adults. We were interested to establish what the young people themselves felt about the information they wanted. We asked them whom they would turn to first if they had a question about sex, contraception or personal relationships, and then we asked them who they thought would be the most likely person to give them the most accurate information about sex and contraception. If this was not the person to whom they would turn first, we asked them why this was so.

It was quite clear from previous studies that friends were a very important source of information or misinformation about sex and contraception. We were interested to know to what extent this remained true for a generation of teenagers who had obviously had considerably more formal education at school about sex, contraception and personal relationships than earlier samples of teenagers.

Tables 46 and 47 must be assessed together. About half the teenagers said that if they had a question about sex or contraception the first person they would turn to would be either their mother or father or both, but with mothers by far the most likely first person to be asked. Forty per cent of teenagers said they would turn first to their mother with a question about sex

137

Table 46 *First person teenager would turn to with question about sex, contraception or personal relationships*

Column percentages

	Re-sex			Re-contraception			Re-personal relationships		
	Total	Boys	Girls	Total	Boys	Girls	Total	Boys	Girls
Mother	41	27	54	40	22	55	42	26	56
Father	5	9	2	8	14	2	5	9	2
Parents	1	2	0	2	4	0	6	10	2
Friends same sex/age	27	25	28	19	20	18	23	20	26
Friends opp. sex/same age	5	7	3	2	4	0	3	5	1
Brother/sister	4	3	5	3	3	5	5	5	5
Teacher	5	8	3	9	12	5	4	6	3
Doctor	2	4	0	5	5	5	0	0	0
Family planning clinic	0	1	0	0	0	0	0	0	0
Older friend	1	0	2	1	0	2	1	0	2
Books only	4	7	2	4	6	2	3	7	0
School nurse	0	0	0	0	0	0	0	0	0
Don't know	3	6	0	5	7	4	5	9	2
Base	(209)	(99)	(110)	(209)	(99)	(110)	(209)	(99)	(110)

and contraception. As far as sex was concerned, a third of the teenagers said that the first person they would ask would be a friend, and over a quarter specified that it would be a friend of the same age and sex. They were not quite so sure about friends and contraception, however, and only a fifth said that they would turn first to a friend with a question about contraception.

Table 47 *Person teenager thought would give the most accurate information about sex or contraception*

Column percentages

	Re-sex			Re-contraception		
	Total	Boys	Girls	Total	Boys	Girls
Mother	33	19	45	23	12	34
Father	6	10	2	8	14	2
Parents	4	6	2	4	7	1
Friends same sex/age	4	5	3	3	3	4
Friends opp. sex/ same age	0	1	0	0	0	0
Brother/sister	3	2	5	3	2	5
Teacher	15	23	7	15	23	7
Doctor	18	21	15	21	20	21
Family planning clinic	2	3	2	7	6	7
Older friend	1	0	2	1	0	2
Books only	2	3	1	3	3	3
School nurse	4	0	7	4	0	7
Don't know	8	5	10	7	7	7
Base	(209)	(99)	(110)	(209)	(99)	(110)

There were striking differences between boys and girls as far as asking their parents was concerned. We have already seen that boys appeared to have far more difficulty than girls in talking to their parents about sex and contraception, and this pattern was repeated here, with 54 per cent of girls saying that they would turn first to their mother with a question about sex and 55 per cent about contraception, compared with only 27 per cent and 22 per cent respectively among the boys. Boys were more likely to ask their fathers about sex or contraception than the girls were, but they were still much more likely to ask their mother than their father about both subjects.

The proportions of both boys and girls saying that they would turn first to a friend of the same age and sex with a question about sex or contraception were very similar, but rather more boys than girls said that they would turn first to a friend of the opposite sex.

But only 5 per cent of the teenagers said they would turn first to a teacher with a question about sex, with rather more boys than girls saying they would, and only 2 per cent said they would turn first to a doctor. Four per cent said they would ask brothers or sisters and a further 4 per cent said they would turn first to books.

Contraception showed a rather different picture, with 9 per cent saying they would turn first to a teacher and 5 per cent to a doctor. It should be noted again that boys were rather more likely to turn to teachers than girls were. In fact, boys were almost as likely to turn to a teacher first as they were to turn to their fathers about sex and contraception, while there was absolutely no question that the girls were much more likely to turn to their mothers than to their teachers. And it should be stressed that girls simply did not appear to consider turning first to their fathers about these matters.

But it was not necessarily for accurate information that the teenagers turned to people with their questions. While mothers were the first person turned to by so many teenagers, they were not thought of so highly as sources of accurate information, although fathers, if they were asked first, appeared to have been asked for the reliability of their information.

But if parents lost some credibility as information-givers, there was absolutely no doubt that friends were very unlikely to be thought of as accurate sources of information on either sex or contraception. Although a third of the teenagers said they would turn to their friends first about sex, only 4 per cent thought they would give the most accurate information about it, and although a fifth said they would turn to friends first about contraception, only 3 per cent thought they would receive the most accurate information from friends.

It was in terms of accurate information that teachers and doctors were regarded as much more reliable contacts, with 15 per cent of teenagers thinking that teachers would give the most accurate information about both sex and contraception. Doctors were thought of even more highly, with around a fifth of teenagers saying that they would give the most accurate information about both sex and contraception. It was interesting that family planning clinics were thought likely to give the most accurate information on contraception by 7 per cent of the teenagers, although none of them would turn to them first, and school nurses were similarly regarded as potentially accurate sources of information, particularly by girls, but, again, none of the teenagers said they would turn to them first.

So why did the teenagers not turn to these well-recognised sources of accurate information first with their questions about sex and contraception, and indeed, why did they not consider turning to them at all, especially when they were so sceptical of the reliability of the information they received from some of their chosen sources, especially their friends?

First of all, teenagers turned to their mothers first because she was there, because they had a close relationship with her and because she was their mother, as this boy of 16 said when he explained why he would not turn to a doctor first in spite of the fact that he thought a doctor would give more accurate information—'Because I think I've got a closer relationship with my mum and I could let my feelings flow more than with a doctor. . .'

And his view was reiterated by a 15-year-old girl from the North-East—'Because parents know you better and to them you are someone special and I would be less embarrassed. . .'—and some teenagers felt that it would in some way be disloyal to their parents if they spoke to a doctor or more reliable source of information first, as this 15-year-old girl explained—'Because it would be a bit sly if I didn't ask my mother first. It would look as though I didn't trust her. . .'

Teenagers certainly tended to have fairly set ideas about the role of doctors, even if they thought they might give them accurate information, as this 15-year-old boy pointed out—'Because it's like going to the top of the ladder to see a doctor. You see someone else first—then you go to a professional. . .' And it should be stressed that some teenagers did not see questions about sex as 'important' enough to consult a doctor about, as this 15-year-old boy from the Midlands pointed out—'If it's just an unimportant question you don't go to a doctor, do you? If it's a real problem doctors are more expert. . .'—and boys in particular were reluctant to 'bother' doctors with such questions, as this 14-year-old boy said—'The doctor would probably tell you off. He'd think you were wasting his time. . .' It did appear that some teenagers were aware that their questions might find quicker solutions than doctors could be expected to appreciate, as this 14-year-old boy who would ask his sister first explained—'It's handier to ask my sister. With a doctor you have to make an appointment. By the time you see him the problem could be over. . .'

The question of familiarity and lack of embarrassment was also the main reason that teenagers asked their friends about sex, as this 14-year-old girl from the North-East pointed out—'I would rather discuss it with friends first and see what they think. They'd probably understand more. . . .' This kind of mutual aid was very common, as this 15-year-old boy said—'Because your friend might have the same problem and be in the same position and might know what to do. . .'

The fact that friends might not know what to do was neither here nor there for a lot of teenagers, but clearly a number of them tried their problems or questions out on their friends first before seeking a second opinion, like this 14-year-old boy—'I'd probably ask my friends' opinions first and if I don't agree, I'd ask my mum. . .'

Teenagers gave very similar reasons for not turning first to a doctor or teacher about contraception, although there was a strong undercurrent of doubt about whether a doctor would be prepared to help, as this boy of 15 explained—'The doctor wouldn't tell you anyway now unless you're 16, and they'd ask your mum first. . .'—and his view was reiterated by this girl of 16—'You have to ask for your mum's permission. . .' Friends with all their unreliability were regarded as more trustworthy and capable of understanding the problem, and in spite of their acknowledged expertise, doctors were not seen as particularly approachable by teenagers, as this 15-year-old boy from the North-East summarised—'I'd rather talk to a friend than someone else. Doctors are busy people and might not have time to listen. . .'

And finally we asked the teenagers whom they would turn to if they had a question about personal relationships. A very similar pattern of behaviour emerged, and it appeared that if teenagers had a good relationship with someone they would turn to them first with questions about sex, contraception or personal relationships, with little regard to the accuracy of the information they were likely to receive. The nature of the relationship and trust were more important factors in seeking information and advice than accuracy. Teenagers were well aware that the information given might be of dubious reliability, but they were able to distinguish the purposes of their conversations. It was interesting that so many pointed out that they regarded the first conversation about a subject as one in which they tried out their feelings and problems, and that if they were dissatisfied with the answer or felt they needed further help, they knew to whom they should turn. Whether they turned to those 'accurate' sources of information was, of course, another matter, but at least they were usually aware of their existence and their expertise.

Parents' and teenagers' assessments of most important sources of information

In assessing the impact of education in sex and personal relationships on the development of young people it is important to know from which source the parents and teenagers thought that teenagers received most information.

Table 48 shows quite clearly that teaching at school was considered the most important source of information about both sex and contraception by both parents and teenagers. The respondents were given the opportunity of naming two sources of information, since it was clear from our piloting that parents in particular found it difficult to cite only one source. It will be seen from the table that it was mainly in answer to the question about the main source of information about sex that parents tended to give two answers, but even so nearly 40 per cent of them just gave one answer. In general, the responses of those who gave only one answer followed the pattern shown in Table 48.

Looking in detail at those who gave two answers to this question, it can be seen that, of the 61 per cent of parents who cited teaching at school as the teenager's main source of information about sex, approximately a third gave this as their only answer, just over 40 per cent combined it with mother or father or both parents, and 22 per cent combined it with friends. In general where two sources of information were given, by both parents and teenagers, the combinations tended to be school and parents, or school and friends. The only other combination mentioned by more than a handful of respondents was that of parents and friends, but this was thought to be the main source of information on sex by less than 10 per cent of parents who gave two answers on this question, and was seldom mentioned in answer to the other questions by either parents or teenagers.

The table shows some interesting patterns. Both parents and teenagers stressed the importance of teaching in school in giving information about both sex and contraception, but clearly many felt it had a relative lack of importance as a source of information about personal relationships. Nevertheless over a third of teenagers, compared with only a fifth of parents, cited school as their most important source of information on personal relationships, and there can be little doubt that the development of teaching programmes concerned with personal and social education, which were so clearly illustrated and commented on by the teenagers we interviewed, had made a considerable impact on them.

Table 48   *Respondents' assessment of where teenager got most information about sex, contraception and personal relationships*

Column percentages

	Parents			Teenagers		
	Sex	Cont.	PR		Sex	Cont.	PR
Teaching at school	61	58	21		63	66	35
Doctor	0	0	0		0	0	0
Family planning clinic/advice centre	0	0	0		0	2	0
Mother *or*	23	16	18		15	6	19
Father *or*	4	3	3	2		2	2
Both parents	17	8	33		5	2	11
Brother/sister	7	3	4		4	1	2
Friends own age/sex	31	18	22		29	20	29
Friends opp. sex	3	0	2		3	2	4
TV	4	1	1		0	1	2
Books	2	2	2		2	3	1
Other media	0	0	1		3	1	2
Older friends	1	2	3		4	3	3
Other relatives	1	0	0		0	0	0
Don't know	5	15	12		0	2	2
Base	(212)	(212)	(212)		(209)	(209)	(209)
2 answers	61%	29%	27%		35%	15%	19%
1 answer	39%	71%	72%		64%	84%	80%

Parents stressed their own importance as a source of information about sex, contraception and personal relationships much more than the teenagers did. Forty-four per cent of parents, compared with only 22 per cent of teenagers, cited parents as the most important source of the teenagers' information about sex. This pattern was followed with contraception, where 27 per cent of parents compared with only 10 per cent of teenagers cited the parents as the most important source of information. Even with personal relationships, where teenagers conceded more parental input, nevertheless over half the parents thought they were the most important source of information, compared with only a third of the teenagers.

It was interesting that parents and teenagers tended to agree on the importance of friends as sources of information, with around a third of both parents and teenagers citing friends of the teenager's own age as the most important source of information on sex, and about a fifth of both samples as the most important source about contraception. Teenagers were, however, more likely than their parents to say that friends were their most important source of information about personal relationships, but nevertheless, nearly a quarter of parents thought that teenagers' friends were their most important source of information on this subject.

As we have seen, teenagers tended to be more categorical in naming only one source as *the* most important source of information on these subjects. It was quite clear that most teenagers thought that school was their most important source of information about sex and contraception, with friends cited as more important about sex than contraception, and parents cited by only a minority as their most important source of information about sex and by only 10 per cent about contraception. Parents, on the other hand, although the majority gave school the same importance as the teenagers, were more likely to combine it with their own influence, particularly as far as information on sex was concerned. But a minority of parents thought that friends were the most important source of information for teenagers on these matters, and there can be no doubt that the importance of friends as reliable or unreliable sources of information on sex, contraception and personal relationships cannot be underestimated.

Perhaps one of the most interesting features of this table is the fact that not only were doctors, family planning clinics or other 'experts' almost never mentioned as the most important source of information about these subjects by either parents or teenagers, but also television and the media, which were thought to have some influence on teenagers' behaviour by the majority of parents, were rarely mentioned as an important source of information.

School, family and friends are clearly the most important sources of information, and although other sources may be thought to have some influence on behaviour, nevertheless information, particularly accurate information, must be the basis of behaviour. If that information is biased or inaccurate there must be cause for concern. It appeared from our interviews with both parents and their children that school has become relatively a much more important source of information for teenagers in the mid-1980s than it was for teenagers only a decade ago, and certainly far more important than it was for our teenagers' parents.

7   ASSESSMENT OF SEX EDUCATION AT SCHOOL

The previous chapters have shown how much education in sex, contraception and personal relationships is given at school and the extent to which parents and teenagers consider this education to be an important source of information for teenagers. This chapter looks in more detail at how teenagers and their parents assessed the importance and influence of the sex education teenagers are receiving at school.

Teenagers' assessment of helpfulness of school sex education
We asked the teenagers what they thought of the education they had received so far on these subjects at secondary school and how helpful they had found it (Table 49).

Nearly 80 per cent of the teenagers found the education they had had at school helpful in learning about sex, with girls more likely to have found it helpful than boys. Nearly 70 per cent of the teenagers had found the education they had received at school helpful in learning about contraception, but it should be noted that nearly 10 per cent of the teenagers said that they had had none. These were mainly 14-year-olds, a fifth of whom said they had had no education on contraception yet. The teenagers were less likely to say that the education they had had at school was helpful to them in learning about personal relationships, but nevertheless 50 per cent of them said they had found it helpful. Again 15 and 16-year olds were more likely to have found it helpful than the younger teenagers, and nearly a fifth of 14-year-olds said that they had had no formal education on personal relationships at secondary school.

There was an interesting area difference, with much higher proportions of teenagers in the South-West area saying that they had found their teaching at school helpful in learning about sex, contraception and personal relationships than teenagers in the other areas. They were also much less likely to say that they had found it unhelpful and in general displayed greater enthusiasm for their teaching at school on these subjects than teenagers in the other areas. For example, 38 per cent of the teenagers in the South-West said that their teaching at school had been very helpful in learning about sex and 31 per cent said it had been very helpful in learning about contraception, in

Table 49 *Teenagers' assessment of helpfulness of education at school in learning about sex, contraception and personal relationships*

Column percentages

	Re sex			Re contraception			Re personal relationships		
	Total	Boys	Girls	Total	Boys	Girls	Total	Boys	Girls
Very helpful	28	26	29	23	22	25	13	16	11
Fairly helpful	51	49	53	45	45	45	37	33	40
Some helpful	1	0	3	1	0	3	2	0	5
Some not very helpful	15	18	12	15	15	15	30	28	32
Not at all helpful	1	1	2	5	7	4	9	14	5
Had none	3	5	2	9	10	8	8	8	8
Base	(209)	(99)	(110)	(209)	(99)	(110)	(209)	(99)	(110)

comparison with the Midlands figure of 18 per cent.

So in what ways did they find teaching at school helpful in learning about these subjects? The main reasons, given by over half the sample of teenagers, were that the teaching at school was informative and taught them things they did not know, in an authoritative, clear and comprehensive manner. Teenagers stressed that they appreciated being taught 'the facts about sex' from a reliable source, as this 15-year-old boy explained—'You know that they are right, and you don't know that when you get information from friends. . ..' They also said that schools gave them the basis of information on which to form their own opinions, as this 16-year-old girl in the North-East said—'They just covered basic ground without going into depth to influence you at all. . .'

Those who found the education on contraception helpful stressed the fact that it covered the subject comprehensively, whereas other information they received was picked up in a much more limited way, as this 14-year old girl pointed out—'It told us all the different kinds of contraceptives people use and gave us various reasons for using different ones. . .' It certainly added to some people's knowledge, as this 15-year-old boy in the Midlands explained—'It was really useful—most things I didn't know had been invented. . .' And teenagers welcomed the knowledge in helping them to discriminate at a later stage, like this 14-year-old boy—'We know how safe or unsafe the different methods are and what is available, so it's quite good. . .'

The importance they attached to learning about the risks of unwanted pregnancy was stressed by a number of teenagers, as this 16-year-old boy showed—'If you didn't learn about contraception a lot of damage could be caused by making people pregnant. . .'

Many teenagers were ready to admit how little they would have known without education at school on these subjects, like this 16-year-old Muslim girl from the South-West:

It was very helpful because it's the only place I've ever learned about it. Besides, it makes you think and to ponder over issues. I might have pondered to myself and gone on knowing nothing about it. For example, none of us had heard of VD before and now we do. . .

It corrected misconceptions and cleared up problems, as this 14-year-old boy pointed out—'Well there were a lot of things I didn't know about . . . Names for things—homosexuals and queers—I didn't know that was the same . . .'

And certainly some teenagers thought that this kind of education at school was a preparation for adult life, like this 15-year-old boy from the Midlands who found it helpful—'To know what to do before you get married—ready for your wedding night. . .'

Teaching by films or other visual aids was found particularly helpful by nearly 15 per cent of the teenagers, and there can be no doubt that the visual presentation of this kind of material helped some teenagers understand more clearly than other methods of teaching, as we saw from their discussion of teaching methods earlier.

It should also be pointed out that some teenagers found teaching at school helpful in talking to their parents about the subject, as this 14-year-old girl explained—'Well I found it easier to turn to my mum about it after learning at school. . .'

Although teenagers were rather less likely to have found school helpful in learning about personal relationships, nevertheless, as we have seen, over half the sample had found it useful, mainly in helping them understand people of the opposite sex and appreciate how they thought and felt about things. Some teenagers stressed that lessons and discussions at school on personal relationships had helped them get along better with other people in general, and it was quite clear that some schools and teachers were very successful in stimulating thought and discussion on the nature of relationships with other people, as this 15-year-old girl in the Midlands explained—'I think I understand now what life is really about. You find a friend you really need and who can understand you. . .'

There was certainly evidence that teenagers found it useful to learn the views of the opposite sex, of which some of them had little experience, like this 14-year-old boy—'We learned about the roles played by different sexes. It made you look at the women's view. . .' And some teenagers stressed how learning about personal relationships in the relatively formal setting of school influenced their behaviour, like this 14-year-old boy—'You'd be impolite to the girls if you didn't have the lessons, and you wouldn't understand them. . .'

Boys in particular often appeared to have little opportunity to learn about the feelings of girls especially if they did not have sisters, and there were many examples of the usefulness boys attached to school in helping them to learn more about girls' feelings and emotions, as this boy of 15 explained—'It was helpful to know how girls were feeling and how to get along with them and to talk about your problems. . .'

But why did some teenagers *not* find school very helpful in learning about sex and contraception or personal relationships? The main reason given was that they had been taught too little about any of these things, or that they had not been taught in sufficient detail. Some of the teenagers thought they were missing something, like this 14-year-old boy—'We haven't been told much at school. We're fourth year now and still the school hasn't told us everything. . .'

Some teenagers were not particularly bothered by the lack of education in these subjects at school, like this 15-year-old girl from the North-East:

> Basically we didn't do that much and by the time people are old enough to learn about this they've already picked it up from parents and friends. . .

And some teenagers did not think that schools put a very high priority on this kind of education, like this 15-year-old boy from the Midlands—'I've not had much of anything. But not many schools have. It's an option. In the fourth year you're given a choice. Sex and contraception won't get you a job so you study something else. . .' This rather functional view of school was reiterated by a 14-year-old girl in the North-East—'You go to school to learn about how to get a job—not to learn all about sex. . .'

Teenagers who had not found school particularly helpful in learning about personal relationships tended to stress that these were personal matters and difficult to cover in a school setting. They often used phrases about personal relationships being an 'individual' thing, and one 14-year-old girl spoke for a number who had not found school very helpful in this respect—'There wasn't much you could learn about that. You have to find out for yourself. . .' There were few comments from teenagers indicating that school sex education had concentrated too much on the biological aspects and not on 'feelings'.

Parents' and teenagers' assessment of quantity of school sex education
We went on to ask both parents and children whether they thought that overall the teenagers had had too much, too little or about the right amount of sex education at secondary school so far.

Table 50   *Parents' and teenagers' assessment of quantity of sex education at secondary school*

Column percentages

| | *Teenagers* | | | *Parents* | | |
	Total	Boys	Girls	Total	Mothers	Fathers
Too much	3	4	3	3	5	0
Too little	22	24	19	12	14	8
About right	75	71	78	53	52	57
Had none	1	1	0	—	—	—
Don't know enough to say	—	—	—	30	29	33
Too much on some/too little on some	—	—	—	1	1	2
Base	(209)	(99)	(110)	(212)	(149)	(63)

We asked all the respondents whether they thought there was anything in particular that there had been too much or too little of. Not more than 2 per cent of the teenagers could think of any particular subject they felt there had been too much of, and the main reason given was that they had found it repetitive, as this 16-year-old girl explained when she said that there had been too much on menstruation and changes at puberty—'Every year we get the same talks—same slides—once would have been enough. . .'

Only 4 per cent of parents had any comments on what they felt there had been too much of in secondary school sex education, and apart from two parents who felt there had been too much of everything, and two who thought there had been too much on childbirth, the rest, representing 2 per cent of the sample of parents, felt there had been too much about sex, as this mother in the Midlands said—'I don't mind the films about periods and growing up but I don't agree with pictures on sex itself and how it happens. I don't think it's good for kids to know. They can find out about it later on. . .'

But her view was, as the figures show, extremely uncommon, and parents were much more likely to stress what they found too little of in secondary school sex education.

Table 51 *Subjects parents and teenagers thought there had been too little of at secondary school*

Column percentages

	Teenagers	Parents
Animal reproduction	0	0
Human reproduction	1	0
Sexual intercourse	6	2
Pregnancy & childbirth	2	0
Changes in a girl's body	1	0
Changes in a boy's body	0	0
Family & parenthood	2	0
Personal relationships	11	7
Guidelines on sexual behaviour	2	0
Contraception/birth control	14	3
Masturbation	3	0
Venereal disease	7	5
Abortion	4	1
Homosexuality/lesbianism	6	0
Everything	5	4
Base	(209)	(212)

There was evidence of great concern among both parents and teenagers that there had been little or no sex education at school, like this 14-year-old boy from the North-East who said—'We've had too little on everything, because we haven't had the lessons and noone has told me the facts of contraception, sex, and everything else on the card. . .' Parents were often worried that the subjects were not taught systematically and these two fathers in the North-East held similar views. One had a 14-year-old daughter—'They should teach it properly as a separate subject —not just bits in this lesson or that. . .' and his view was reiterated by the father of a 15-year-old daughter—'I think it should be a proper lesson, with regular specialists attending to give lectures and do the follow-up. . .'

The concern by teenagers on having too little education about contraception was often that they had not learned about it in enough detail, as this boy of 16 complained—'They just didn't show it in any detail at all. They just went through it all quickly so as to get it over like—that's how it seemed. . .' And another 16-year-old boy stressed the importance that a number of teenagers attached to the preventive aspect of sex education. He thought he should have had more on contraception—'So we know when we get older. We don't want to get girls pregnant, do we?' And there were some teenagers whose parents were also concerned, as this 16-year-old girl in the North-East explained—'They don't teach you anything about contraception, perhaps because it's an RC school. Dad taught me instead because he doesn't want me to come to any harm. . .'

Some parents also thought there had been insufficient detail about contraception, as this mother of a 15-year-old in the Midlands said—'I told her about the pill and she didn't know about it. If they told them at school there wouldn't be so many girls getting into trouble. . .'

But both teenagers and their parents were concerned that there had been too little about personal relationships, summed up very succinctly by this 15-year-old boy from the North-East—'We only had one lesson on that compared to eight on contraception, so we knew how not to get pregnant, but not how to get on with each other. . .' Sometimes teenagers felt that the school did not consider personal relationships very important, as this boy of 14 explained:

> We've only done childbirth and contraception and not really learned anything else about personal development. I don't know very much. I suppose they have to stick to a set syllabus, but I wish I knew more. . .

Some parents felt even more strongly about what they perceived to be too little about personal relationships at school, like this mother of a 14-year-old boy in the North-East:

> They have covered everything but not thoroughly. I just don't think they go into it deep enough. I think they should have a one-hour lesson a week and go into everything like relationships deeper. It's all so rosy but you have to work like mad to make anything work. . .

It must be remembered that nearly one-third of our sample of teenagers were not living with both parents, and there was some evidence in the comments of parents on the need for more education in personal relationships that they

151

were concerned about their children's future relationships in the light of their own experience.

Some parents were concerned that the teenagers were being told about the mechanics of sex and bodily changes without learning about relationships. But these parents were not saying that sex education should cover relationships without covering the biological side. In many cases they felt that the education did not go far enough in general, as this mother of a 14-year-old boy said:

> They don't go into personal relationships. It's mostly films about the body. They don't go into feelings—or things like masturbation—to be told that it's normal to feel that way otherwise they have guilt feelings. Perhaps teachers find it embarrassing or perhaps the school feels it should be left to parents. . .

We have seen how difficult most parents found it to talk to their children about masturbation and, indeed we have seen how difficult many children found it to talk to their parents about any of these subjects. There was certainly an assumption by many of the parents who felt that their children had had too little on these subjects that it was the school's responsibility to teach them more. As we have seen, 27 per cent of parents interviewed preferred all sex education to be left to the school, and the majority of parents wanted the school to be involved. Certainly some schools and teachers might have been surprised at how much the parents wanted them to teach the children about sex, contraception and personal relationships. This father of a 15-year-old was surprised that he had had to 'take over':

> He hasn't had enough sex education generally. He has seen films and they discuss things but they don't really teach him much about sex itself. He usually comes home and asks me about what they are supposed to have been teaching him. . .

Both parents and teenagers who thought there had been too little on some of the other subjects tended to stress the need for education at school to help prevent certain consequences. A 16-year-old girl in the North-East wanted to know more about abortion and homosexuality:

> We don't really know anything about those. You might need an abortion or be a homosexual and get very worried because you know nothing at all. At secondary school you need to know these things. Teachers should cover all the subjects. How do they know what you need to know about?

And her view of the need for more information on certain topics was stressed by a number of teenagers as far as VD was concerned as well, as this boy of 14 said:

> There was quite a lot missed out on VD. I've read the papers they gave

me and you can die from it. I don't know, there just wasn't enough. It's an important subject and you don't want to get it, do you?

Parents also thought that schools should give more information on subjects like venereal disease and homosexuality, which, as we have seen, were often subjects which parents felt handicapped in talking to their children about since they felt they did not know enough themselves. But it was not only information that some parents thought the school should give, as this mother of a 16-year-old in the South-West pointed out—'It's important they know if they've got VD. And if they're gay in any way they should be told not to be embarrassed and ashamed of it. . .'

But teenagers often felt that the school could not cope with 'difficult' subjects, as this 16-year-old girl from the Midlands explained:

We haven't talked about relationships or things or about masturbation or homosexuality. Maybe they don't think teaching relationships is very important and I don't think the head-mistress would think it right to talk about masturbation and homosexuality. . .

It was noteworthy that hardly anyone thought that there had been too little education at school on guidelines on sexual behaviour, although one or two parents considered that the 'moral' component of sex education was sacrificed to the biological, as this mother of a 14-year-old girl said—'Teenagers are given the information on contraception or how they can avoid having a child during intercourse, when more emphasis should be placed on the self control aspect rather than on birth control. . .' But teenagers sometimes presented a different picture of sex education at school, as this 15-year-old girl pointed out when she said there had been too little on guidelines of sexual behaviour:

We've had too little on the problems of having sex if you're too young— if you get pregnant what to do—or which pill is best or other contraceptives. We haven't really had help if we did want to have sex. They just say it's best not to. . .

Teenagers' and parents' views on guidance at school on sexual behaviour
We asked the teenagers and their parents specifically if they thought that teachers should give children in secondary schools guidance or help on how to behave in sexual matters.

It was striking that nearly twice as many parents as teenagers thought that teachers should give guidance on these matters. There was virtually no difference between the different age-groups of teenagers, but teenagers in the North-East were much more likely than others to say that teachers should give guidance. Nearly 50 per cent of the North-Eastern teenagers thought they should, compared with only a quarter of teenagers in the South-West and only 18 per cent of those in the Midlands. Parents in the Midlands too

Table 52   *Teenagers' and parents' views on whether teachers should give guidance or help on how to behave in sexual matters*

Column percentages

	Teenagers			Parents		
	Total	Boys	Girls	Total	Mothers	Fathers
Yes	33	33	32	61	62	59
No	55	57	54	34	34	37
Don't know	12	10	15	4	4	5
Base	(209)	(99)	(110)	(212)	(149)	(63)

were less likely than others to think that teachers should give guidance on these matters, but 70 per cent of parents in the South-West thought they should, and so did two-thirds of the North-Eastern parents.

None of the teenagers attending single-sex schools thought that teachers should give guidance, compared with a third of those attending mixed schools.

It was rare for parents to stress the 'moral' component of sex education but to lay far more stress on the need for teachers who gave guidance to be trained, willing to take on this responsibility and able to communicate with teenagers. Parents were sometimes worried about teachers with one-sided views giving guidelines on sexual matters, like this father of a 15-year-old girl:

> Some guidelines would be beneficial but it's difficult to stereotype people into set groups. I would want to know that the teacher wasn't bigoted. . .

And his view was presented in a rather different way by the mother of a 14-year-old boy—'I think it might help if it was handled in the right way, but it's like politics that what is right for one is wrong for another and it's difficult to teach. . .'

Some parents thought it a good idea in principle but were not sure that children would want to talk to their teachers about these matters or take any advice they might have to give. Other parents thought that it was a good idea only if children could not talk to their parents, but there were parents who felt that teachers had more influence than they did, like this mother of a 15-year-old boy in the North-East—'They can talk to them better than I can. . .' while others felt out of touch with their children, like another mother of a 15-year-old boy in the North-East—'They know them better than we do. . .'

Teenagers, although far less enthusiastic about the idea than parents, nevertheless gave a rather different emphasis to the subject when they said they thought it was a good idea for teachers to give guidance on sexual matters, like this 14-year-old boy from the North-East who stressed the preventive nature of teachers' guidance:

> If they didn't talk to you about sexual behaviour all the kids would be going round looking for lasses just to have sex. It does help a lot. . .

And another boy of 16 agreed—'If you're not taught you wouldn't think to buy contraceptives and you could get someone pregnant. . .'

One 14-year-old boy had clearly been influenced by what he interpreted as guidance by a teacher 'About role playing. It makes you not be a sexist chauvinist. . .'

But the minority of parents who thought that teachers should not give guidance about sexual matters often felt very strongly that it was the parents' role, as this mother of a 16-year-old girl in the North-East said:

> I want my children to learn from me. I can tell them all they need to know. I wouldn't like my children to talk to someone else about sex and things. . .

Other parents thought that it was not the teacher's job and that teachers were there to 'teach', while others thought that not every teacher 'practised what they preached'. Teachers were not always held in very high esteem by parents—'Kids don't respect them enough today. At my son's school they treat everything as one big joke. . .'—and one mother went further:

> They need help and guidance themselves. Generally they have a lot of hang-ups. They're a profession with a lot of hang-ups. They're people in one sense and in another sense they're bound up by professional etiquette. If they're my age—at school in the sixties—they're no wiser than me. . .

And as we have seen, the majority of teenagers thought that teachers should not give guidance on these matters, mainly because they did not see it as the teachers' role, but also because some felt teachers could not be trusted not to gossip and some preferred to get this kind of guidance from their parents.

Teenagers and sexual behaviour
We asked the teenagers whether they felt that knowing the facts about sex, contraception and personal relationships had affected their own behaviour in any way.

Younger teenagers were more likely than older ones to say that they did not know whether it had affected their behaviour or not. It was clear from our piloting that it was too early for many of these teenagers to say whether their knowledge had affected their behaviour, and some of them, of course, felt their knowledge was limited, so we asked them whether they thought that knowing the facts might affect their behaviour in the future.

Taken together, these tables indicate that 49 per cent of teenagers thought that knowing the facts about these matters had affected or would affect their behaviour, with girls (55 per cent) much more likely than boys (42 per cent) to say that it had or would.

Table 53   *Whether teenagers felt that knowing the facts about sex, contraception and personal relationships had affected their behaviour in any way*

Column percentages.

	Total	Boys	Girls
Yes	21	14	26
No	72	81	64
Don't know	7	4	10
Base	(209)	(99)	(110)

Table 54   *Whether teenagers felt that knowing the facts about sex, contraception and personal relationships might affect their behaviour in future*

Column percentages

	Total	Boys	Girls
Yes	36	33	40
No	48	51	44
Don't know	15	14	16
Base—all those who thought that knowing the facts had not affected their behaviour so far	(165)	(84)	(81)

But what effect had knowing the facts had on their behaviour already and what effects did they think it would have? The main effect cited by the teenagers was that it had made them or would make them more cautious. Girls were more likely than boys to say that knowing the facts had made them understand the risks more, and to behave differently at an earlier stage in a relationship, like this 16-year-old in the South-West—'It has made me more cautious as to how involved I get with boys. I know I could be used. . .'— and this 14-year-old in the North-East—'I'm more careful when I'm with boys. I don't want to get the boys going. . .'—and another 14-year-old girl in the North-East—'It's made me a little more cautious when talking to lads— especially certain types—the wilder sort. . .'

It certainly put some girls off certain behaviour, as this 16-year-old said—'Well I wouldn't jump into bed with anyone in case I got pregnant or VD. I want to be in love before I do that. . .' —and it had put some girls off altogether, like this 14-year-old—'I think about it all. I'm put off—getting married and having a family. It puts you off. . .'

Boys, as we have seen, were less convinced that knowing the facts had affected their behaviour and they were more likely to interpret the question slightly differently, as this boy of 16 from the Midlands said—'You know how to act with decorum in situations and what to do if you're going to have sex. . .'

If girls had been made more cautious, it was interesting that boys tended to stress different aspects, like this boy of 16 in the Midlands—'I understand most of it and it's made me more mature towards people. . .' And, although the approach of some was less than mature, nevertheless it was clear that a certain basis of factual knowledge was necessary for a responsible approach, as this boy of 15 indicated—'I'm more cautious. I'll think twice before I do it—knowing you could easily get a baby or fertilise an egg. . .'

Only three teenagers, 1 per cent of the sample, said that knowing the facts about these matters had made them want to experiment with sex, but it was, of course, impossible to say whether they had experimented, and if they had, to what extent this was due to their knowledge. It should be stressed that the vast majority of the replies by teenagers to this question stressed very firmly that knowledge of the facts had discouraged rather than encouraged experimentation in sex.

This was also true of the teenagers who said that although knowing the facts had not affected their behaviour so far they thought it would in future. Again, the main effect they thought it would have was in making them more cautious about sex, about casual sex and about rushing into relationships. It appeared that girls again had taken notice of the risks of casual relationships, as this 14-year-old from the North-East pointed out—'It teaches you not to rush into things—to do things with the boys that ruin your life, like having a baby too soon. . .'—and certainly it seemed that knowledge of the possible consequences of sexual activity had made a big impression on some girls—'It would make me more cautious. When you know the awful things that can happen you are much more careful. . .'

Some of the teenagers stressed specifically that their knowledge would make them use reliable contraception, as this girl of 16 pointed out:

I'll know more about contraception than my mother did. She had seven of us. Because of 'Child Care'—when they told us what age to have children, I'll probably have mine at that age. . .

None of the teenagers who thought that knowing the facts would affect their behaviour in future said that it might make them want to experiment. Looking at the answers to these questions as a whole, it can be seen that although half the teenagers thought that knowing the facts had not affected their behaviour and was unlikely to affect their behaviour—for whatever reason— half thought that it had or would, with over one-third of the sample saying spontaneously that it had or would make them more cautious about their sexual behaviour, while the majority of the rest thought it would make them behave in a more mature or wise manner or help them form better relationships and understand the opposite sex better.

8 ASSESSMENT BY PARENTS AND TEENAGERS OF EFFECT OF SCHOOL SEX EDUCATION ON SEXUAL BEHAVIOUR

The effects of education in sex and personal relationships in schools have been widely discussed. Widely conflicting claims have been put forward about the results of 'sex education', ranging from those who think that '. . . sex education, as presently practised, is a mass of misinformation, misrepresentation, and outright fraud . . .'[21] to those who feel that only through 'sex education given by every school to every child . . . can contemporary man be helped to come to an intelligent understanding of his own sexuality'[22]. 'Sex education' has been held to encourage promiscuity and early sexual experimentation on the one hand and to discourage early experimentation and encourage caution on the other. It has been suggested by some that sex education puts too little emphasis on the values of marriage and the family, while others suggest that it encourages the development of mature and caring relationships between the sexes.

Very little evidence has been put forward to support these conflicting claims, and this is not particularly surprising. Behaviour is the result of all the influences in a person's life. It is quite impossible to pull out one influence or another and say that it alone has made someone behave in a certain way. This study has indicated the enormous number of influences at work on the behaviour of adolescents, among which education at school is only one. It is also quite impossible to make any generalisation about 'sex education', as has been clearly illustrated in this report. The provision and methods of teaching in the different schools attended by the teenagers in the three areas we studied varied enormously, and any assessment of 'sex education' at school would have to take account of the fact that this variety will be repeated up and down the country.

Nevertheless, this study offered the opportunity of asking parents and their teenage children what they thought about the effects of 'sex education' at school. We were concerned throughout the investigation to establish the facts and to ask for opinions. The questions were always neutral and balanced, and we always asked for reasons for the answers. The report has clearly shown the value placed by both parents and teenagers on sex education at school, but we wanted to ask a very specific question about what they felt to be the effects of sex education at school on the early sexual behaviour of young people.

In our pilot study we asked the question, 'Some people say that having sex education at school makes young people more likely to experiment with sex at an early age. What do you think about that?' The answer to this question showed quite clearly that those who disagreed with the proposition often added that, on the contrary, they felt that sex education at school made young people more cautious. We therefore decided to put both propositions in our main study, so that parents and teenagers could give their assessment of both. We present the results below and discuss the implications of both questions together.

Table 55 *Parents' and teenagers' assessment of whether sex education at school makes young people more likely to experiment with sex at an early age*

Column percentages

	Teenagers			*Parents*		
	Total	Boys	Girls	Total	Mothers	Fathers
Agree strongly	1	0	2	4	5	0
Agree	25	29	21	16	16	14
Depends/some might possibly	11	9	14	18	16	24
Depends/probably not/only a few	5	7	3	10	7	16
Disagree	40	37	43	41	43	35
Disagree strongly	14	11	17	9	9	10
Don't know	3	6	1	2	3	0
Base	(209)	(99)	(110)	(212)	(149)	(63)

Before we discuss these figures, it should be pointed out that there was evidence of both teenagers and their parents agreeing or disagreeing with both propositions, in other words, saying that sex education at school could make young people more likely to experiment *and* more cautious, *or* that it made them neither more likely to experiment *nor* more cautious. In addition, some respondents thought that it was impossible to generalise about either proposition and that it depended on the individual and the circumstances in both instances. Table 57 shows the proportion of parents and teenagers who gave the same answer to both questions.

One-fifth of the parents and a quarter of the teenagers thought that sex education at school made young people more likely to experiment with sex at an early age, although, as we can see from Table 57, teenagers were more

Table 56 *Parents' and teenagers' assessment of whether sex education at school makes young people more cautious about experimenting with sex at an early age*

Column percentages

	Teenagers			Parents		
	Total	Boys	Girls	Total	Mothers	Fathers
Agree strongly	3	4	3	2	2	3
Agree	55	53	56	31	32	29
Depends/some might possibly	11	9	13	30	28	35
Depends/probably not/only a few	1	1	1	1	1	3
Disagree	22	26	18	25	29	17
Disagree strongly	1	0	2	4	4	3
Don't know	7	7	7	5	5	6
Base	(209)	(99)	(110)	(212)	(149)	(63)

likely than their parents to say that it made young people both likely to experiment *and* to make them more cautious. Girls were less likely than boys and fathers less likely than mothers to think that sex education at school made young people more likely to experiment.

Table 57 *Proportion of respondents giving same answer to questions on whether sex education at school makes young people more likely to experiment or more cautious at an early age*

Column percentages

	Teenagers			Parents		
	Total	Boys	Girls	Total	Mothers	Fathers
Makes young people more likely to experiment *and* more cautious	11	12	11	3	1	6
Does not make young people more likely to experiment nor more cautious	14	12	15	15	17	11
'Depends' to both questions	4	5	4	16	11	29

So why did teenagers think that sex education made young people more likely to experiment, and what was their evidence for this assertion? In fact those who thought it made young people more likely to experiment seldom gave much reason for thinking so. Sometimes, but rarely, they referred to their own behaviour, like this 14-year-old girl in the South-West—'It influences them, yes. They are bound to go out and try it, aren't they? Well, *I* did. . .'—and her view was reinforced by a 15-year-old boy from the South-West—'It's true, because when the teacher tells you something you go out and do it. . .'

But nearly 60 per cent of teenagers disagreed with the idea or thought that only a few might be influenced to experiment. Some of the teenagers— nearly a fifth of the girls in fact—disagreed strongly with the very idea and expressed their views forcibly, like this 15-year-old boy—'Rubbish—they think all teenagers are sex-mad and they are not. Most of them are scared stiff. . .'—and this 15-year-old girl from the Midlands—'Load of rubbish. Just because you talk about it it doesn't mean you're going to go out and do it. . .'

Many of the teenagers stressed the fact, which had been emphasised throughout the study by teenagers, that sex education at school made them aware of the risks, and this 15-year-old girl from the Midlands explained— 'Most of the people who do experiment didn't listen properly to what they were taught—the situations they could get themselves into—pregnancy and catching VD. . .'—and her view was shared by a 15-year-old boy from the same area—'No way—it puts you off it—all the bad things that can happen. . .'

A number of teenagers and their parents who disagreed with the proposition felt that sex education at school did not make much difference to people's behaviour, as this boy from the Midlands said—'That's stupid. If they're going to experiment they will. They don't have to have somebody tell them how to do it first. . .'—and a girl of 15 from the North-East agreed— 'If they're going to experiment I think they would if they had sex education or not. . .'

A number of teenagers thought that lack of sex education at school was more likely to cause experimentation, as this 16-year-old girl from the North-East pointed out—'Once they know about the facts I don't think they will. They're more likely to experiment if they don't know. . .' And the varying provision of sex education at school was highlighted by a 14-year-old girl in the Midlands who said tersely—'It doesn't. They don't teach you enough to experiment. . .'

The parents were less likely to think that sex education at school encouraged early sexual experimenting, as we have seen, although rather more thought that it depended on the circumstances and that some young people might. It was rare for parents to say that sex education at school put ideas into young people's heads or 'brings out their curiosity' as one mother said. Those who agreed with the proposition were more likely to say that it depended on how and how much they were taught. It was difficult to see how some parents thought that children should be taught 'properly' but it often appeared that these parents did not think that schools stressed the risks of early sexual experimentation sufficiently.

Over a quarter of the parents thought that it depended on the individual child and the circumstances and this mother of a 15-year-old boy in the North-East expressed the view of many parents in this category—'It depends on how it is put across. Some children will try it anyway, whether they're taught or not—they will do it regardless. . .'—and this father of a boy of 14 from the Midlands agreed—'If a child is going to experiment he will. What he learns at school won't affect it. You can't blame the schools for it—nor the parents either—it's human nature. . .'

But, like the teenagers, the majority of parents disagreed with the proposition, as this mother of a 14-year-old girl explained—'No—if they learn as they grow up and are taught the full facts I don't think they'll experiment. It's when they're not taught the full facts that they will. . .'—and other mothers applauded the efforts of schools, like this mother of a 16-year-old girl in the Midlands—'I don't think so at all. It's good for them to know about it—better than dirty-minded things in their heads. . .' Sex education at school was often seen as a balance to 'other pressures' around them, as this father pointed out—'I think there's a good chance it will balance that which they've picked up from their friends, most of which is inaccurate anyway. . .' Some parents thought that schools were necessary to teach children the risks, as this mother of a 14-year-old girl said—'I think they experiment anyway and at least they learn how to experiment safely. . .'

Teenagers were more likely than their parents, however, to agree with the proposition that sex education at school made young people more cautious about experimenting with sex at an early age, while parents were more likely to say that it depended on the situation. Nearly 60 per cent of teenagers said that it made young people more cautious and a further 11 per cent thought that it made some more cautious, compared with a third of parents who thought it made young people more cautious and a further third who thought it made some more cautious.

As we have seen, teenagers tended to stress the risks that they had learned about at school, particularly as far as pregnancy and venereal disease were concerned. This boy of 15 had become more cautious—'If I had not been taught at school I wouldn't have known about contraception and VD and might take unnecessary risks. . .'—and the advantage of seeing films at school in instilling caution was frequently stressed, particularly by boys, like this 14-year-old from the North-East—'The film on VD puts them off because they are a bit wary after that. A lot of them have tried it out earlier and after the film they get scared and stop doing it. . .'

Teenagers often used words like 'wary' in describing how teenagers were affected by school sex education, as this 14-year-old girl said—'The teacher can explain all the problems and what can happen and make you more wary. . .' And several teenagers used the word 'damage' to explain what could happen to their lives, like this 15-year-old girl—'They are shown what damage can be done with pregnancy and disease and it can put them off. . .' Education in itself was thought to be a good thing by many teenagers, even if they did not think it necessarily made teenagers more cautious, as this 15-year-old boy in the North-East said:

> Not more cautious, but it makes them more aware of the things that could happen—unplanned babies, VD, those sort of things. . .

It sometimes appeared that some teenagers took the preventive aspect of sex education more seriously than the schools themselves might have intended. We have already seen that films on childbirth were not always seen as encouraging, and this came up again in answer to this question. The horrors of venereal disease as portrayed on films were certainly thought by many teenagers to instil caution, and some teenagers appeared to have lodged certain pieces of information away in their minds in a way which was perhaps not intended, like this 14-year-old boy in the North-East who thought school sex education did make young people more cautious—'They don't want to get pregnant too early do they? And the lads who've done it don't want to have blood tests to find out if they are the father, do they?'

Parents too tended to stress the preventive aspects of sex education at school, although not as much as the teenagers. Some of the parents echoed the comments of the teenagers, like this mother of a 15-year-old boy:

> I would agree with that. It makes them understand how dangerous it can be especially with VD. By knowing there are danger signs—like being tied down at an early age if they get a girl into trouble. . .

The consequences of early sexual activity were stressed by a number of parents, some of whom were very hazy, as we have seen, about what was actually taught at secondary school, like this mother of a boy of 14 who thought that sex education did make young people more cautious—'Well, it makes them understand. They should be taught why they shouldn't experiment at an early age. If they know what it leads to they'll understand why they shouldn't do it. . .' Some parents advocated various shock-horror techniques, including a surprising one from a mother of a 14-year-old boy in the North-East—'If they showed an actual act of sexual intercourse it would put them off. . .'

But, as we have seen, a third of parents tended to think that it depended very much on the individual and the circumstances, stressing that there were many more influences on young people than simply sex education at school, as this father of a 14-year-old girls said:

> Good education will help them come to terms with their sexual development. For some it will make them more cautious, some more confident. It will vary considerably. . .

But for over a quarter of parents there was no doubt in their minds that sex education at school did not make young people more cautious about sexual experimentation, like this father of a boy of 16—'I don't think it would. If a child's imagination is fired by what he or she has already learned, by the time there's some formal instruction that formal instruction won't modify the desire to experiment. . .' Some parents felt that they had evidence to the contrary, like this mother of a 16-year-old girl—'Statistics prove that it doesn't. There's a lot of abortions and unwanted babies about in spite of having the pill. . .'—and parents often had plenty of anecdotal evidence, like this mother of a 15-year-old girl—'Rubbish. I've got a sister—20 in October. A friend of hers who had some sex education lessons has been pregnant twice. I can't understand it. . .'

And the difficulty that parents recognised in educating young people in these matters was underlined by the mother who said—'Some might be more cautious but a lot won't be. Look at drinking and driving. . .'

School sex education and personal relationships

'Sex education' at school has been criticised in the past for laying too much emphasis on the biological or mechanical aspects of sex and not helping children develop a social and personal awareness so that they can grow up as mature individuals capable of forming loving and responsible relationships with others. Much of the curriculum guidance and discussion in recent years has encouraged the development of programmes in secondary schools of personal and social education, and it was quite clear from our interviewing that many of the teenagers attended schools where these programmes had been introduced, particularly in the fourth and fifth years. At the same time, an increasing emphasis in schools on the importance of pastoral care, especially by senior staff, has also led to more awareness of the importance of developing social skills and awareness and the ability to form relationships with other people and respect their views.

Many teenagers interviewed in this study had emphasised how much they valued discussions at school as a way of learning about sex, contraception and personal relationships. We were interested to know whether their sex education lessons or discussions had helped them understand better how people of the opposite sex felt about things, and whether they felt a need for more insight into the feelings of people of the opposite sex. Since discussions about personal relationships often brought up matters such as emotions and feelings, we were interested to know how useful the teenagers found this type of discussion.

There was a marked age difference here, with 15- and 16-year-olds more likely than 14-year-olds to say that they had been helped to understand better how the opposite sex felt about things. This was perhaps not surprising in view of the fact that they were more likely to have had a programme of personal and social education of some sort. But girls had obviously found it more useful than boys, and this was not related to age.

Table 58 *Teenagers' assessment of whether school sex education had helped them understand better how people of the opposite sex felt about things*

Column percentages

	Total	Boys	Girls	14	15	16
Yes	44	39	47	36	46	51
No	51	53	49	56	47	49
Don't know	6	8	4	8	7	0
Base	(209)	(99)	(110)	(75)	(81)	(53)

The vast majority of the teenagers who said that they had been helped by lessons or discussions at school to understand the opposite sex better said that they had found it useful. We were interested to know how they had been helped.

Some of the teenagers found it difficult to articulate exactly why they had found it helpful, but girls found it useful to hear what the boys felt about things. There was clear evidence throughout the interviews with teenagers that, without the relatively formal structure of having discussions in 'lessons', boys and girls rarely exchanged views and opinions on 'relationships' and 'feelings' in the way that they did with people of their own sex. A girl of 14 expressed the views of a number of girls in saying what she found useful about these discussions:

> It gives you a balanced view about what the boys feel about something and about what the girls feel about things. . .

Some teenagers stressed that these discussions helped to correct misconceptions they had about the views of the opposite sex, as this girl of 15 in the North-East pointed out—'We used to think that boys preferred girls to be slags but now I know that's not true. . .'—and a boy of 14 in the Midlands talked about what he had learned about girls through discussions on personal relationships at school:

> I can't explain it really. They don't like being rushed into things. If, like, you want to go out with a girl and you want her to come out with all your other friends and she doesn't want to, you have to wait and ask her gradually. . .

It was this gradual development of social skills and the ability to appreciate the feelings and emotions of the other sex which teenagers felt they had learned through this kind of education at school. A lot of it was clearly learned in an 'incidental' way, but there were many references to discussions covering a wide range of personal relationships, as this boy of 14 in the Midlands said when talking about discussions at his school—'About how a man always expects a woman to do the housework and other things, and it really shouldn't be that way. . .'

We asked all the teenagers whether they would like to know more about how people of the opposite sex felt about things. Overall, 45 per cent of teenagers said that they would, but it was striking that nearly 50 per cent of the boys said they would, and so did the same proportion of 14-year-olds. It appeared that these groups had perhaps not benefited as much as older teenagers and the girls from the education they had had so far. It should also be noted that most teenagers at single-sex schools wanted to know more about how the opposite sex felt about things. It should be stressed, however, that half the teenagers had not felt that they had been helped by education at school to understand better how people of the opposite sex felt about things, and half of them did not want to know more about how the opposite sex felt!

But what did the teenagers want to know more about? About a fifth wanted to know what the opposite sex felt about everything, and about a fifth wanted to know what they felt about relationships with the opposite sex.

It should be emphasised that some of the things that teenagers wanted to know might appear to be very naive, but it must be remembered that, in spite of their apparent sophistication and knowledge, some of these teenagers were very immature. By this time in the interview, many of them had established a trusting relationship with the interviewer and there was a certain poignancy in some of the comments made by the young people, like this wish of a 14-year-old in the North-East, who summarised the views of many of his age:

I'd like to know how to talk to girls and how not to put them off. How they feel about things and how to know if they like you. . .

There was evidence among boys of great insecurity in approaching girls, in spite of the apparent bravado and 'macho' qualities that parents thought they affected. This 16-year-old boy was quite clear on what he wanted to know—'If I could know what they're thinking just by looking at them, I'd know if to play it cool or what. . .'

Girls were often more articulate about feelings and emotions, and this 16-year-old from the Midlands tried to explain what she wanted to know:

I'd love to know what they're thinking—if it's the same as you and why they behave the way they do. I'd like to know about differences in emotions and why they become mardy when things happen like breaking up. They get emotional in different ways from girls and they keep things inside and get strung up. Girls tend to talk to friends but boys keep quiet. . .

Boys, on the other hand, sometimes reiterated the functional view they had shown throughout the interviews, like this 14-year-old boy—'If you know their reactions, you know how they feel. It might come in handy in

166

later life. . .'—and this 15-year-old from the Midlands—'What they think about contraception and things like that. It would be useful if I had a special girlfriend to know how she felt about it. . .'

Eighty per cent of parents thought it was a good thing if schools tried to help young people understand better how people of the opposite sex felt about things. Parents felt very strongly about this matter, and similar proportions of mothers and fathers stressed its importance.

Why did they feel it was so important? Parents gave a variety of answers but there were three main reasons given—that they felt it would lead to a better understanding between the sexes in general, that boys and girls were different and had different emotions and feelings and that these should be discussed, and that school was the best place in which to learn about these things under the guidance of a teacher, since they were better trained than parents, and, perhaps surprisingly, because children would take more notice of these matters if they learned about them at school.

One mother explained why she felt it necessary for teenagers to learn about these things at school:

I think it's important to understand how the other sex feels how girls develop and about periods, and why boys' voices break and not to laugh at one another. To help understanding between the sexes. . .

Some parents saw it as a preparation for life, like this father of a girl in the North-East:

In the wider sense it's a matter of interpersonal relationships. I think it will prepare them for maintaining a good relationship after leaving home when they are away from the influence of their parents and coping with life outside. . .

Others thought that school could correct the effect of certain other influences which not everyone found desirable, as this mother in the North-East explained:

The boys and girls at her school learned about their bodily differences— the physical side, that is. They have done roles within the family a bit as well. People tend in the North-East to think of the man as breadwinner and mother at home, so perhaps it has helped her to see the difference in the sexes and their roles.

But it was on this question that so many parents stressed that teenagers could perhaps learn more at school than at home, as this mother of a 15-year-old boy pointed out—'It's good for the types of people like me who can't talk to him, whereas at school he would *have* to sit and listen and it would maybe do him some good. . .' It certainly appeared that parents in the North-East were very much concerned with this subject, as this father of a 15-year-old boy said—'He will sit and listen at school and can't say he hasn't time. He won't be able to dash off somewhere. He'll *have* to stay and listen. . .'

167

The expertise of teachers was stressed on this subject, which was perhaps surprising since it appeared that there was little technical knowledge required in discussing personal relationships. But parents were quite clear on what they wanted from the school, as this father of a 15-year-old boy said—'I think they can explain it more than we could. The children take more notice of school things. . .'—and his view was reinforced by a mother from another area—'They have a better way of putting it and have a lot more understanding. The child would take more notice of someone at school as they could explain it more. I'm not saying he would take no notice of me, but the teachers have got the right attitude. . .'

It was clear that parents were concerned that their children should learn about the opposite sex so that they could form happy relationships, as this father of a 15-year-old boy from the North-East said:

> I hope they do teach them that at school. It makes them more caring and understanding and would help with marriage. It might also make them more cautious about sex before marriage. . .

Some of the heartfelt comments in answer to this question suggested that we had touched a chord in the parents which questions about specific subjects had not touched. The importance which parents attached to the need for help from school in learning about personal relationships was summarised by this father from the North-East:

> They should learn at school because of the misunderstandings that can happen. You learn to see the other sex's point of view. Seeing the other bloke's point of view helps in work as well as relationships with women. It's good to learn about other people. . .

But did parents know much about what their children had learned at school about these things? A third of the parents said that their children's school had in fact helped them to understand better how the opposite sex felt about things, but 16 per cent said it had not, and 51 per cent said they did not know. More fathers than mothers thought the school had helped in this respect, and this father of a 15-year-old in the North-East pointed out:

> Yes, he knows about periods and how girls feel at that time of the month. He understands some of the problems of being a woman and giving birth, and he knows that marriage is an equal partnership and there shouldn't be one dominant partner. . .

And this mother of a 14-year-old girl in the South-West knew quite clearly what her daughter had learned:

> In child care and development she learned about how everything starts from two people loving one another and caring for each other—sharing things generally, and that it's not just lust. . .

In general, parents who thought that the school had helped stressed that it had deepened their children's knowledge and understanding of the opposite sex in a variety of ways. But it was perhaps surprising that more than half the parents had no idea what the school did about encouraging understanding of the opposite sex, and, considering it was a matter of such concern to parents, it appeared that schools could do much more to let parents know what they were attempting to achieve. Parents know little enough about the school's actual teaching on concrete matters, so possibly it was not so surprising that they did not know exactly what was going on in rather less tangible discussions. Nevertheless, schools should be aware of the tremendous support they would get from parents on this particular matter, and should foster this contact.

Discussions on feelings and emotions

Since so much emphasis was laid by teenagers on the importance of discussions in learning about sex, contraception and personal relationships, we were interested to know how useful they found it to have discussions at school about things like emotions and feelings. Two-thirds of the teenagers thought it was useful, again with older teenagers more likely to find it so. Indeed over 70 per cent of the 16-year-olds said they found it useful.

The value of hearing 'other people's point of view' was again the most important reason given. We had thought that perhaps teenagers might feel more inhibited about discussing feelings and emotions than more factual aspects of 'sex education', but clearly many schools integrated the discussions on facts with discussions on feelings and emotions, thus refuting the charge that children were taught in too mechanistic a way without taking into account feelings and relationships.

Feelings of mutual support and not being isolated from the world were very important for some teenagers, as this 15-year-old boy from the Midlands indicated—'You sometimes think only you feel like that and it's nice to know other people feel that as well. . .' And sometimes the feeling of mutual support went even further, as this girl of 16 in the Midlands said—'It helps you to cope with the situation. If you were going out with a boy and he packed you in you could talk about it at school. . .'

Simply sharing problems was thought to be important by many teenagers, as this 15-year-old boy from the Midlands showed: 'Some people might have problems and they'd just want people to talk with them. If they don't talk about it with people they just worry about it. . .' It was clear that discussions at school of this kind were geared to sorting out all kinds of personal relationships, as this girl of 14 in the South-West explained—'If you're going through a bad patch with your parents and someone else is going through the same thing then someone else can help someone else. . .'

Teenagers were quite open about the value of discussions of emotions in understanding relationships between the sexes, as this boy of 16 in the North-East said in describing what he found to be the value of discussions about emotions and feelings at school—'In case they get a girlfriend and they fell out. They want to cry their eyes out. They'll understand the emotions. . .'— and his view was reinforced by a girl from the same area—'Maybe it might make other people wary—both boys and girls. Girls get hurt and boys just leave them and go on to another girl, and it would let them know how you feel. . .'

The importance of group discussions in helping to develop an insight and self-awareness was put succinctly by some teenagers, like this 15-year-old girl from the South-West—'It's useful because we can understand why we feel like we do—why we feel angry about things or sad. . .'

And, perhaps most important, teenagers wanted to know simply how to get along with people, of the same sex and the opposite sex. They felt that class discussion helped—'So you don't say the wrong things to upset people. It helps you to understand them. . .' It appeared that an organised forum for discussion such as that provided in the personal and social education lessons at school often gave teenagers the opportunity for self-exploration and understanding of others which they could not find elsewhere.

But some teenagers did not find it useful to have discussions at school about things like emotions and feelings, and a third of the boys said it was not helpful. Boys tended to say that these things were too 'personal' and that others might laugh at them, as this boy of 15 in the South-West pointed out— 'I don't think it would be taken seriously and you would be laughed at and called a "weirdo". I don't think they have much feeling about it. . .' And the privacy that many teenagers cherished was expressed by both boys and girls, as this boy of 14 said—'You should discuss these things at home. Your mates and teachers might spread it around—not keep it secret.'

Girls tended to stress their own individuality and to see no point in sharing—like this girl of 15 in the Midlands—'Because you have your own emotions and feelings and you have your own way of looking at things—because everyone isn't the same. . .' And others felt that they could not express themselves about these matters in a group at school, like this 15-year-old girl—'I couldn't really talk in front of the teachers. I would get all tongue-twisted. I just turn to my friends who understand more. . .' Maturity and understanding were thought to be lacking in some, as this girl in the North-East explained—'Most lads laugh and some lasses are too young to understand. They try to act mature but they're not. . .'

But some teenagers denied any need for this kind of discussion at all, like this girl of 14 from the North-East—'Because they don't have anything to do with us. You don't have emotions at my age. . .'—and this boy of 16 from the same area—'It's a bit sloppy. I don't go in for emotions. . .'

But most teenagers did, and interviews with teenagers were remarkable for the evidence they gave of the value so many of them attached to the discussions, both formal and informal, they were able to have at school about feelings, emotions and personal relationships. If the aim of educators and teachers in introducing programmes of personal and social development into schools has been to make children more aware of the feelings of others, to share views and opinions and to develop a responsible attitude to the opposite sex, then there is plenty of evidence from teenagers in this report that they have been successful.

General assessment by parents of teenagers' sex education at school
We asked the parents how satisfied they were in general with the sex education their son or daughter had had at secondary school, and Table 59 summarises their views.

Table 59   *Parents' satisfaction with the sex education received by teenager at secondary school*

Column percentages

	Total	Mother	Father
Very satisfied	15	16	11
Fairly satisfied	48	48	49
Not very satisfied	6	6	6
Not at all satisfied	2	3	0
Don't know	29	28	33
Base	(212)	(149)	(63)

This table confirmed the evidence collected throughout this investigation. It showed that there was a generally high level of satisfaction with what the school was providing teenagers in sex education, but that there was a certain lack of knowledge among a substantial minority of parents. One third of the fathers and over a quarter of the mothers said that they did not know whether they were satisfied with the sex education their son or daughter had had at secondary school, mainly because they felt that they did not know enough about it.

Only 17 parents (8 per cent) said that they were in any way dissatisfied with the sex education their children had received, and it should be stressed that over a third of these said that their children had not had enough sex education in general, and a further third thought there had not been enough on specific subjects such as contraception, venereal disease or personal relationships. Four parents were dissatisfied with the *way* that it had been taught, for example by a male teacher or in a group, while only two parents—1 per cent of the total sample—were dissatisfied because they thought sex education should not be given at secondary school at all.

These are, in fact, very low levels of dissatisfaction among parents on secondary school treatment of a subject which has been the topic of so much controversy. It must, therefore, be asked whether this controversy has been artificially contrived by people who are completely out of touch with what the majority of parents of teenage children think and feel.

9 SEX EDUCATION—WHOSE RESPONSIBILITY?

The aim of this report has been to establish the facts about the present provision of sex education in secondary schools, to look at this provision against the background of all the other influences on the development of teenagers, and to put it into the context of the education on these matters given to teenagers at home. It has been asserted that education about sex and personal relationships should not be given at school and should only be given at home. We asked both parents and teenagers what they thought about this to try and establish their views on a matter on which they were, in fact, the people most affected. We asked the following question: 'Some people say that giving sex education to children and young people should *only* be the responsibility of the parents and that schools should play no part in it. What do you feel about that?' The responses are presented in detail in Table 60.

It will be seen quite clearly that the overwhelming majority of both parents and their teenage children were of the opinion that sex education should be provided at school. Two per cent of parents and 1 per cent of teenagers thought that sex education should not be provided by either school or parents, and 2 per cent of parents and 4 per cent of teenagers thought only parents should provide sex education. Ninety-six per cent of parents and 95 per cent of teenagers thought that schools should provide sex education to children and young people, at least to some extent, and the provisos are given in the table and discussed below. It should be noted that Christine Farrell found in 1974[1] that 96 per cent of parents interviewed thought that sex education should be provided at secondary schools, so the findings of this study should not be regarded as surprising.

It was firmly felt by a quarter of both parents and teenagers that both schools and parents should provide sex education to young people and that it should be a joint responsibility. Parents often used the words 'joint responsibility' or 'joint effort', and their views were summarised by this mother of a 15-year-old boy in the Midlands:

Table 60 *Parents' and teenagers' views on the proposition that sex education should only be the responsibility of parents and that schools should play no part in it*

Column percentages

	Parents	Teenagers
Both schools and parents should provide/joint responsibility	23	24
Schools should provide:		
—because some parents can't/don't talk to children re SE	19	31
—no reason given	13	11
—because give more accurate information/facts/better equipped	9	12
—because part of education/that's what there for/children listen more	9	2
Parents should have main responsibility backed up by school	6	3
Schools should have main responsibility backed by parents	4	1
Schools should provide:		
—as long as teachers qualified/taught properly	3	0
—because some children can't/don't talk to parents re SE	3	7
Parents ideally but not all parents/children can talk to each other	3	1
Schools should provide:		
—because children hear more points of view/more discussion	2	2
—because parents prefer them to—less embarrassing for parents	2	3
Sex education should *not* be given by either parents or school	2	1
Parents should/their role/teachers not suitable	1	2
Only parents should provide—no reason given	1	2
Depends on parents' and children's preference	1	0
Schools should but not at primary school	0	1
Base	(212)	(209)

I think both should have responsibility. The teacher will tell him one side of the story which is right and the parents can also tell them. Some children will take it more from the parents and others from the teacher. . .

And her view was repeated by a father of a 14-year-old boy in the South-West:

Schools should play a part. It's half the battle. Two heads are better than one. If the parent doesn't care about the child—is not interested— at least the child will get some. . .

And teenagers agreed, as this 14-year-old boy in the Midlands summarised—'I reckon it should be at school and at home. Some parents can't tell you everything and some teachers can't. . .'

Nearly a third of the teenagers thought that schools should provide sex education because some parents could not or did not talk to their children about these matters, sometimes because they did not know enough themselves. This view was shared by a fifth of the parents, and this mother of a 14-year-old girl in the Midlands summarised what many parents said about the statement that sex education should only be the responsibility of parents—'I don't agree at all. A lot of parents can't even talk to each other about sex, so there's no way they'll learn how to discuss it with their kids. A lot of parents don't know the facts about sex themselves. . .' It was common for parents to relate this to their own experience, like this mother of a 14-year-old girl who wanted to make sure that children did not miss what she considered to be an important part of life—'It's not right. Some parents can't talk to their children, so if the schools don't give them sex education they will all grow up like I was. . .' And parents often stressed their lack of faith in the ability of other parents to talk to their children about these matters, like this mother of a 16-year-old boy in the South-West:

I don't agree. If it was left to the parents we'd have the most ignorant lot of teenagers. The schools should do it because some parents can't or won't do it. . .

And her view was reinforced by such a parent, the mother of a 15-year-old girl in the South-West—'No, I definitely don't agree with that. If it was left to parents like me a lot of children wouldn't get any sex education. . .'

Teenagers felt this most strongly, as this 16-year-old girl from the South-West pointed out:

The school has got to have some say in it. You might have parents who are too embarrassed to tell you about it and by the time they do pluck up courage it might be too late. You might end up going through life knowing nothing about it. . .

Some teenagers spoke from their own experience, like this 16-year-old boy in the Midlands—'It's wrong. You should learn at school as well. A lot can't talk to their parents, especially if it's your father's second wife like me. She's always busy with the younger children. . .' and other teenagers stressed that their own parents had not been able to tell them anything, like this 15-year-old boy from the Midlands—'Well my parents never told me anything, so I found out from friends. It should be taught in schools because friends don't always know all the risks and stuff. . .'

Teenagers certainly knew that the information received from friends was not reliable, as we have seen, and this view came up in answer to this question, as this girl of 16 from the North-East said:

> Some parents don't tell their children because they are embarrassed, and they're just going to learn off other children and that could be wrong and what they tell them might not be right. . .

while others thought that it was not only friends who might give inaccurate information, like this 15-year-old girl who thought the school should give sex education—'Because parents might get embarrassed and so give misguided facts. There should be some back-up of this. . .'

It was felt by both parents and children that teenagers were more likely to receive accurate information at school rather than from parents, as this father of a 14-year-old boy in the North-East said forcibly—'Some parents couldn't teach their children to eat properly, never mind sex education. The child must be taught properly. . .'—and his view was shared by another father in the North-East—'I don't agree that it should just be the parents' responsibility—nothing worse than passing on your own ignorance. . .'

Teenagers agreed and passed on the consumers' view, like this 16-year-old in the North-East—'Schools should do most of it. Teachers do it better—make it more plain and less embarrassing and use the right words and it's more like a lesson. Parents feel a bit queer about it I think. . .' Teenagers tended to stress that schools presented them with reliable facts and a comprehensive picture in an unbiased way, as this boy of 14 from the Midlands pointed out:

> School gives you a professional view of it and helps you understand the workings of the body, whereas a parent only talks about an opinionised version of it and not a general idea. . .

It was also pointed out, as it had been throughout the interviews with teenagers, that schools were better equipped to present the information in a way which made it easy to understand, as this 15-year-old boy from the North-East said—'You go to school to learn and that includes sex education. They have films, videos and slides to help you get it all straight. . .'

Parents were more likely than teenagers to say that sex education was part of general education and that children would take more notice if it came from school. Nearly 10 per cent of parents gave this as their main reason for saying that they disagreed with the statement that only parents should give sex education, as this father in the North-East said—'Children spend six hours a day at school, so they must learn more at school than at home. I have no objections to teachers teaching them about sex the same as they do about maths or any other subject. . .' And his view was shared by parents from other areas, like this mother from the Midlands—'It is part of education. Schools are there to learn your children on every subject—sex should come into it. . .'

We have already seen the difficulty that some parents said they had in actually getting their children to listen to them at all, and how they found particular difficulty in talking to them about sex. Pinning the children down to listen was thought to be something at which the school was better, as this father of a 15-year-old boy explained—'At school they have to sit down and listen. They can't get up and go out of the room. . .' and a mother from the North-East agreed—'I think schools should (give sex education) because the kids have to listen in school and it's just like an ordinary lesson. For people like me it's a godsend. . .'

Although few teenagers gave this as their main reason for approving of sex education at school, nevertheless this boy of 14 from the Midlands confirmed the suspicions of parents in other areas—'Silly—of course the schools should play some part in it as you spend so much time at school. Most of the time you only see your parents at weekends. . .'

It was chiefly parents who thought that the main responsibility should rest with the parents, but that it should be backed up by the school, but nevertheless it can be seen that only 6 per cent of parents held the view expressed by this mother of a girl of 15—'I think that it should be almost wholly the parents' responsibility but that the school should reinforce what they've learned at home. . .' while 4 per cent of parents thought that it should be the main responsibility of the school, backed up by parents, who could give the 'social or moral guidance' as one father put it.

This was also the view of two girls—both from the Midlands—one of whom said—'I think the school should play an important role in the sex education of a child. At school you are supposed to learn things, and sex education has a high factual content and is better taught by teachers, and your parents can teach you the emotional side. . .'—and her view was echoed by the other—'Schools should definitely play a part. They can give you all the difficult instruction and then parents can join in later. . .'

Three per cent of parents thought that schools should provide sex education as long as it was taught 'properly' by qualified teachers and using expert outsiders as back-up. Seven per cent of the teenagers and 3 per cent of parents thought that schools should provide it because some children could not talk to their parents, as this mother of a boy of 16 said—'I think it should be 50:50 because when they get to 14-15 years old they don't ask their parents any more. . .' Some parents felt that this was not only because of the child, as this mother of a 14-year-old boy pointed out—'I feel the school should do it as some children can't speak to their parents, especially if they are a bit strait-laced and think everything going on around them is disgusting—then a child won't talk to the parents. . .'

And even parents who thought that it should ideally be the parents' role recognised that school sex education was necessary, as this mother of a boy of 15 in the North-East explained—'I *really* think it should be the parents but it's a good thing the schools are there to teach them because *I* couldn't. . .'

One mother of a 15-year-old boy in the South-West thought that it was necessary to have school sex education even though she was of the opinion that it ought to be primarily the parents' role:

It depends what the parents are like. There may be no communication at home—that's why I don't agree with Mrs Gillick. I would prefer it within the family unit, but failing that the schools should teach it but out of the classroom. It's too sensitive a subject in class. There should be some degree of intimacy to it. . .

Some parents and children stressed the need for children to hear the different points of view they were likely to hear at school to 'give them a balanced view', as one teenager put it, and also simply because some parents preferred it because they themselves were too embarrassed to give sex education.

And finally there were the 4 per cent of parents and 5 per cent of teenagers who thought either that sex education should not be given by either parent or school or that it should *only* be the responsibility of the parent.

This mother of a girl of 16 in the Midlands spoke for some—'I think it's best for them to find out for themselves and ask questions at home about it. Thirty years ago there was none of this education and now 90 per cent of them at school are doing things they didn't ought to. . .' Her view was shared by a 14-year-old girl in the North-East—'The school shouldn't (give sex education). They're there to teach you but not about sex. It's up to your own parents. If they want to tell you they will, and if they don't they won't. . .' We found that it was mainly 14-year-olds who shared this view, like this girl from the South-West—'I think it should be the responsibility of the parents. They know best when a child is ready to learn about these things. . .'

It was quite clear from the answers to this final question that there was no doubt in the minds of the overwhelming majority of both parents and their children that schools should provide sex education. A view held by 95 per cent of teenagers and 96 per cent of parents really cannot be brushed aside by those who hold the opposite view. The careful thought and argument, based on first-hand experience, of both parents and their teenage children has been presented here in detail to show their reasons for holding their views, and the results simply speak for themselves, both literally and in statistical terms.

DISCUSSION OF FINDINGS

The most striking finding in this study was the extent to which the overwhelming majority of parents and teenagers approved of the provision of education in sex and personal relationships at school. Ninety-six per cent of parents and 95 per cent of their teenage children thought that schools should provide sex education. Indeed, 27 per cent of the parents interviewed preferred the school to take sole responsibility for all aspects of the education of their teenage children on how the body works, sex, contraception and personal relationships. The majority of parents were in favour of education being given to children in primary schools on topics such as reproduction, preparation for puberty and family and parenthood, and virtually all parents were particularly concerned that primary schools should be involved in telling children of the dangers of going with strangers.

It should be stated immediately that the wish by parents for secondary schools to provide their children with the facts about reproduction, puberty, pregnancy and childbirth, contraception, abortion, venereal disease, homosexuality and so on was reinforced by their wish for the schools to provide their children with education on such matters as family and parenthood, personal relationships, feelings and emotions and understanding the opposite sex. It was quite clear that parents and teenagers were aware that there was far more to 'sex education' than simply knowing about the mechanics of sex, and this report presents clear evidence that both parents and their children welcomed the involvement of schools in providing education of a very wide-ranging nature on these topics. There were, in fact, many indications that not only did parents welcome the involvement of the schools in this type of education but that they expected it, and there were many more criticisms by parents of the inadequacy of the coverage of the sex education programmes in schools than of any over-provision.

This study in three local authorities in very different areas of England shows what an enormous increase there has been in the provision of education in sex and personal relationships in secondary schools in comparison with the last major study of sex education which was carried out in 1974 with a nationally representative population of 16–19-year-olds who had been at secondary school in the early 1970s[1]. But what has *not* changed is the extent of parental support for sex education at school. It must be stated again that Christine Farrell found in 1974 that 96 per cent of parents interviewed thought that sex education should be provided at secondary schools.

Over the last ten years there has been much emphasis on developing the pastoral care given in schools and a great deal of work on the curriculum, especially in encouraging an awareness of the needs of others and the changing society in which we live. The interviews with teenagers in this report often give glimpses of the success of such programmes of personal and social education, not only in the sensitive comments they made about the feelings of others but also in their descriptions of some close and trusting relationships with teachers.

We found widespread evidence that the topics covered in education in sex, contraception and personal relationships were firmly integrated into the curriculum as a whole over all the years the children were at secondary school. The topics could arise in more than one subject in any year and were likely to be discussed in more than one lesson in that subject. 'Sex education' was no longer a 'special' subject taught in only one or two lessons by a biology or science teacher or an outsider, but was regarded as covering a wide variety of topics which could be treated in a number of ways in a number of subjects and in different ways at different ages. It was clearly nonsense to talk about 'sex education' as though it could be removed 'at a stroke' from the secondary school curriculum. We also found clear evidence that schools had become aware of the importance of ensuring that teenagers could relate bodily functions to the world of emotions and the wider social and family context in which they lived.

Teenagers talked a great deal about the variety of ways in which they had been taught about these matters, and there had clearly been an enormous increase over the past ten years in the use of visual material such as films, videos, television programmes and slides in presenting these topics. Some of these had made a clear and lasting impression on teenagers and there can be no doubt that the visual treatment of these topics presented simply and in great detail was much appreciated by the children. There had also been a big increase in the use of books and pamphlets and diagrams in teaching about these topics compared with the early 1970s.

But perhaps the most interesting development had been the increasing use of class discussion in education on these topics. Teenagers showed great enthusiasm for these discussions and over 90 per cent thought it was a good idea to have discussions in class about these matters, mainly to hear a variety of views which gave them a wider and less biased understanding of the problems and issues which faced them all in growing up. There were many indications that they appreciated the organised forum for discussion provided in the classroom under the guidance of a teacher which gave them the opportunity for self-exploration and understanding of others which they could not find elsewhere. This was particularly true in helping them understand the feelings and attitudes of the opposite sex, about which many of the teenagers were woefully ignorant and had little opportunity to learn in a family setting. There was clear evidence that boys and girls rarely exchanged views and opinions about feelings and emotions in the way that they could with their own sex and that the classroom setting provided the opportunity to do so.

It was interesting that girls were much more likely than boys to have had some sex education in single-sex groups, mainly in learning about menstruation and changes in girls' bodies at puberty. They were also more likely than boys to express a preference for having some discussions in single-sex groups. There was evidence that boys were still given less education in some of the matters than girls in some schools, and this worried some boys, who thought they might be missing something. The concern of the 14-year-old boy in the North-East who said, 'The girls were told about body changes whilst we boys did revision. I think that's stupid. We need to know too. . .' should be shared by everyone who thinks that men and women should take equal responsibility in developing loving and caring relationships.

Parents were certainly concerned about this and there was overwhelming support among parents for schools to help young people understand better how people of the opposite sex felt about things. Parents laid a lot of stress on the importance of schools discussing personal relationships, and their continuing concern about these matters throughout the interviews reflected the fact that nearly one-third of our sample of teenagers were living with only one of their natural parents. There can be little doubt that many parents were concerned about their children's future relationships in the light of their own experience.

Some people who claim to speak for parents have said that education in sex and personal relationships should be the responsibility of parents only, and that schools should play no part in it. It has been conclusively shown in this report that this view was not shared by the overwhelming majority of parents and children interviewed. In spite of the fact that many parents and children had very good and close relationships with one another, there was considerable evidence that they frequently found it difficult to talk to each other about very personal matters, particularly about sex. Parents often did not see themselves as good 'sex educators' for a variety of reasons. They stressed that they often had little expertise in certain matters, that they did not know how to express themselves, that their teenage children were shy and embarrassed or that they themselves were shy and embarrassed. These views were expressed by parents of both sexes, all classes and all ages, but fathers in particular appeared to have difficulty in talking to their teenage children about these matters and their children had even greater difficulty in talking to their fathers.

At the same time there was a great desire among parents that teenagers should receive 'proper' education on these topics. Parents were often very critical of the complete inadequacy of their own sex education, and, indeed, as their comments showed, some parents had been left in total ignorance of even the most basic bodily functions, often to their great distress. It was difficult to imagine, in reading some of the accounts given by women in particular, that these were people who had been teenagers in Britain in the 1950s and 1960s. It was, perhaps, hardly surprising that they were determined that their own children should not suffer in the same way. However, this very lack of education in their own adolescence also made many parents feel very ill-equipped to give such education to their own children, and there was no doubt that many welcomed the contribution of the school for this reason.

It was also quite clear from interviews with both parents and teenagers that there were certain areas which were difficult for them to discuss with each other. This was particularly true of matters which directly related to the teenager's own emerging sexuality or could in any way be related to the parents' sexual activity. It should be remembered that 58 per cent of the boys and 31 per cent of the girls said that they had never spoken to their mothers about *any* of the topics covered in the interviews, and 72 per cent of both boys and girls said they had never spoken to their fathers about any of these topics. Although parents were more likely to say that they had discussed these matters with their teenage son or daughter, nevertheless over a fifth of the mothers and nearly 40 per cent of the fathers said that they had never talked about *any* of the subjects to their children.

These findings were surprising, and it is quite clear that it would be utterly wrong to assume that parents will automatically give their children any information, let alone discuss these matters which are so much part of life. Even on matters such as changes in girls' bodies at puberty, a subject on which some mothers gave horrifying accounts of their own lack of knowledge as teenagers, there was widespread evidence from both mothers and daughters that no information had been given and no discussion had taken place in the home. It was perhaps even more alarming that discussions at home with boys about any of the topics were considerably less commonly reported, both by boys and their parents, than discussions with girls.

Nevertheless, parents were very concerned that their children should be educated in these matters, and that this education should be well-informed and comprehensive. Parents displayed anxiety about the influence on teenagers of the media, of videos and of the teenagers' peer-group. Their main worries were that the teenagers could be receiving inaccurate or biased information from these sources on matters of fact, and that their attitudes towards sex and the opposite sex could be affected by the way in which the subjects were treated. It should be reiterated that although many parents felt that the example of the home was important, nevertheless many recognised that their teenage children needed more information and more guidance than they themselves felt able to give in order to counteract what they thought were strong and misleading influences.

There was considerable emphasis throughout the interviews with parents on the important role that schools played in giving a balanced and unbiased education on matters concerned with sex and personal relationships, and that a certain status and formality was given to these subjects when they were part of the school curriculum. There was no doubt that many parents were particularly concerned about the possible distortion of sex roles as presented in the media in general and about the violent or brutal depiction of sex and relationships between men and women in videos. They felt unable to counteract on their own what they saw as undesirable influences, and it was clear that many of them felt that the school had an essential role to play in correcting misinformation and unacceptable attitudes. It was quite apparent that many teachers and educationists have completely underestimated the trust and faith that so many parents put in schools in educating their children on these topics.

The question of greater contact between parents and school about all facets of education has come increasingly under scrutiny in recent years, and it has been encouraged both at central and local level. Certainly much more information is available for parents about schools than was the case ten years ago, but nevertheless parents in this study remained very hazy about what their children were being taught about sex and personal relationships, and often seemed to know very little about the educational films and videos seen at school which had made a considerable impact on their children, according to the information the teenagers gave our interviewers. Similarly parents seemed to have little awareness of the importance the children attached to discussion in class about personal and social development and the value placed by the teenagers on class discussions in learning about the feelings and anxieties of others. They also often appeared to know little about the good relationships their children had with some members of the teaching staff.

It is clear that, although relationships between parents and their teenage children may be very close and trusting, the nature of these relationships during adolescence may be subject to constant shifts, particularly as the teenager develops independence. Many parents demonstrated in these interviews that there were certain areas which they recognised as being particularly sensitive, and it was interesting to find that, although the majority of parents said that they themselves did not find it difficult to talk to their teenage children about sex, for example, they were much less likely to think that their teenage children found it easy to talk to them on the subject, and certainly the teenagers themselves found it even less easy. Therefore, it is not surprising that the parents did not hear too much from their children about what they were learning at school. It is notoriously difficult to obtain information on school work in general from many teenagers, and it is even less likely that adolescents will volunteer information on what they are learning at school about subjects which they have difficulty in discussing with their parents in any case.

It should perhaps be stressed that many parents were not concerned about this lack of information, and, indeed, it should not be forgotten that, when given the opportunity of attending either the children's primary or secondary school to hear how and what their children were being taught in these subjects, only a minority went, and among those who had not been invited, there was evidence of considerable lack of interest. But there were parents who were very interested in knowing what was going on, often so that they could learn how to communicate on these subjects with their children, and there can be no doubt that schools could do more to inform and involve parents in the teaching of these very important topics. It certainly appeared that parents who were in any way dissatisfied with the schools in the provision of 'sex education' were more concerned about the possibility of their children being taught too little rather than too much.

The teenagers showed themselves to be much more cautious and level-headed than many of their parents feared. They were much more sceptical of the potential influence of the media than their parents were, and even if they thought that young people were influenced by magazines or television, they often displayed considerable maturity in their assessment of the possible influence on 'other people'. The viewing of sexually explicit videos was thought by teenagers to have much more effect than magazines or television, and there was also surprising evidence that some teenagers had viewed these videos in the home with their parents. The impact of such viewing can only be a matter of conjecture, but, as the report points out, it puts a different perspective on the demands of those who say that sex education should be the sole responsibility of parents.

Teenagers were less likely than parents to say that they felt under pressure to have a boyfriend or a girlfriend or to have sex at an early age, and the 14-year-old boy who said, 'I've never really bothered. I've got other things that interest me. I'd rather go fishing. . .' was by no means atypical of the teenagers interviewed. Indeed, parents were much more concerned about pressures on teenagers than the teenagers themselves were, although there was evidence that the peer-group could make life very uncomfortable for some sensitive teenagers who felt that others knew more and did more than they did.

There were many indications that teenagers valued relationships with the opposite sex for friendship and companionship, and teenagers had far more conventional views on love and marriage than many of their parents or teachers might have thought. Certainly, their comments on the value they placed on learning how others felt about things from discussions in class would confirm the importance educationists have placed on the need for curricular development of a personal and social education programme.

It was clear too that teenagers were able to discriminate between their need for informal discussions with friends about sex, contraception and personal relationships and their assessment of the accuracy of the information likely to be given by friends. In this respect, teenagers appear to have come a long way from their counterparts of ten or twenty years ago. The teenagers interviewed in this study were well aware of the fact that the information on these matters that they were likely to pick up from friends, and even parents, was less likely to be accurate than information from school or from doctors or other professionals. Nevertheless they felt a need to turn first to informal sources for a preliminary discussion, even if they knew that the reliability of the information likely to be given was of a more dubious quality than that from school or a professional source.

It was particularly interesting that the majority of both parents and teenagers thought that the teenagers got most of their information about both sex and contraception from school, although parents tended to link their own contribution as information-givers with that of the school much more than teenagers did. Both teenagers and their parents still stressed the importance of friends as sources of information on these matters, but, as we have seen, teenagers had a healthy scepticism about the accuracy of this information.

Teenagers certainly valued the contribution of school to their understanding of sex and contraception and the vast majority had found school helpful in learning about these subjects. Although there was widespread evidence of the extent to which schools were now concerned with personal relationships and social awareness, and many teenagers found discussions on these matters particularly helpful, there was still concern among both parents and teenagers that not all schools were equally good at teaching teenagers about these matters. They are, of course, not easy to 'teach', and there are many other influences which play their part, not only at home and among friends but also in the playground. Nevertheless, the words of the boy of 15 from the North-East must not be forgotten. In talking about personal relationships he said, 'We only had one lesson on that compared to eight on contraception, so we knew how not to get pregnant, but not how to get on with each other. . .'

We have seen that many parents thought that schools had an important part to play in teaching teenagers about personal relationships, particularly in helping them recognise that life was not all 'rosy' and romantic, but that relationships needed to be firmly based in reality and that life with other people could be difficult. Parents also stressed far more than teenagers their wish for schools to emphasise the preventive side of 'sex education'. There was considerable evidence of parents being concerned that their children should be warned of the dangers of sex without contraception and of venereal disease. It was rare for parents to mention the 'moral' component of sex education, but they were much more likely than their children to say that teachers should give guidance or help on how to behave in sexual matters. It was noteworthy how few parents and their teenage children said that they had discussed this at home and, again, many parents appeared to assume that it was a suitable role for the school to take on. It should be noted, however, that a substantial minority of parents considered guidance in sexual matters not to be a role for teachers, even if they thought that schools should give sex education, and those who held this view often held it very forcibly.

As we have seen, teenagers were much less likely to welcome guidance from teachers on sexual matters, however much they valued teachers as sources of information, as discussion-leaders and, so often, as people to be trusted with problems about sex, contraception or personal relationships. Many teenagers gave evidence of close and trusting relationships with teachers which would have considerably surprised many people of their parents' generation. The value the teenagers placed on the expertise, approachability and friendliness of some of the teachers they described was both matter-of-fact and very touching, and there can be little doubt that schools have come a long way in terms of pastoral care from the schooldays of these teenagers' parents. However, there was also clear evidence of some very poor relationships between some teachers and some of the teenagers interviewed, and certainly evidence that some teachers were not trusted with confidential information.

Well over half the teenagers said that there was a member of staff whom they thought they could ask an informal question about sex and contraception, with both boys and girls expressing a preference for asking a teacher of their own sex. Nearly half said that there was a member of staff they felt they could turn to with a problem about personal relationships, with boys and girls more likely to prefer a female teacher, although it was clear that personal qualities were often more important than the subject taught or the sex of the teacher concerned. There was evidence of good relationships built up with pastoral staff, and certainly some of the more senior staff, particularly if they were responsible for the personal and social education programme, were rated very highly by both boys and girls.

Nevertheless there was still felt to be a need for a special person in every secondary school whom children could go and talk to if they had problems or questions about sex or personal relationships. Just under 80 per cent of the teenagers thought it would help if there were someone special in the school who fulfilled this role. It was particularly interesting that about half thought this should be a teacher, but about half thought it should not be, and it should be noted that over 40 per cent of the girls thought that this 'special' person should be a school nurse. Although so many teenagers were able to talk freely to teachers, not everyone trusted teachers to maintain confidentiality, many did not see teachers out of an instructing role, and some doubted their expertise in these matters. We have seen how difficult many teenagers found it to talk to their parents about problems of this kind, and it did appear that there was a need for a friendly, non-judging, information-giving, reassuring kind of person at school to help teenagers.

In saying why they would not consider turning to a doctor or clinic with a question about sex, contraception or personal relationships, teenagers often said that their question was not 'important' enough, or that they would feel as though they were wasting a professional's time. It did appear that some teenagers felt a need for an 'expert' opinion from someone who did not teach them, was not related to them, was more reliable than their friends, and yet who was not a professional with whom one had to make an appointment and with whom an informal question was turned into a formal consultation. It appeared that boys were more likely to accept a teacher in that role than girls. There was no doubt that the strong preference of girls for confiding in someone of the same sex was reflected in their preference for a school nurse. Some of the teenagers interviewed had complicated family patterns, and it sometimes appeared that some of them would welcome a 'mother' figure or 'father' figure rather than a 'counsellor'.

The use of outsiders in discussing sex, contraception and personal relationships with schoolchildren has changed somewhat over the past ten years or so, and there has been encouragement for teachers to take as much responsibility as possible themselves in integrating all aspects of health education into the school curriculum. There can be little doubt that the great increase in the use of visual material such as films and videos has helped teachers present material with which they might have felt ill-at-ease and has also provided the expertise which they might not have had. In this respect films and videos have to a certain extent replaced outside speakers, and, of course, can provide a high level of consistency and professional presentation.

However, both teenagers and their parents, in spite of the relatively low involvement of outside speakers in their schools on these subjects, were very much in favour of the use of outsiders, both for their presumed expertise, and, interestingly enough, because they were not known to the children. Although there were many teenagers who preferred to talk to people they knew, there were many who preferred to talk to strangers about these matters. In many respects, the enthusiasm of teenagers for having outsiders talk to them reinforced the impression they gave of welcoming a variety of methods of teaching them about these subjects, and boys in particular, who were much less likely than girls to have had outside speakers, yet again stressed their anxiety not to miss anything and to learn from a variety of sources.

Although there can be little doubt that the education of boys about sex and personal relationships has come a long way from the dismal picture painted by Michael Schofield twenty years ago which showed a very low level of sex education for boys, nevertheless there were a number of indications in this report that boys still received less education in these matters than girls did, both from school and particularly from home. Although some of the reported lower involvement of boys in school sex education programmes might have been due to girls being more likely to have had talks on menstruation in single-sex groups, there were still rather disturbing indications that girls were being given information while the boys 'did revision'. Certainly the 'options' system in most secondary schools in the fourth and fifth years means that girls are much more likely to choose 'child care' or 'child development' than the boys are, and that family roles and personal relationships are more likely to come up in 'child care' than in woodwork.

Nevertheless there were reassuring signs that both boys and girls were receiving a programme of education in personal and social development, and even though girls were more likely to say that they had had lessons covering family and parenthood and personal relationships than the boys were, nevertheless almost equal proportions of boys and girls said that they had covered such topics as human and animal reproduction and contraception.

But if boys were almost as likely as girls to receive a comprehensive programme of education in sex and personal relationships in school they were certainly much less likely to receive any at home, and it should be remembered that nearly 60 per cent of the boys interviewed, compared with under a third of the girls, said that they had never discussed any of the topics with their mothers, and nearly three-quarters of them had never discussed any with their fathers. Although, as we have seen, girls were equally unlikely to talk to their fathers, at least they were more likely to talk to their mothers.

Again, although boys found it as easy as girls to talk to their mothers about most things, nevertheless they found it more difficult than girls to talk to their mothers about personal problems and considerably more difficult to talk to them about sex. Neither boys nor girls found it very easy to talk to their fathers about sex. Mothers clearly overestimated the extent to which their sons found it easy to talk to them about sex, although there was evidence of good and easy relationships on other matters, and fathers certainly overestimated the extent to which either their sons or their daughters found it easy to talk to them about sex.

Boys did appear to be at a grave disadvantage in learning about sex and personal relationships, and the importance of school in the sex education of boys cannot be overemphasised[23]. Any thought of increasing the number of single-sex discussion groups, which some of the girls seemed to prefer, must be counterbalanced by the obviously pressing need for the boys to have a forum in which they can learn from others as well as express their own views. It was perhaps not surprising that so many of the boys were worried that they might be missing something.

In looking at the impact and effect of school education in sex and personal relationships, it must be asked what it is all for. There are those who say that it should not be given at school at all but should be the sole responsibility of parents. We have seen that parents utterly refute this view. In any case, as this report has shown in great detail, it is an oversimplified view based on the assumption that there is a separate entity which can be defined as 'sex education'. It would be very difficult to remove many topics covered in 'sex education' from the curriculum without making nonsense of the biology syllabus, for example, and it is clear that other aspects are an integral part of any programme of personal and social development such as has been encouraged in successive government publications.

It is also quite clear that if education in sex and personal relationships were left to parents alone many adolescents would receive no education in these matters from any authoritative source. Not only would there be the danger of a return to the widespread distribution of misinformation from friends and the general horrifying ignorance such as that described by parents interviewed in this study, but there could also be the even worse result of teenagers picking up much of their information, views and attitudes from pornographic videos depicting brutal sex and violence as the norm.

Education in Sex and Personal Relationships

Much of the interest in education in sex and personal relationships in the 1960s and 1970s was spurred by an increasing teenage pregnancy rate and suggestions that young people were sexually active at an earlier age than their parents' generation. Prevention of pregnancy was a very strong motivating force among 'sex educators', and certainly a lot of attention was paid to the need for teenagers to be aware of contraceptive methods and the desirability of preventing unwanted pregnancies.

The emphasis in sex education has now changed and it is generally accepted that it should be part of a wider programme of personal and social development. The preventive aspect has not been neglected, but more stress has been laid on ensuring that sex should be part of a loving and equal relationship between mature people. Nevertheless there have been claims that sex education has no 'moral' element and that it encourages promiscuity by giving teenagers information on 'how to do it'. This study examined this claim since it appears to attract a completely disproportionate amount of attention.

It was quite clear that the majority of parents and teenagers thought that sex education at school made young people more cautious about experimenting with sex at an early age. Teenagers in particular stressed how education in these matters at school made young people more aware of the risks of pregnancy and venereal disease, and, although there has been a slight shift in emphasis away from the preventive nature of sex education, nevertheless there was strong evidence of teenagers saying that they had become more 'wary' as a result of their education. But it was not only wariness about the simple fact of becoming pregnant that had been communicated to teenagers, but also an awareness of the consequences of an unwanted pregnancy. Parents and teenagers alike often talked about the 'damage' that an unwanted pregnancy could do to a teenager's life, and there was considerable evidence that parents wanted their children to have a better, more successful life than they had had. It was perhaps not surprising that parents often wanted schools to stress the preventive aspects of sex education.

It is interesting to note that teenage pregnancy rates are in fact dropping, particularly among older teenagers, and there is some evidence that there are influences at work in society today which encourage a more responsible attitude towards sex and early pregnancy. It is difficult to say to what extent the widespread adoption of education at school in sex and personal relationships integrated into a programme of personal and social development has affected these rates. However, it is perhaps important to quote from an assessment of teenage pregnancy undertaken in 37 developed countries by the American Alan Guttmacher Institute. Detailed case studies took place in five countries which were similar to the United States in general cultural background and stage of economic development and yet which had rates of adolescent pregnancy considerably lower than that of the United States: Canada, England and Wales, France, the Netherlands and Sweden.

In summarising the position in these countries compared with that of the United States, the authors write:

> By and large, of all the countries studied, Sweden has been the most active in developing programmes and policies to reduce teenage pregnancy. These efforts include universal education in sexuality and contraception; development of special clinics—closely associated with the schools—where young people receive contraceptive services and counselling; free, widely available and confidential contraceptive and abortion services; widespread advertising of contraceptives in all media; frank treatment of sex; and availability of condoms from a variety of sources. It is notable that Sweden has *lower* teenage pregnancy rates than have all the countries examined, except for the Netherlands, although teenagers begin intercourse at earlier ages in Sweden. It is also noteworthy that Sweden is the only one of the countries observed to have shown a rapid decline in teenage abortion rates in recent years, even after its abortion law was liberalised[24].

It is clear that Britain does not have the same attitude towards sex education as Sweden but certainly there has been a considerable acceptance by teachers, doctors, politicians and parents that schools have an important part to play in informing teenagers about the need to reduce the incidence of unwanted teenage pregnancies.

As we have seen in this study, 94 per cent of the 16-year-olds interviewed, 85 per cent of the 15-year-olds and 65 per cent of the 14-year-olds said that they had covered contraception or birth control at secondary school. If this pattern is repeated throughout the country, it appears that very few teenagers will leave school in Britain today without some accurate knowledge of contraceptive methods. Coverage of reproduction, pregnancy and childbirth and changes at puberty was almost universal, and the vast majority of teenagers had had some education about family and parenthood, personal relationships, venereal disease and abortion by the time they were sixteen. Teenagers in the three areas that we looked at were certainly well-informed on the whole about the risks of early sexual activity and there was widespread evidence that they felt able to assess the information they had been given. There was no guarantee that possession of information would affect their behaviour. It has been shown with all health education programmes that information alone does not necessarily change behaviour patterns which are formed by a myriad of other influences. But certainly the way in which many of the teenagers in this study had received this education at school had encouraged them to think responsibly about the issues.

Finally, we should end this report on an optimistic and realistic note. There was considerable evidence in this study of teenagers who were not 'sex-mad', who were concerned about the feelings and emotions of others, who were interested in a wide variety of academic and sporting pursuits, who were balanced and deeply responsible individuals with strong affection for their parents, loyalty to their friends and good relationships with their teachers. There was evidence of caring and loving parents who stressed the openness of their relationships with their children, but who nevertheless acknowledged that they found it difficult to cope with their children's emerging sexuality, particularly in the light of their own inadequate sex education. And we found evidence of teachers who could strike up good and trusting relationships with teenagers, who could lead discussions on personal relationships of a very sensitive nature, and who could make children aware of the need for tolerance and humanity in dealing with people both of their own sex and of the opposite sex.

Parents in this study stressed above all their wish that their children should be happy and should be able to form relationships which were meaningful and which could last. Many of the children interviewed came from familes in which they were living with only one of their parents. There is clearly much more to 'sex education' than learning the mechanics of sex, and there is plenty of evidence in this report that schools have come a long way in the past ten years in laying the foundations for a better understanding of other people.

SUMMARY

1. The main aim of this study was to look at how far the present provision of education in sex and personal relationships in schools was meeting the needs of secondary schoolchildren and their parents, the extent to which this education was thought to be delivered in an acceptable form and how it was thought to affect the behaviour and attitudes of the children. The views and experience of teenagers and their parents concerning other influences and sources of information on sex and personal relationships were sought in order to put into perspective the education received by the teenagers at school.

2. The study was based on interviews with representative samples of teenagers aged 14-16 years and their parents in three cities in England, one in the North-East, one in the Midlands and one in the South-West. Interviews were carried out with 209 teenagers—99 boys and 110 girls—and 212 parents—149 mothers and 63 fathers. Interviews took place in 205 households with both a parent and a teenager.

3. After being prompted about specific topics, 89 per cent of teenagers and 78 per cent of parents said that the teenager had had some education at primary school about sex, personal relationships and how their bodies worked. 82 per cent of teenagers and 61 per cent of parents said that this education had covered the topic of 'not going with strangers'. Parents knew very little about other topics covered at primary school, although mothers were much better informed than fathers. 27 per cent of the teenagers said that they had covered changes in a girl's body as she grows up, 20 per cent changes in a boy's body as he grows up and 23 per cent said they had covered animal reproduction, but otherwise not more than a fifth of teenagers mentioned any other topic. Memory clearly played a part in recalling primary school education since 14-year-olds mentioned more topics than older teenagers.

4. Two-thirds of the teenagers said that they had watched some kind of visual presentation of these topics at primary school, and films, television programmes or videos were usually followed by explanation by a teacher. Over a fifth said they had used books and 11 per cent had used worksheets in

learning about these topics. Only a quarter of the parents knew whether their children had seen films at primary school and few knew that they had seen a film on 'not going with strangers' which had often made a lasting impression on the children.

5.   The overwhelming majority of parents (91 per cent) thought it a good idea for children to have education on not going with strangers in primary school, and the majority thought it a good idea to have education on animal and human reproduction, changes in boys' and girls' bodies at puberty, and family and parenthood, while nearly half thought pregnancy and childbirth should be covered at primary school. A recurring theme throughout interviews with parents was the fact that children took these matters more seriously if they learned about them at school, and parents stressed that they wanted their children to be taught 'properly' and to regard these matters as 'natural'.

6.   43 per cent of parents said that they were satisfied with the education their children had received on these topics at primary school, while 16 per cent expressed some dissatisfaction and 39 per cent said that they did not know enough to make a judgement. The main reason for dissatisfaction was lack of knowledge about what had been taught, and only a tiny minority expressed dissatisfaction with the content of the education.

7.   Although the majority of teenagers who had had education at primary school on these topics had found it informative or useful, over 40 per cent thought it could have been improved by giving more facts or details. Nearly 60 per cent of teenagers thought it a good idea to have education on these matters at primary school, but a substantial minority thought that primary schoolchildren were too young to cover certain topics.

8.   We asked the teenagers and parents about fourteen topics at secondary school. More than 90 per cent of teenagers had had some education on human reproduction and pregnancy and childbirth at secondary school, and over 80 per cent had covered changes in boys' and girls' bodies at puberty, animal reproduction, sexual intercourse and contraception. These topics had been covered by virtually all the 16-year-olds interviewed. Around 70 per cent of teenagers had covered family and parenthood, personal relationships and venereal disease, nearly 60 per cent had covered abortion and over 50 per cent had covered guidelines on sexual behaviour. 37 per cent had covered masturbation and 28 per cent had covered homosexuality or lesbianism. Sixteen-year-olds were more likely than younger teenagers to have covered all these topics, and indeed 94 per cent of 16-year-olds had learned about contraception at secondary school.

9.   These topics had been covered in a wide variety of subjects in different

years and were likely to come up in more than one lesson in more than one subject in more than one year. There was evidence that 'sex education' had been firmly integrated into the curriculum as a whole rather than treated as a 'special' subject, and it was increasingly part of a programme of personal and social development led by teachers within the school rather than by outsiders.

10. Visual presentation of these topics was widespread and nearly 90 per cent of the teenagers had seen a film, video or television programme on at least one of these subjects. They were very enthusiastic about this form of visual presentation and in the vast majority of cases films were followed up with classroom discussion and explanation.

11. Teenagers also expressed considerable enthusiasm for class discussions on these subjects, mainly so that they could hear a variety of views and opinions to give them a wider understanding of the issues which faced them all in growing up. They felt that class discussions with a teacher present could help to correct inaccurate information while at the same time problems could be shared and embarrassing issues could be brought into the open. They welcomed hearing the views of the opposite sex, although girls were more likely than boys to express a preference for some discussion in single-sex groups. There was evidence that girls were sometimes given more education on these topics than boys were, and some boys were concerned that they might be missing something.

12. Written work on these topics was almost universal, mainly in the form of notes, and the vast majority of teenagers had used biology textbooks when learning about these topics. Nearly 60 per cent of the teenagers had had at least one pamphlet or leaflet about some aspect of education in these topics.

13. Nearly all teenagers thought that diagrams and pictures were useful methods of teaching these subjects and most said that they always understood them. However, they were less likely always to understand the words that teachers used, and 14-year-olds in particular showed a lack of understanding of 'proper' words, expressing a preference for using both 'proper' words and the words that young people used to describe things.

14. Just over half the teenagers had heard an outside speaker on these topics at school, but girls were very much more likely than boys to have heard one, mainly because the talks or discussions had usually been given by a nurse of some kind, on the subject of menstruation or pregnancy and childbirth. Teenagers were interested in outside speakers whether they had heard them or not, mainly because they were thought to have expertise, knowledge and experience, and some teenagers thought that it was easier to talk to a stranger, although some thought it was less easy.

15.   Nearly half the teenagers thought that the topics should be presented in a mixture of ways at school, although 14-year-olds were more likely than older teenagers to prefer visual presentation.

16.   The topics which teenagers remembered most were contraception and birth control, pregnancy and childbirth, venereal disease and changes at puberty. A quarter of the 16-year-olds said that the lessons on birth control had stuck in their minds most.

17.   55 per cent of the teenagers said that there was a particular member of staff at school whom they felt they could ask informally if they had a question about sex or contraception, with girls in particular preferring to ask a teacher of their own sex. 40 per cent of teenagers said that there was a particular teacher they could talk to if they had a problem with personal relationships, with both boys and girls more likely to turn to a female teacher. Teenagers were particularly concerned about confidentiality. Approachability and friendliness were more important than the subject taught by the teacher, and senior pastoral staff were often well-regarded.

18.   Just under 80 per cent of teenagers thought it would help if there were someone in every secondary school whom teenagers could go to with problems or questions about sex and personal relationships. About half thought it should be a teacher, but over 40 per cent of the girls thought it should be a school nurse. Teenagers who thought it should *not* be a teacher often expressed concern about lack of confidentiality, or had fears that teachers did not have enough expertise in these matters.

19.   Parents appeared to know more about the experience of their teenage children at secondary school than at primary school, although they were still rather vague about the actual content of the lessons. Mothers consistently knew more about the topics being taught than fathers did. There were striking differences between the knowledge of the parents and the experience of the teenagers, however, with 40 per cent of the parents not knowing whether their children had covered pregnancy and childbirth at school, while over 90 per cent of the teenagers said that they had. Although nearly 60 per cent of parents said that their children had seen a film on one of the topics at secondary school (compared with nearly 90 per cent of the teenagers who said they had), they were fairly hazy about the subject matter. Similarly they often knew little about any outside speakers on these subjects at the schools, although, like the teenagers, they expressed enthusiasm for the use of outside speakers not only because of their assumed expertise and knowledge, but also because a substantial minority thought that teenagers would take more notice of outsiders.

20. There was evidence that parents had little contact with either primary or secondary schools about programmes in education in sex and personal relationships. 11 per cent of parents had been invited to a primary school meeting and 14 per cent to a secondary school meeting to hear how these topics were being treated, but only in 5 per cent of cases did one or other parent go to the primary school meeting and in 6 per cent of cases to a secondary school meeting. Of those not invited to either, more than half said they would like to have been invited, but a third said they would not and 10 per cent said they did not know whether they would or not. Those who wanted to know more said they would have liked to know what was being taught and how it was being taught, mainly so that they could reinforce it at home or so that they could learn how to communicate on these topics with their children. One-third of parents said they had had a letter from the secondary school and one fifth from primary school, usually to ask their permission for their child to see a film on a particular topic, but giving little information. There was a desire for more written information from the school on these topics. Three quarters of the parents remembered having received a booklet or brochure about the secondary school, but only 13 per cent remembered whether it said anything about the treatment of sex education at school. There was a widespread feeling among parents that they could find out more if they wanted to, and considerable evidence of trust in the school to exercise responsibility in teaching these matters. There was also evidence of very lukewarm interest among a substantial minority of parents.

21. Only 70 per cent of the teenagers interviewed lived with both their natural parents (only two-thirds of the girls). 25 per cent lived with their mother but not their father, and 4 per cent lived with their father but not their mother. There was evidence of some very complicated family patterns. If the teenagers lived with only one parent, nearly two-thirds said they rarely or never saw the other parent. This was especially true in cases where the parent with whom they were living had not remarried.

22. Discussion between parents and teenagers on the fourteen topics was relatively limited. 43 per cent of the teenagers (58 per cent of the boys and 31 per cent of the girls) said that they had never spoken to their mother about *any* of the topics, and 72 per cent of the teenagers (equal proportions of boys and girls) said that they had never spoken to their father about any of the topics. (This question was only asked of boys and girls who were living with the parent concerned or who saw them frequently.) The most frequent topic discussed with mothers was pregnancy and childbirth - reported by 37 per cent of the teenagers (20 per cent of the boys and 51 per cent of the girls), and the second most frequently discussed topic was changes in a girl's body at puberty, discussed by 57 per cent of the girls but only 9 per cent of the boys. The most frequently discussed topic with fathers was personal relationships, reported by only 11 per cent of teenagers.

23.   Parents reported more conversations with their children on these topics, but nevertheless 26 per cent said that they had talked to the teenager about *none* of the subjects (21 per cent of the mothers and 37 per cent of the fathers). Only two topics were said to have been discussed by more than 50 per cent of mothers—pregnancy and childbirth and changes in a girl's body at puberty. 42 per cent of parents said that they had talked to their teenage son or daughter about guidelines on sexual behaviour, but this was recalled by only 10 per cent of teenagers. Both parents and teenagers agreed that masturbation was almost a taboo subject, with less than 10 per cent of both samples saying this had been mentioned.

24.   27 per cent of parents said that they preferred the school to take full responsibility for teaching their children about *all* these topics, 11 per cent said they preferred to take the full responsibility themselves and 60 per cent said that teenagers should learn from both home and school. Parents were particularly keen that schools should take responsibility for teaching the teenagers about masturbation, venereal disease and homosexuality, even if they thought the education should be a joint responsibility in general.

25.   Over 70 per cent of teenagers thought their mothers approved of their having sex education at school and over 60 per cent thought their fathers did, but most of the rest said they did not know whether their parents approved or not. They thought their parents wanted them to be well-informed so that they would not make 'mistakes' and that they laid some stress on the 'preventive' nature of sex education but were often too embarrassed to tell them themselves.

26.   Teenagers, particularly girls, found it easier to talk to mothers than fathers. The majority (78 per cent) of both boys and girls found it easy to talk to their mother about most things. Girls (69 per cent) found it easier than boys (53 per cent) to talk to their mother about personal problems and considerably easier (55 per cent) than boys (28 per cent) to talk to their mothers about sex. Boys were more likely to find it easy to talk to their father about most things (69 per cent) than girls (53 per cent); they found it a bit easier (39 per cent) to talk about personal problems than girls (33 per cent), and 26 per cent of the boys found it easy to talk to their fathers about sex compared with only 15 per cent of the girls. There was widespread evidence of good mother-daughter relationships which often excluded fathers.

27.   Although it appeared that parents reflected the views of the teenagers, with 79 per cent saying that the teenagers found it easy to talk to them about most things, 54 per cent saying they found it easy to talk to them about personal problems and 43 per cent saying they found it easy to talk to them about sex, nevertheless mothers were much more likely than fathers to say that the teenager found it easy to talk to them about personal problems and

sex. However, mothers tended to overestimate the extent to which their sons found it easy to talk to them about sex, and fathers overestimated the extent to which either sons or daughters found it easy to talk to them about sex. Parents thought that teenagers found it difficult because they were embarrassed or shy, and nearly 10 per cent said the teenagers (especially boys) were too young. Fathers thought children found it easier to talk to their mothers about these matters, and mothers often drew attention to 'barriers' between daughters and fathers on the subject of sex.

28.   Parents thought that they themselves had no difficulty in talking to their children about sex. 70 per cent said they had had no difficulty nor did they expect any, mainly because they said that the atmosphere at home was 'open' and these matters were treated as 'natural'. But some thought teenagers were too shy or embarrassed, some found it difficult to talk to their children about these matters without intruding on their child's developing sexuality or acknowledging their own, while others had a lot to say but found that their children did not want to stay and listen. Parents were less likely to have tried to talk to their children about contraception, but again the majority expected no difficulty and stressed the need for teenagers to know about it especially to prevent teenage pregnancy. Parents felt more comfortable talking to their children about personal relationships, but, nevertheless, 14 per cent found it a difficult or potentially difficult subject.

29.   Even if parents themselves said they did not find it difficult to talk to their teenage children, nevertheless 62 per cent thought parents in general found it difficult to give sex education to their teenage children. The main reason given was embarrassment on the part of the parents, coupled with a lack of knowledge or the ability to find the right words to put it over. Many emphasised that they found it difficult because of the way they had been brought up themselves, and cited particularly their own lack of sex education which was often said to have provided them with a totally inadequate basis for giving their children sex education.

30.   Parents had a very low opinion of their own sex education when young, both at school and from their own parents. 80 per cent said that their own sex education at school had been non-existent or very poor and over 70 per cent said the same about the sex education received from their parents. 57 per cent said they wished they had been given more or better sex education when young (63 per cent of the mothers and 41 per cent of the fathers) from both parents and school. There was some horrifying evidence from women in particular of ignorance of the most basic facts of life, including menstruation. Over 10 per cent of the mothers said that they had known little or nothing about periods, and for some the onset of menstruation had been a traumatic experience. Over one-fifth of the mothers said they had known nothing about sex when teenagers, or even when they got married, and many

197

felt that this ignorance had adversely affected their lives and they were determined that their own children should not suffer in the same way. Fathers in particular stressed their lack of education and knowledge about personal relationships.

31.   22 per cent of parents (26 per cent of mothers and 11 per cent of fathers) thought they needed more information now on certain topics, particularly venereal disease and homosexuality, and to a lesser extent birth control methods and information for discussing guidelines on sexual behaviour. They wanted this information mainly from books, magazines or pamphlets.

32.   Nearly 30 per cent of the teenagers thought that people of their own age knew more about sex than they did, but the 14-year-olds (32 per cent) and 15-year-olds (31 per cent) were more likely to think this than the 16-year-olds (19 per cent). This represented equal proportions of boys and girls, but children living with only one parent and those attending single-sex schools were more likely to think this. Two-thirds said they were not bothered by this, but some felt very rejected and left out by their peer-group.

33.   43 per cent of teenagers and 53 per cent of parents thought that young people today were under pressure to have a boyfriend or girlfriend. Sixteen year-olds (53 per cent) were much more likely to think this than 14-year-olds (32 per cent). Pressure was thought by both teenagers and their parents to come mainly from friends of their own age and sex. Teenagers hardly mentioned any influence other than friends but parents were much more likely to mention television, radio or magazines. Parents stressed that the pressure started early and over two-thirds thought that it started at the age of thirteen or younger. Parents were concerned that the pressure could lead to unhappiness among teenagers, and this concern was reflected among some teenagers who expressed fears that there was something 'wrong' with them if they did not have a boyfriend or girlfriend. Although the majority of teenagers said that it was not important to them whether they had one or not, nevertheless over a third of the boys, compared with only a fifth of the girls, said that it was important to them.

34.   51 per cent of the parents, compared with only 31 per cent of the teenagers, thought young people were under pressure to have sex. Girls were more likely to think this than boys, and tended to think that the pressure came from boyfriends, while boys thought it was more likely to be exerted on them by other boys. Again parents cited the potential influence of television, radio and magazines which were hardly mentioned spontaneously by teenagers. Parents expressed concern that the pressure to have sex started at too young an age, and were worried that their children could be missing out on the 'fun' of growing up.

35.   It was quite clear that teenagers thought that sex was acceptable at an earlier age than parents, with 16 per cent of the boys and 7 per cent of the girls saying that it was 'all right' for a girl to have sex at fifteen or under and 18 per cent of the boys and 12 per cent of the girls saying that it was 'all right' for a boy to have sex at fifteen or under. Only 3 per cent of the parents agreed about this age for boys and only 4 per cent agreed about girls. One-third of the teenagers (similar proportions of boys and girls) thought it was all right for both boys and girls to have sex at sixteen, compared with 20 per cent of the parents. Teenagers almost never stipulated that people should wait until they were married to have sex, while over a tenth of parents did. One-fifth of teenagers and one-third of parents said it was impossible to set an age for when it was 'all right' to have sex, but that it depended on the individual and the circumstances.

36.   Three-quarters of the parents but only 58 per cent of the teenagers thought that young people were influenced about sex and personal relationships by magazines. Girls were thought more likely to be influenced by 'teenage' magazines, and boys by pornographic magazines. Parents were worried that girls might pick up over-romantic views of life and love, but the girls themselves expressed some scepticism on whether this was so. Boys were thought by parents to be less influenced than girls but there were worries that they might be influenced by pornographic magazines into copying what they saw. There was concern among both mothers and fathers that these magazines gave boys the wrong 'image' of women and girls which might lead them to develop a stereotypical picture of a girl as a sex object or submissive. There was particular concern that these magazines encouraged a 'macho' type of behaviour among boys.

37.   77 per cent of parents but only 56 per cent of teenagers thought that young people were influenced about sex and personal relationships by television. Teenagers stressed that they did not believe everything they saw, while parents were more concerned that teenagers might copy or be encouraged to experiment and that television programmes tended to make out that life was easy and romantic.

38.   Videos were much more likely to be regarded by teenagers as having an influence on attitudes towards sex and personal relationships, and indeed more teenagers (70 per cent) than parents (68 per cent) thought this. There was no doubt that teenagers were thinking of explicit sexual or pornographic videos but parents were more likely to be concerned about 'video nasties' than teenagers. Girls and parents were worried about the effect on boys and their relationships with girls and expressed concern about the possibility that such videos encouraged rape, violence and stereotypical thinking. Parents in particular pointed out that these videos often portrayed relationships between men and women in a brutal and violent way.

39. 42 per cent of the teenagers said that they had seen a video of an explicitly sexual kind, although it is possible that 'explicit' sex might have different meanings for different people. This was true in all areas and among all ages, but boys (52 per cent) were more likely to have seen one than girls (33 per cent). Over half the teenagers with only one parent had seen at least one. Thirty-eight per cent said that they had seen a video at home and 72 per cent at a friend's home. 25 per cent of those who had seen one said they had watched it with their parents (representing 11 per cent of the total sample), 22 per cent with brothers and sisters, nearly half had watched with friends of their own sex (especially boys) and 34 per cent with friends of both sexes. The report suggests that these findings cast a new light on recommendations that sex education should be the sole responsibility of parents.

40. About half the teenagers said they would turn first to their mother or father or both parents with a question about sex or contraception, about a third said they would turn first to a friend with a question about sex and about a fifth with a question about contraception. But boys and girls were very different, with 54 per cent of girls saying they would turn first to their mother about sex and 55 per cent about contraception, compared with only 27 per cent and 22 per cent respectively among the boys. Only 5 per cent of teenagers said they would turn first to a teacher and only 2 per cent to a doctor with a question on sex and 9 per cent to a teacher and 5 per cent to a doctor with a question on contraception. However, although teenagers were not sure whether their parents were likely to be accurate sources of information on these matters, they were quite clear that friends were not, and indeed only 4 per cent of teenagers thought that friends were likely to be the most accurate sources of information on sex, in spite of the fact that one-third said they would turn first to friends if they had a question on the subject. Similarly only 3 per cent thought their friends would give them the most accurate information on contraception but one-fifth said they would turn to friends first for advice. Teachers and doctors were thought to be much more reliable sources of information. Teenagers did not turn to the most reliable source of information first because the nature of the relationship and trust and confidentiality were more important factors than accuracy in seeking information and advice. However, there was evidence that teenagers knew to whom they should and could turn for reliable information, having first tried out their questions on people who were close to them.

41. Teaching at school was thought by both parents and teenagers to be the most important source of information for the teenagers on both sex and contraception. Over 60 per cent of both parents and teenagers thought that teenagers had got most information about sex from school, two-thirds of teenagers and nearly 60 per cent of parents thought they had got most information on contraception from school, but only one-fifth of parents, compared with over a third of teenagers, thought that school was the

teenagers' most important source of information on personal relationships. Parents were much more likely than teenagers to link their own importance as a source of information with that of the school. Friends were thought to be the most important source of information about sex by about a third of both parents and teenagers and about contraception by about one-fifth of both samples. However, teenagers were more likely than parents to cite friends as the most important source of information on personal relationships. Teenagers were less likely than parents to name more than one important source of information. Doctors, family planning clinics and other professionals were almost never cited as the most important sources of information on these matters, and neither were the media.

42.　Nearly 80 per cent of the teenagers said that the education they had had at school had been helpful in learning about sex, nearly 70 per cent found it helpful in learning about contraception, (although nearly 10 per cent, mainly 14-year-olds, had had no education on this topic), and 50 per cent had found school helpful in learning about personal relationships, especially the 15 and 16-year-olds. They had found their education helpful in that it had been informative and taught them things they did not know in an authoritative, clear and comprehensive manner. They stressed the reliability of the 'facts' they learned at school in comparison with the information received from other sources and emphasised that the visual presentation of topics and discussions in class were particularly helpful. Those who had not found it helpful said they had been taught too little or in insufficient detail.

43.　75 per cent of teenagers and over half the parents (53 per cent) thought that the quantity of sex education the teenagers had had at secondary school had been about right, but 22 per cent of teenagers and 12 per cent of parents thought there had been too little, while 3 per cent of both samples thought there had been too much, with teenagers saying that it had been repetitive. However, 30 per cent of parents said they did not know enough about it to judge. Some teenagers thought there had been too little on contraception and personal relationships.

44.　Over 60 per cent of parents but only a third of teenagers thought that teachers should give guidance or help on how to behave in sexual matters. Teenagers in the North-East were much more likely than other teenagers to think that they should. It was rare for parents to stress a 'moral' component in this guidance, but they wanted teachers to be trained, unbigoted, willing to take responsibility and able to communicate with teenagers about these matters.

45.　Nearly 50 per cent of teenagers thought that knowing the facts about sex, contraception and personal relationships had affected or would affect their behaviour in future. Girls (55 per cent) were more likely to think this

201

than boys (42 per cent), mainly in making them more cautious, particularly about casual sex because they knew more about the risks. Boys were more likely to say that it would make them act in a more mature and responsible manner.

46.   One-fifth of the parents and a quarter of the teenagers thought that sex education at school made young people more likely to experiment with sex at an early age. Nearly 60 per cent of teenagers and a third of parents thought sex education at school made young people more cautious about experimenting with sex at an early age, although a further third of parents thought that it might make some more cautious. Teenagers stressed that they had learned a lot at school about the risks of pregnancy and venereal disease, which made them more cautious and 'wary'.

47.   44 per cent of teenagers (47 per cent of the girls and 39 per cent of the boys) said that school sex education had helped them understand better how people of the opposite sex felt about things, with 16-year-olds much more likely than 14-year-olds to say this. There was evidence throughout the report that the relatively formal structure of classroom discussions was one of the only ways in which boys and girls exchanged views and opinions on relationships and feelings. 45 per cent of teenagers (50 per cent of boys) said that they would like to know more about how the opposite sex felt about things.

48.   80 per cent of parents thought it was a good idea if schools tried to help young people understand better how people of the opposite sex felt about things, and thought that it would lead to a better understanding between the sexes. They thought that school was the best place to learn about such things, particularly because many felt that children took more notice if they learned about these matters at school.

49.   Two-thirds of the teenagers thought that it was useful to have discussions at school about things like emotions and feelings, again stressing the desirability of hearing a variety of views, offering mutual support and sharing problems. Teenagers who did not find it useful emphasised the need for privacy and confidentiality, and it was clear that some teenagers did not particularly enjoy group discussions.

50.   63 per cent of parents expressed satisfaction with the sex education received by the teenager at secondary school, 8 per cent expressed dissatisfaction, but nearly 30 per cent said they could not judge because they did not know enough about it. The main reason for dissatisfaction was that there had been too little sex education given or that it had been taught in insufficient detail. Only 1 per cent of parents were dissatisfied that it was taught at all.

51.   96 per cent of parents and 95 per cent of teenagers said that schools should provide sex education to children and young people, 2 per cent of parents and 1 per cent of teenagers thought that sex education should be provided by neither school nor parents, and 2 per cent of parents and 4 per cent of teenagers thought that only parents should provide sex education. A quarter of both parents and teenagers thought that sex education should be a joint responsibility of both parents and schools. School sex education was thought necessary because it was said that some parents could not or did not talk to their children about these matters, because schools gave more accurate information and were better equipped with films and teaching aids, because it was considered part of education in general, because children took more notice of information given at school and because some children found it difficult to talk to their parents about these matters.

CONCLUSIONS AND RECOMMENDATIONS

1.   Education in sex and personal relationships at school is welcomed by the overwhelming majority of parents and school-children. It should be the aim of all secondary schools to follow the pattern established in certain local education authorities and schools of integrating these topics into a programme of personal and social education for all pupils in secondary schools. These programmes of education should emphasise to schoolchildren the importance of relating bodily functions to the world of emotions and personal relationships and the wider family and social context in which they live.

2.   These programmes should be given to both boys and girls, and although there may be limited advantages in some discussions in single-sex groups, it should be ensured that both boys and girls cover the same material. Boys receive much less education than girls on these topics at home, and the same is true of some schools.

3.   Schools should ensure that all pupils understand the *words* used in teaching or discussing these topics. Younger teenagers in particular do not always understand technical words, and the use of the vernacular in addition to 'proper' words aids understanding.

4.   Schools should make as much use of visual presentation of these topics as possible. Diagrams, films, television programmes and videos were very much appreciated by schoolchildren in learning about these topics.

5.   Discussions in class or in smaller groups on these topics under the guidance of a teacher should be encouraged and extended. Teenagers found discussions of this kind particularly helpful in relating facts to relationships and stressed the value they placed on learning from others through hearing a variety of views. They found it particularly helpful in learning about the feelings and attitudes of the opposite sex. Parents too stressed the important role played by schools in helping young people understand the opposite sex better, thereby laying the foundation for loving, caring and equal relationships in later life.

6.   The discriminating use of outsiders giving talks or leading discussions at schools should be encouraged. Both parents and teenagers were in favour of 'outsiders', not only because of their presumed expertise and knowledge, but also in some cases because they were strangers. Many teenagers expressed a wish to learn from as wide a variety of sources as possible. The status of outsiders should always be clearly identified to children.

7.   Schools should be encouraged to inform parents in detail about their programmes of personal and social education and to adopt a less defensive attitude towards the discussion of these subjects at school, since the vast majority of parents are supportive of their aims and objectives. Although many parents displayed complete confidence in schools to handle these matters with care, some parents were concerned that too little was being taught in too little detail. A substantial minority of parents were ill-informed about what and how their children were being taught and would have welcomed more information.

8.   Although many schools have an excellent pastoral care system, others do not. There was a strong desire on the part of the vast majority of teenagers for a special person to be available in the school who could be approached with problems or questions on sex or personal relationships. In many schools this function may be performed already by a teacher or teachers, but girls in particular expressed a preference for a school nurse. Senior pastoral staff were particularly highly thought of by schoolchildren, and it is suggested that they might stress their availability for consultation by younger pupils. Every teacher should be made aware of the importance of complete confidentiality in dealing with the personal problems of schoolchildren.

9.   Primary schools should provide an introduction to the personal and social education programmes of the secondary schools. All primary schoolchildren should be given education on not going with strangers, and the majority of parents think that primary schools should cover animal and human reproduction, changes at puberty and family and parenthood.

10.   There was evidence of some pressure on teenagers, particularly from their peer-group, to have a boyfriend or a girlfriend or to have sex. Schools should make sure that such pressures are discussed openly and frankly with teenagers and that young people are encouraged to develop personal independence and responsibility.

11.   Explicitly sexual or pornographic magazines and videos were thought by both teenagers and parents to have a potentially damaging effect on boys in particular, by glorifying violent or brutal sex and by portraying relationships in which women were submissive or regarded as sex objects. Schools should regard it as an important part of their role to correct the influence of

such videos and magazines, since many parents feel themselves inadequate to do so, and, in any case, there was evidence of children watching such videos with parents.

12.   Priority should be given to training teachers in the skills needed to handle these topics in the classroom and when approached on an informal basis. This training should be part of all teacher-training courses and should be available and encouraged as part of in-service training for teachers. Both men and women teachers should be encouraged to undertake such training, particularly in view of the relatively poorer provision of sex education for boys both at home and at school.

REFERENCES

(1)   Christine Farrell, *My Mother Said . . . the way young people learned about sex and birth control*, Routledge and Kegan Paul, 1978.
(2)   Statutory Instruments 1981 No.630, *Information relating to individual schools to be published by an Education Authority or by or on behalf of the governors of an aided or special agreement school*, The Education (School Information) Regulations, DES, 1981.
(3)   Julia Field, *Education in Sex and Personal Relationships Technical Report*, Social and Community Planning Research, 1985.
(4)   DES, *The School Curriculum*, HMSO, 1981.
(5)   *House of Commons Hansard*, 28 October 1982, Vol. 29, No.174, col.554.
(6)   DES, *A Survey of Health Education in Fifteen Primary Schools in Avon*, (A report by HM Inspectors), DES, 1984.
(7)   National Council of Women of Great Britain, *Sex Education / Whose Responsibility?* NCW, 1984.
(8)   *Report by Working Party on Sex Education in Schools*, Nottinghamshire County Council, Education Department, 1979.
(9)   DES, *Health Education in Schools*, HMSO, 1977.
(10) DES, *Curriculum 11-16: a review of progress*, HMSO, 1981, (pp.109-119: Sex education).
(11) Kenneth David, *Personal and Social Education in Secondary Schools*, Longman for Schools Council, 1983.
(12) Richard Pring, *Personal and Social Education in the Curriculum*, Hodder and Stoughton, 1984.
(13) DES, *Aspects of Secondary Education in England: a survey by HM Inspectors of Schools*, HMSO, 1979, (pp.206-240: Personal and social development).
(14) Donald Reid, 'School sex education and the causes of unintended teenage pregnancies—a review', *Health Education Journal*, Vol. 41, No.1, 1982.
(15) K. Fogelman, *Britain's sixteen-year-olds*, National Children's Bureau, 1976.
(16) *Children and their primary schools*, (The Plowden Report), HMSO, 1967.
(17) Lesley Campbell, *The Language of Sex Education: A Communication Problem?* M.Sc. Unpublished dissertation, University of London, 1983.
(18) Isobel Allen, *Counselling Services for Sterilisation, Vasectomy and Termination of Pregnancy*, Policy Studies Institute, 1985.
(19) Judith Bury, *Teenage Pregnancy in Britain*, Birth Control Trust, 1984.
(20) Michael Schofield, *The Sexual Behaviour of Young People*, Longmans, 1965.
(21) Professor Thomas Szasz, 'The Case Against Sex Education', *British Journal of Sexual Medicine*, December 1981, quoted in The Responsible Society, *Sex Education in Schools— what every parent should know*, 1982.
(22) Rex S. Rogers, *Sex Education: Rationale and Reaction*, Cambridge University Press, 1974.
(23) Dilys Cossey and Joanna Chambers, 'Sex Education and Boys', in *Men, Sex and Contraception*, Birth Control Trust and Family Planning Association, 1984.
(24) Elise F. Jones *et al.*, 'Teenage Pregnancy in Developed Countries: Determinants and Policy Implications', *Family Planning Perspectives*, Vol. 17, No.2, March/April 1985.

APPENDIX A
SUMMARY OF METHODOLOGY AND TECHNICAL INFORMATION

1.   The fieldwork for this study was carried out by Social and Community Planning Research (SCPR) under the direction of Julia Field. A full description of the survey design and fieldwork, together with further tabular information and the questionnaires used with teenagers and parents, has been published by SCPR[3]. The fieldwork was conducted between mid-February and mid-April 1985.

2.   *Survey design*
The study was designed to achieve a sample of 200 teenagers aged 14, 15 and 16, together with one parent of each teenager, aiming at approximately equal numbers of mothers and fathers to be randomly selected (when both parents were present in the household). The aim was to interview 200 teenagers and 200 parents, giving 400 individual interviews. Three cities were selected in different parts of England. Within each city the aim was to concentrate the interviewing in three or four wards to reflect different types of district, for example, inner city, suburban and residential, and forming the main catchment areas for individual secondary schools. The cities and wards were selected purposively rather than by random methods. The cities were in the North-East, Midlands and South-West, to give a broad geographical spread. They were recognised as having developed comprehensive programmes of personal, social and health education. Electoral registers were used as the source for systematic random sampling of addresses. The number of selections allowed for ineligible households (those with no teenagers of the required ages) and nonresponse (refusal and other reasons for nonparticipation by eligible households).

Teenagers aged between 14 and 16 form a very small proportion of the total population—5 per cent nationally (1981 Census)—and are therefore difficult to sample in a systematic way. As a result it was decided to use a procedure called *focused enumeration*, often employed in screening for minority groups. Addresses were selected from the Electoral Registers in blocks of six adjacent addresses. Interviewers call at two of the six addresses to enquire about the presence of the target group there and at the two addresses on either side.

Because areas had been purposively selected, the samples for each ward would be independent samples and in the strict technical sense not additive to form a single whole which could be said to be properly representative of the three areas combined. The results are therefore not necessarily representative of the country as a whole, nor of the regions from which they come. Education policy and practice is very much a local authority concern and the differences we found within wards and within cities indicate that a much larger sample would be necessary to provide a fully representative national picture of sex education.

3. *Questionnaires*

The questionnaires were fully structured, in that questions were asked in predetermined sequence and using identical wording for each interview. A fairly high proportion of questions were open-ended, requiring the interviewer to write down verbatim responses and to probe for further information or elucidation of responses where necessary. Interviews lasted an average of 63 minutes with the teenagers and 50 minutes with the parents.

4. *Response*

4,176 addresses were issued to interviewers and 338 households were found to contain an eligible teenager (8.1 per cent). Interviews with both a teenager and a parent were achieved in 205 households, which is 61 per cent of those eligible and 4.9 per cent of all addresses covered—slightly lower than the estimated 5-6 per cent. A further seven interviews were carried out with a parent only and a further four interviews with a teenager only.

Response rate	%
Parent and teenager interviewed	61
Parent only interviewed	3
Teenager only interviewed	1
Sub-total: interviewed	65
Parent refused	22
Teenager refused	3
Both refused	6
Other reasons (away, ill, inadequate English, non-contacts, etc.)	5
(Base: all eligible households)	(338)

The response varied considerably from ward to ward and/or by interviewer. Substitution of an unwilling or unavailable parent was allowed, and in 11 per cent of cases mother was substituted for father and in 7 per cent of cases father was substituted for mother. Overall over two-thirds of the parents interviewed were mothers and under one third were fathers. The imbalance was due mainly to the preponderance of mothers where the teenager was living with only one (natural) parent, but in addition more mothers than fa-

thers were willing or available to be interviewed and there was some imbalance in the way the random selection procedures operated in practice.

5. *Achieved interviews*

209 teenagers were interviewed—99 boys and 110 girls—and 212 parents
were interviewed—149 mothers and 63 fathers. 205 pairs of parents and teenagers were interviewed with the following distribution:

Parent and teenager pairs	%
Mother and son	32
Mother and daughter	39
Father and son	16
Father and daughter	13
(Base: all paired interviews)	(205)

The following tables give the distribution of the teenagers interviewed by sex,
age and area and the parents interviewed by sex and area.

Characteristics of teenagers interviewed

Column percentages

| | Total | AGE | | | AREA | | |
		14	15	16	SW	Midl.	NE
Boys	47	52	44	45	47	49	47
Girls	53	48	56	55	53	51	53
(Base: all teen-agers inter-viewed)	(209)	(75)	(81)	(53)	(45)	(76)	(88)

Area of residence of parents interviewed

Column percentages

	Total	SW	Midlands	NE
Mothers	69	79	77	61
Fathers	31	21	23	39
(Base: all parents)	(212)	(47)	(74)	(91)

6. *Schools and present educational status of teenagers*

One of the purposes of the study was to identify a sample of schools through the samples of teenagers, and this was one of the reasons for restricting the interviewing to three to four wards within each city. We asked the teenagers the name of their present or most recent school.

Type of school attended by teenage respondents (most recently)

Column percentages

	Total	Boys	Girls	SW	Midl.	NE
Comprehensive	94	96	93	91	93	97
Grammar	1	0	1	2	0	0
Independent (fee-paying)	5	4	6	7	6	3
(Base: all teenagers)	(209)	(99)	(110)	(45)	(76)	(88)

The teenagers reported a total of 50 schools as their present or most recent school. In the North-East area they attended 13 schools, in the South West they attended 11 schools, but in the Midlands areas they attended 26 schools. In both the North-East and the South-West, the four schools most frequently mentioned were attended by 80 per cent of the teenage respondents, but in the Midlands area the four schools most frequently mentioned were attended by 51 per cent of respondents, with the rest of the teenagers widely scattered at schools in the city and surrounding areas.

Ninety-five per cent of the teenagers were at local authority or voluntary-aided secondary schools, including 7 per cent at Roman Catholic secondary schools (10 per cent in the North East) and 3 per cent at Church of England secondary schools. Five per cent were at independent fee-paying schools, mainly at day schools.

Ninety-four per cent of the teenagers were at mixed schools—97 per cent of the boys and 91 per cent of the girls. Of the 13 teenagers attending single-sex schools, ten were girls and three were boys.

We asked the 16-year-olds what they were doing at the moment and the following table gives details.

Present educational status of 16-year-old respondents

Column percentages

	Total	Boys	Girls	SW	Midl.	NE
Still at school	79	83	76	92	74	78
At a 6th form college	6	4	7	0	4	11
At another type of college	6	0	10	0	13	0
Working	4	4	3	8	4	0
On a youth train- ing scheme	6	8	3	0	4	11
(Base: all 16-year- olds)	(53)	(24)	(29)	(12)	(23)	(18)

7. *Religion of respondents*

Column percentages

	Total teenagers	Total parents
Church of England/other protestant	63	77
Roman Catholic	11	14
Hindu/Muslim/Sikh	3	3
None	23	6
(Base: all respondents)	(209)	(212)

8. *Social class*

We asked the parent respondents about their own occupation and that of their spouse. This meant that we were able to assign a socio-economic group-ing classification and social class to the parents. However, because of the relatively high proportion of single-parent respondents, mainly mothers, and the extent of remarriage, we decided against using any analysis of the ma-terial by social class, since the results on a sample of this size could be misleading.

APPENDIX B
THE DEVELOPMENT OF SEX EDUCATION IN BRITISH SCHOOLS: A REVIEW OF THE LITERATURE BY MARIE-ANNE DOGGETT

Introduction

Although the term 'sex education' is widely used in the British educational system today, it would nevertheless appear to be an uncertain shorthand for a wide range of differing concepts. Writing in 1972, Dallas[14] (p.9) defined sex education as 'a wide, all embracing and all but meaningless term', and Hierons [43] stated that 'sex education is not a subject: it is a way of life, an attitude of mind'.

The pioneering work in young people's attitudes to sexuality was that of Schofield[64] in the mid-1960s. He found that schools were more concerned with providing sex education for girls than for boys and that their emphasis was very much on the provision of biological information. He reported signs that teenagers were 'not altogether content' with what little sex education they had been getting and concluded that his research showed 'a lively demand for information about sex' which was not being fulfilled.

Ten years later, Farrell's crucial study [28] demonstrated that the question was no longer whether or not young people received sex education in schools, but rather whether it was presented at an appropriate stage in their development. In comparison with Schofield's study, she found that boys were more likely to have had some sex education in schools although the position for girls had not appreciably changed. For both sexes she concluded that schools were still not filling the gap left by parents and that there was 'room for improvement' in the age at which lessons were provided, the amount of detail and the topics discussed, and the presentation by many teachers. Although reactions to sex education provision were 'as varied as the provision itself', 48 per cent of the young people in her sample were seriously critical or made apathetic comments on it. Nevertheless, most parents and children alike were in favour of increasing the amount and extending the range of sex education in schools.

The characteristic picture which still emerges of the provision of sex education in schools is 'too little too late'[35] (p.321). The Goldmans conclude that home-based and media teaching should also start at an earlier age, and their study provides some insights into the extent of modern provision [35] (pp.300-303). However, the evidence collected by the Joint Working Party on Pregnant Schoolgirls and Schoolgirl Mothers [48] showed that 'the picture is one of very uneven provision', with 'examples of serious concern and dedicated effort' alongside 'inactivity and indifference'[48] (para. 32) Rogers[63] (p.9) feared that this variability stemmed in part from 'the very autonomy of individual schools', while the DES[18] (p.238) blamed 'lack of leadership and agreed policies' and expressed concern at the 'wide differences in the extent to which admirable general intentions have been translated into effective practice'.

Objections to sex education in schools are often given much prominence, even though they are regarded by many as an 'anachronism'[13]. Ten years ago Schofield[64] expressed a very real concern that 'inoffensive' courses were usually also 'ineffectual' and, more recently, another expert[71] has warned that the influence of the anti-sex-education lobby is 'almost certainly greater than their numbers' because of their tendency to join pressure groups.

Despite the very obvious need for such data, we still lack the information about sex education in the school curriculum which Rogers commented on in 1974[63] (p.9) and we still lack evidence of any improvement in its quality as Reid pointed out in 1982[61]. Official bodies, such as the World Health Organisation[76] (p.21), may emphasise the value of research 'as an important tool in changing attitudes and creating public and official awareness of problems', but in Britain there is still a dearth of significant research results on which to base recommendations.

In 1977 the DES[20] recognised that there are no 'standard answers' to the Who? When? What? and Where? of sex education. This review attempts to survey the available evidence on the development of sex education and attitudes to it within the framework of these questions, and as a background paper to the main study.

HISTORICAL PERSPECTIVES

Brief summaries of the historical development of sex education in Britain can be found in several publications[36,58] (pp.3-5) [63] (pp.37-40).

Examples of very early courses (held during the 1940s) are described by Tuchler[69,70], who concludes that the boys were 'interested, attentive and well-behaved', that there was 'no silliness, giggling, or blushing', and the 'mothers did not complain of the course'.

The changing aims of sex education
In the early 1930s, Barry[3] considered that the main aim of sex education was

the prevention of illegitimacy. With the outbreak of the Second World War, the emphasis changed to the prevention of VD, described by Dallas[14] (p.11) as a 'negative objective'. During the 1950s, a general reduction in population growth was seen as the prime purpose[3], which, by the 1960s, was also incorporating an attempt to reduce the guilt and shame so much associated with sex[3].

Programmes in the late 1960s and 1970s were primarily concerned with sex education and contraceptive advice[17], and during that period Pearson and Lambert[60] detected a considerable increase in the breadth of teaching, and in satisfaction with information received on reproduction and contraception.

Moving into the 1980s, Reid[61] states that sex education is increasingly regarded as a component of social education, whose aims include improving decision-making skills, raising self-esteem, clarifying values, and an increasing awareness of the consequences of actions and sensitivity to the needs of others. Went[73] (pp.19-20) feels that the very wide scope of sex education programmes makes it difficult to summarise the aims of a whole course, the objectives of which should relate to knowledge, attitudes, communication skills, decision-making processes, sensitivity to others and so on. She goes on to list the aims of sex education as follows:

(i)   To combat ignorance and increase understanding. To provide full, honest information about the physical, emotional and social aspects of human sexual development from conception to old age, including the nature of love, personal relationships and family life, which may enable people to have a positive and happy acceptance of their own sexuality, thus increasing self-value and esteem. To increase sensitivity to the sexual nature of oneself, and members of both sexes, so that insight may be gained into the potential for fulfilling sexual relationships and enjoyment.

(ii)   To reduce guilt and anxiety. To provide knowledge and acceptance of the variety and variability of human sexual behaviour, and by seeking not to establish unrealistic 'norms', to improve the quality of sexual relationships, and encourage better mental health.

(iii)   To promote responsible behaviour. To increase individual responsibility for sexual behaviour so that neither one's own nor one's partner's body or feelings are hurt. This includes not passing on sexually transmitted diseases, initiating unwanted pregnancies, nor forcing unwanted sexual activity on other people.

(iv)   To combat exploitation. To promote an awareness of the misuse of sex, both for commercial profit, and in personal relationships, so enabling people to protect themselves from exploitation. To become aware of dual codes of sexual behaviour, and work towards their elimination.

(v)   To promote the ability to make informed decisions. To help young

214

people develop the ability to determine their own values within a moral framework, and to make decisions about their behaviour which will be beneficial to themselves and their partner, and to enable children to recognise the pressures on groups of individuals to behave in certain ways, and develop strategies for coping with them.

(vi) To facilitate communication on sexual matters. To provide an acceptable vocabulary for discussing sex, and to enable this to be used without embarrassment in a group, class or clinic situation.

(vii) To develop educational skills for future parents and child carers. To further understanding of the sex education needs of small children, so that parents, nurses, doctors, police, social workers, friends or relations can provide explanations of sex without embarrassment, and at the right level for the child concerned. As in all health education we are working for attitude and behaviour changes away from negative damaging ones, towards positive helpful ones. This involves the most difficult skills ever required of teachers, and as some of the changes will be slow, they are often difficult to evaluate in the short term. It is important not to lose heart at the enormity of the task, but do the best possible under the circumstances, and be aware of the many variables involved, some of which are quite out of the control of the school[73].

More succinctly, the WHO has declared that the emphasis should be on 'understanding, mutual tenderness, delight and responsibility'[76] (p.21), while the IPPF states that such education should 'aim to increase young people's understanding of themselves and the world they live in, be relevant to specific age groups, social, cultural and environmental conditions, and emphasise the benefits of avoiding early pregnancy'[45].

Official Reports
In 1943, the Board of Education issued a pamphlet entitled 'Sex education in schools and youth organisations', which recognised for the first time that schools have a responsibility in this area; it is briefly summarised in the DES publication 'Health education in schools'[20] (p.109). Although it gave a far-sighted lead at that time, its provisions were not really acted upon for some twenty years, until the slow change in the climate of public opinion allowed it[43].

Between 1959 and 1967, three reports of the Central Advisory Council for Education were published. They were the Crowther Report in 1959, the Newsom Report in 1963 and the Plowden Report in 1967. Summaries of the main features of all these reports, as far as school sex education is concerned, can be found in three publications[20] (pp.109-10); [58] (pp.3-4); [63] (pp.35-36). Over a period of great change, these reports reveal the concern which was shown about responsible presentation of the problems of sexual development.

They were followed in 1977 by the DES's 'Health education in schools'[20] and the DHSS's 'Prevention and health', which emphasised the need for a coordinated policy in both primary and secondary schools, in which sex education would be most effective when forming part of a programme of education in lasting personal relationships, seeking to relate factual knowledge to an individual sense of personal responsibility[58] (p.4)

Curriculum guidance

By 1980 sex education was specifically mentioned in the Education Act, in which the Publication of Information [Section 8] requirements are that local education authorities should publish details about each school within their jurisdiction, including information on 'the ways and context in which sex education is provided'[73] (p.16).

The following year, the DES produced 'The School Curriculum' which identified sex education, along with moral education and preparation for parenthood/family life, as essential constituents more likely to feature in a variety of courses distributed throughout the curriculum than to be 'subjects' in their own right[58] (p.5).

Finally, the important work of the Schools Council and the Nuffield Foundation in producing working papers (for example, [65]), reports on activities and revisions of the content of school courses must not be overlooked. They are described in Dallas[14] (pp. 42-52) and in Rogers[63] (pp.38-40).

Parliamentary concerns

A selection of parliamentary questions asked and answered between 1977 and 1985 reveals some of the main preoccupations of those years. The government is often pressed to include sex education as part of the core curriculum and to support or condemn particular teaching materials produced by independent groups. Concern is expressed about sex education in primary schools and about parental rights. The usual response by Ministers is to re-iterate that it is up to individual education authorities and schools to make their own arrangements, but that these should always include the fullest possible consultation with parents.

A recent White Paper, entitled 'Better Schools' draws attention to the fact that government would expect to see sex education taught 'within a moral framework', and this is further interpreted as being without undue emphasis on the physical aspects at the expense of a deeper understanding of the responsibilities of parenthood and family life in general[23].

LEA responsibilities and the lack of government policy

There are many who agree with Judith Bury when she writes: 'For sex education in schools to become more effective, it needs to be made national policy with government backing'[8] (p.65). A commonly agreed core curriculum is often suggested, though the proponents of such might lend an ear to Schofield's remarks about 'the dreary sort of standardised sex education syllabus that would emanate from the DES'[64].

Without guidance from 'above', few education authorities or individual heads have regarded sex education as a priority area, and many schools have 'officially' ignored the subject, while 'unofficially' allowing those staff who feel comfortable and concerned enough to approach it as they see fit[22].

An IPPF Survey in 1975[46] described the British educational system as 'a complex system of local autonomy, with central government checks and balances'[46] (p.39). This meant that both within authorities and within schools, the patterns of curriculum were very 'local' affairs. Some LEAs developed special courses which had a national reputation, while others might exert a powerful influence on local schools, but might not be known even in a neighbouring locality[46] (p.42). Local authorities tended to be 'against' premarital sex, considering that 'sex life may be taken up before marriage, but only if it grows from love for the other person, and even then only after a considerable time'[46] (p.41). In both the public and private sectors, school sex education was only 'sporadically' implemented, while the DES was characterised as 'friendly and neutral'[46] (p.40).

The virtual autonomy of the LEAs in curricular matters had resulted in much diversity of practice and content[35] (p.54). Examples of LEA schemes are outlined by both Rogers[63] (pp.43-48) and Schools Council[65] (pp.62-76). More detailed accounts of individual approaches can be found elsewhere, for example, Redbridge[1], Borehamwood[3], London[12] (pp.19-23), Lancashire[29], Glasgow[42], Hertfordshire[62], Nottinghamshire[69,70] and Gloucestershire[14] (pp.60-62).

CURRICULUM DEVELOPMENT
School sex education courses cannot be designed without reference to the framework of sexual and moral codes currently pertaining. In the past sexuality was seen as an innate 'animal passion', whereas the more modern view is that of human socio-sexual development as a 'learning process'[63] (p.3). Today's perspective should set human sexuality 'firmly in the context of caring relationships and an understanding of the importance and validity of our sexual feelings[2].

Even in the 1940s, Tuchler[70] was expressing the view that, for children aged 14 and over, almost every subject should lend itself to the inclusion of 'moral' (and therefore 'sexual') education. Dallas summarises the work of John Wilson in clarifying what is meant by 'morality', as opposed to 'moralising'[14] (pp.14-15) before a firm basis for deciding objectives in sex education can be reached.

More recent official policy documents renew the emphasis on the importance of 'moral education' in schools—now often replaced by the word 'ethics'—and the report from the National Council of Women points to the wide variety of curricular areas which this concept will cover[58] (p.24). Previously, Rogers had underlined the potential dangers of separating 'moral education' from the concrete facts and realities of everyday (sexual) life, whilst appreciating that successful integration must depend on an individual teacher's ability to avoid 'introduction' of a particular morality[63] (p.5).

From biology to personal relationships

Tuchler's 'controversial' and 'experimental' sex education course at a boys' secondary school in Nottingham during the 1940s was part of the science syllabus for 2nd year boys aged 12 + . Basic biology of frogs, cats and rabbits led to a consideration of human reproduction, but emotional aspects were only dealt with 'on a rather elementary level'[69]. Elsewhere, Dallas has described this approach to sex as 'similar to that used when dealing with maps of the coalfields'[14] (p.10).

With the 1960s came much greater recognition of the importance of emotional elements, so that Dalzell-Ward, Medical Director of the Central Council for Health Education, was able to write in 1965: 'Our overall aim is the promotion of community health through the promotion of emotional maturity in the individual'[15]. At classroom level this meant that the 'facts of life' were regarded as more complex than merely imparting biological knowledge[29].

Later in the decade and into the following one, many saw the main emphasis of sex education as being on contraception for the prevention of unwanted pregnancy[17]. However, by 1977 the DES was 'doubtful if wider knowledge of methods of birth control would significantly reduce pregnancies among girls below the school leaving age' and expressed the view that 'whatever the phrase, "sex education", may mean, it is certainly inextricably bound up with the physical, emotional and mental development of children, especially in adolescence'[20] (pp.114-115). Education in personal relationships was now considered to be an 'implicit function of all communities, including all schools', though several schools felt that their formal curriculum did not 'adequately deal with aspects of education likely to make a particularly important contribution to personal development' and were seeking ways 'of making the curriculum as a whole more responsive to personal needs'[19] (p.34). By 1984, the Health Education Council was able to claim that 'the need to enhance the personal and social development of pupils in schools and colleges is now made explicit through the establishment of pastoral care systems and the curriculum itself'[39].

Some of the most recent writers on the subject emphasise that today's sex education must be made more personally relevant to pupils, must underline choice, responsibility and affection in relationships, and not merely impart factual information in a classroom atmosphere that is unlikely to affect personal awareness[8]. Others feel that we need to look at the whole area of human relationships—personal, professional, social, economic, political and individual—and that the way forward lies in giving young people 'a broad enough appreciation of the way they fit into and relate to the world for them to act in significant and meaningful ways'[54] (p.148).

Perhaps this is an appropriate moment at which to recall Dallas's earlier warnings that the interpretation of sex education was becoming 'sharply polarised' between 'anatomical diagrams and bold explanations of physiological processes' on the one hand, and the 'vaguer realms of personal relationships' on the other[14] (p.9). She found it uncommon that the two approaches were integrated, largely because those who 'feel securely expert in one approach feel very inadequate in the other'. Such integration, however, is implicit in the declared aims of sex education as perceived by organisations such as the IPPF[45] i.e. increased understanding of oneself and one's world, avoidance of early unwanted pregnancy and awareness of the social, emotional and psychological implications of sex.

The question of a core curriculum
The WHO states, quite unequivocally, that sex education should be 'an integral part of education in every school system, to be implemented before puberty and enforced by legislation'[76] (p.22). This view is shared by many in this country, who feel that 'to see all schools giving sex education is a viable goal, whereas to see all parents instructing their children is not'[63] (p.8). In its recent report[58] (p.33), the National Council of Women gave as its very first recommendation that 'A programme of personal and social development, including health education, sex education and education about parenthood, should be an essential constituent of the curriculum for children of all ages and abilities and both sexes'.

The same authors believe that such programmes should be part of the core curriculum of every school in order to avoid the problems of duplication or omission which otherwise tend to arise[58] (p.29). In this regard, an earlier report from the Joint Working Party on Pregnant Schoolgirls and Schoolgirl Mothers[48] (p.13) had particularly singled out the problem of those 'more academic pupils' who may be debarred from non-core classes on the grounds that their rigorous timetables do not allow space for 'non-academic subjects'.

In practice, though, the DES's inspectors found that very few schools were giving sufficiently detailed attention to the contribution of the curriculum. They pointed out that the very existence of a programme would convey messages to the pupils and influence their attitudes to certain parts of their education, and that the distribution of resources and staff might indicate values held by the school in a way that was not necessarily perceived or intended[18] (p.208).

The context of sex education courses
The consensus view, as represented by the National Council of Women in 1984, is that sex education should be set 'within the context of a planned programme for personal, social, moral and health education, including preparation for parenthood and an adult role in social and family life'[58] (p.29). This integration into a truly 'interdisciplinary' programme is seen as the ideal by Went[73] (p.10) and by the WHO, which declares that 'sex educa-

tion that is integrated throughout the school curriculum from preschool level to primary school and secondary school is preferable to a single course of instruction'[76] (p.11).

Smith[66] acknowledges that the integration of sex education into the curriculum in British schools has been severely restricted by factors outside the control of individual teachers. They may have accepted the need to provide such education, but the DES is cautious about the extent to which 'more personal education may require the development of new and separate courses, and how far these needs may be better met by shifts of emphasis and content within existing subjects'[18] (p.42).

The debate between the various advantages and disadvantages of the 'specialist' and 'integrated' approaches to the problem is well-documented by the Schools Council in its 1976 Working Paper[65] (pp.14-20).

The spread across the curriculum
Writing in 1965, Dalzell-Ward[15] considered that 'the most important public health problem of our day' was that of 'population' and that young people could be interested in this problem through their religious, geographical, economic and civic studies. Ten years later, in their survey on the status of sex education in European countries, the IPPF found that, in Britain, the subject entered very many areas of the school curriculum, encouraged by 'present methods'[46] (p.42). 'On the whole, sex education is not taught as a separate subject, but is dealt with mainly under the heading of biology, but also, and importantly, under such subjects as health education, domestic science, home economics and physical education, which tend to deal with the physiological and hygiene aspects. Other areas are explored in religious education, English literature, social studies, mathematics, general studies, geography, and history etc.'[46] (p.41).

Dallas considered that this duplication arose basically from the inability of schools to integrate their physical and emotional approaches to the subject[14] (p.9), while Leathar and Bostock pointed to the dangers of omission, which could arise in the cases of pupils who were not 'doing' the particular subject which included sex education, particularly biology[53] (p.15).

In the late 1970s, HMIs discovered that many schools had well-conceived courses designed to encourage pupils to meet life as young adults outside the school with greater confidence, but that in a large number of schools these courses were included in the option system and were expressly intended for the less able pupils[18] (p.211).

More recently, Gingell paints an entertaining sketch of sex education in 1981—'dropped into the laps of the biology or religious knowledge teachers, in the hope that training has given them some miraculous protection against the burns of this hot potato'[34], while Lee is amused to find herself, as a sex educator, 'listed' under domestic science, general studies, social studies, home economics, childcare, general science, biology, health care, and sixth form options[54] (p.143).

Watson[71] suggests in 1983 that many teachers prefer not to use the words 'sex education' on a timetable, selecting instead headings such as 'personal relationships', 'preparation for life', 'learning to live', 'child development' etc, and that, although health education is sometimes used as a euphemism, such courses frequently do not contain any sex education at all.

The need for coordination

With such a plethora of courses and subject areas which could include sex education, it would seem obvious that coordination is essential if wasteful duplications and/or damaging omissions are to be avoided. Yet in 1984 Dixon[22] observed that 'few schools appear to have any policy discussions on sex education and teachers are unsure'.

Dallas felt that there was a strong case for a coordinator to spend much time 'just becoming familiar with the mass of material' and producing a synthesis best suited to the school'[14] (p.42).

Who should be such a coordinator, and *what* their role should be is well covered by the Schools Council[65] (pp.24-27).

Counselling and pastoral care

The developing emphasis on the emotional side of sexual activity and on the evaluation of personal relationships has been paralleled in schools by the introduction of more formal systems of care and guidance[16]. HMIs found that 'schools placed much greater emphasis on fostering the personal development of their pupils through pastoral care than through their curriculum'[18] (p.208). On the grounds that sexuality is part of the total life experience and should not be consigned to special lessons[44], the practice of counselling in schools aims primarily to help pupils learn how to deal with the problems or tasks which have led them to seek help[18] (p.221).

The need for such individual counselling is reflected in the types of questions asked by pupils during sex education classes[11] and in the evidence of increasing sexual activity revealed in many surveys[58] (p.22). Holden[44] also suggests that counselling might compensate for changes in the structure and significance of the family and the effect of television on social value judgements.

However, in the late 1970s only 14 per cent of schools surveyed by the HMIs had a teacher with special responsibility as a counsellor, and there were problems which militated against effective provision, for example, lack of time, inadequate accommodation, poor communication and ill-defined roles[18] (pp.221-222).

Pastoral care in schools should provide a bridge between sex education[65] (pp.21-22) and the academic/curricular system[58] (p.31), with which it should have equal emphasis and importance[18] (p.239). Where such care is divorced from the academic system, or is inadequate, the interrelationship between the academic and personal development of pupils is likely to be poor[18] (p.221).

WHOSE RESPONSIBILITY?

School or parents

Although the National Council of Women[58] (p.5) speaks for many in re-iterating that parents should bear the main responsibility for the personal, social and moral education of their children, its members point to the fact that many people do not realise the difficulty most parents have in ensuring that their children know all they need to know in the 'right way' at the 'right age'. Between the mid-1960s and the mid-1970s, Pearson and Lambert[60] detected an increase in the use of parents as satisfactory sources of information, though responses to the 1982 'Woman' survey[47] indicated that fewer than 1 in 10 readers thought that sex education should be left entirely to parents. Over 90 per cent felt that the responsibility should be *shared* with the school, and most studies have shown that schools are considered appropriate places in which sex education should take place[35] (p.321), [73] (p.10).

Parental involvement in school sex education

Full consultation with parents is strongly advocated by most authorities[45,61] since programmes are felt to be more effective with parental support[8] (p.56). The DES[20] (p.118) sees sex education as 'an area of teaching in which co-operation between parents and schools is not only essential but often highly effective in encouraging mutual understanding and trust'. The report continues:

> Teachers are wise to give parents the opportunity to examine and discuss with them innovatory courses of sex education or personal relationships. Parents are wise to realise that schools can neither avoid references to the broader issues by other boys and girls nor confine the mention of sexual matters to a programme of sex education.

Bury[8] (p.56) welcomes the new law which obliges schools to inform parents of the 'manner and context' of their provision for sex education, although Williams[75] draws the distinction between informing parents and consulting with them. Whereas 44 per cent of the schools in his survey kept parents informed of the content of their programmes, only 18 per cent consulted parents in their preparation.

Overall, there would appear to be a lack of integration between parents and schools[53] (p.15), with a 'significant number' of schools only providing the legal minimum in the way of informing and consulting parents[58] (p.7). All LEAs and individual schools should be urgently looking at ways in which parents, pupils, teachers and the community can come together in co-operative schemes, such as that run by Dudley LEA[58] (p.9). Went[73] (pp.29-30) offers guidelines on parent-teacher meetings about sex education, which she sees as a 'very rewarding approach'.

Much prominence is given to parental 'rights' in sex education, particularly the right to withdraw a child from classes[58] (p.11). The Schools Council[65] (p.29) urges that 'attention should be paid to minority views', but the National Council of Women did not feel that all teachers reacted with sufficient insight or understanding of deeply-felt parental fears and anxieties[58] (p.10). Both agree that withdrawal of a child should be reluctantly permitted, after full discussion, though this is not generally felt to be in the child's best interests and can usually be avoided if all parents are aware of the content and presentation and have met the staff involved[73] (p.11).

Other influences
Perhaps the most extensive survey of the sources of children's sex education, other than parents and schools, is that of the Goldmans[35] (pp.308-9, 309-313), who nevertheless concluded that 80 per cent of sources were, in fact, mothers, teachers or the media(p.321).

Reid[61] and Clarke[11] express the view that 'input' from peers, family and the media can 'dilute' the impact of school sex education in the long term, and that initial attitudes and/or information from friends may carry more weight than information given at school. The dangers of 'erroneous, inaccurate or misunderstood' information are highlighted in the National Council of Women's report which also draws attention to the increasing use of books, magazines, films, papers, TV and video for the children of today[58] (pp.11-12).

Outside speakers in schools
There is much debate on the desirability and/or usefulness of using speakers from outside agencies in the classroom. In Scotland, 'these outside agents were more favourably regarded than teachers'[53] (p.15) and Clarke[11] showed that such visitors can be of great value.

Many would agree with Went[73] (p.40) that they can 'add variety and interest to the programme and offer specialist knowledge and training and a different approach . . . and a link with "real-life situations"'. The Schools Council[65] (p.32) emphasises that the 'thoughtful use of outside experts as part of a carefully planned course can be of great value' and presents guidelines for the use of such visiting speakers.

Their advantages and disadvantages must vary according to the circumstances in individual schools, which are urged to be selective and to ensure supervision of the speakers' ability to communicate with teenage pupils and to present a balanced view of contentious issues[58] (p.31). They may have more in-depth knowledge of their subject matter, but they cannot know the personalities or achievements of the pupils and this can tend to isolate sex education from other parts of the curriculum[1,34]. To this end, many advocate a partnership between outside speakers and teachers, who can ensure continuity[34] and use outsiders as an aid, not a substitute, for themselves[1].

Pupils may feel freer to ask an outside speaker a question, especially where these are anonymous and the visitor is not seen as part of the authoritarian establishment[73] (p.40). However, many visitors are not necessarily trained communicators with good teaching skills; contacts with teachers are therefore essential[73] (p.40).

However, the subject of teachers' own training in sex education skills has also given rise to much comment, as the next section shows.

The training of teachers

The consensus view is that training in sex education, though vital[45], is still rather inadequate in this country[8] (p.66). Teachers identify sex education as the topic in which they feel they have the most serious lack of expertise and which is therefore the most difficult to teach[58] (p.32). Williams[75] has undertaken an entire project on what has happened in the initial training of teachers, but particular concern is expressed about the need for in-service training[8,76] (p.13) and the lack of male teachers who undertake the work[58] (p.32).

Dallas[14] (p.92) believed that 'a variety of teachers, young and old, mature or immature, demonstrating a variety of attitudes, methods and roles, both communicative, informative and authoritative, provides the ideal situation for sex education in its widest sense rather than searching for any one ideal teacher', and that, on the whole, 'teachers select themselves' for the work. Earlier, Dalzell-Ward[15] had reported an imprecise knowledge as to the qualities required in teachers, although there was an awareness that the most enthusiastic were not necessarily best. Similarly, there was uncertainty about the length of preparation required and its content.

The WHO[76] (p.12) shows itself more positive:

> Training should include knowledge of the basic facts of human sexuality and an understanding of developmental, psychological and social factors, but should also provide a setting for the acquirement of the communication skills needed to transmit that knowledge, and develop empathy and understanding of the needs of the students. Sex educators should be given the opportunity to develop an awareness of their own sexuality, its needs and expression, and recognise their particular inhibitions and areas of discomfort.

However, since British establishments concerned with teacher training are to a large extent autonomous, with decisions about curriculum content left to the teaching staff of the individual institutions[73] (p.49), it would seem likely that there is as great a variety in the training of teachers for sex education as in the teaching itself in our schools. Both government and LEAs are urged to provide more, and not merely as an 'optional extra'[58] (p.32).

WHEN SHOULD SEX EDUCATION BE TAUGHT AND TO WHOM?

International agencies are quite emphatic in insisting that sex education should be age-specific[76] (p.21; 45), although the DES is at pains to point out that particular stages of a child's development are not accurately indicated by age[20] (p.116). The basic core of information should be adapted to the different age or developmental groups and repeated at different levels[58,76].

Some papers try to suggest the particular topics which might best be dealt with at certain ages[46] (p.41; 57), but Dallas[14] (p.16) prefers to make the overall comment that the needs of the various age, ability and cultural groups must be considered and that the paramount factor is the reduction of anxiety, guilt and shame.

'Boys too'
Nearly all commentators express concern that boys can be a very deprived group as far as sex education is concerned. Goldman[35] (p.321) found that a sizeable proportion of boys felt that they could not ask questions of their parents, teachers or friends, while the Joint Working Party[48] (p.13) commented on the fact that few boys' schools provide a curriculum which includes sex education.

At a time when we are calling for more shared responsibility between the sexes in matters concerning reproduction[58] (p.23), there are those who are seeking more 'positive discrimination' in favour of the sex education of boys[12] and increased efforts to educate young men in responsible relationships, parenthood and family life[45].

Many feel that it is a good thing for boys and girls to be taught together[8,57] and Went[73] (pp.39-40) offers a comprehensive summary of the advantages and disadvantages of mixed-sex classes.

Younger children and primary school provision
Since most children are believed to have picked up 'some outlines' by the age of 9[29], there is strong support that sex education should begin 'in the early years of life'[45] and even 'before school age'[76] (p.21). Many countries begin their sex education classes at 13-14, but this is considered too late for a large number of children[14] (p.32) who would benefit from such education at an earlier age[58] (p.14).

Goldman[35] (p.321) reports that 'most' children in his study wanted sex education in primary schools and Rogers[63] (p.123) overviews the valuable arguments in favour of the long-term effectiveness of primary school provision, i.e. that a higher sexual knowledge amongst first year pupils at secondary schools can be associated with the classes they had at primary school. Dallas[14] (p.34) feels that it is 'indefensible' to leave young children 'vulnerable to the impact of sex education from adverts, television and prurient school friends'.

However, the available evidence suggests that only around 50 per cent[37] or less[35] (p.321) of primary schools are actually providing sex education, although nearly all undertake health education[37]. Many schools still gave none at all[14] (p.37) in 1972.

The situation in British primary schools was reported in 1966 by Chanter[9] and again ten years later by Rogers[63] (pp.41-42). More recently, Hagerdorn[37] reports considerable changes in the 1980s (although it is still difficult to get a coherent programme into all primary schools), and feels strongly that to leave all sex education until secondary school should be 'a thing of the past'.

Several writers comment on the influence of radio and TV programmes developed especially for use in primary schools[43], 20 per cent to 30 per cent of which make use of them[61]. Rogers' book contains several chapters reporting on the various broadcasts[63] (pp.197—250) and his own summary of the effects of televised sex education at the primary school level (pp. 251-264).

Finally, we are reminded by Dallas[14] (p.35) that in primary schools 'more important than the transmission of facts is the provision of a climate of communication where children feel happy to ask questions and where a worried child can find supportive counselling from a reassuring adult'.

THE CONTENT OF SEX EDUCATION

According to the WHO, guidelines for sex education programmes should be laid down in written form 'so as to provide a framework to safeguard the dignity and integrity of both student and teacher'[76] (p.21). In Britain, education authorities are now statutorily required to publish particulars 'of the manner and context in which education as respects sexual matters is given'[67].

Bury[8] (p.65) emphasises the importance of accurate information, which should be given precisely and honestly, while Clarke[11] found that the teenagers in her study had definite ideas about the content of their courses and recommended that these should be taken more fully into account when planning future courses. Others point out that courses should always take into account the questions children ask[58] (p.12), and Goldman[35] (pp.313-321) devotes several pages to a consideration of what children want to know about sex and what they receive, observing that there is often a 'shortfall' between the two.

In 1975, the IPPF[46] (p.40) drew attention to the fact that there was often a difference in Britain between what might be stated in a curriculum and what was in fact taught in the classroom. They discovered that, where a curriculum did exist, it tended to include the nature and hygiene of menstruation for girls (though seldom for boys), the structure and functioning of male and female sex organs, though seldom the techniques of fertilisation and coitus, the symptoms of VD, though rarely the treatment, while topics such as masturbation, nocturnal emission, homosexuality, pornography or group sex were not usually included at all. They also commented that neither the methods nor principle of contraception were often included.

It is interesting to contrast this with the recommendations laid down recently by the WHO Regional Office for Europe[76] (p.12):

> The curriculum should include information about the male and female body and its functions, changes that occur at puberty and variations in both the timing of the event and in outcome of physical development that might lead to anxiety. Reproduction, conception and contraception, pregnancy and childbirth would be included. An understanding of the sexual spectrum and the place of homosexuality, masturbation and sexually transmitted diseases should not be overlooked.

The balance between the physical and emotional aspects of sex

The same source summarises the basic content of every sex education programme as 'information on human anatomy, reproductive physiology, family planning and emotional aspects'[76] (p.22). Programmes are most effective if 'time is given to deciding what factual matter should be included to give adequate knowledge of mental, physical and emotional factors, and how responsible attitudes towards sexuality could be developed'[76] (p.11). 'Sex education should be part of a broader programme that builds an understanding of the moral values needed to provide rational bases for making decisions, develops objective and understanding attitudes towards sex in its various manifestations, and fosters an appreciation of the positive satisfactions that honest and considerate relationships can bring'[76] (p.12).

In reality, studies have shown that the physiological aspects of reproduction are more likely to have been covered at school than other topics[30] and that students are critical of the emphasis on the physical aspects at the expense of emotional aspects, moral values and interpersonal relationships[53] (p.15).

Nevertheless the ideals are still presented as worth striving for. The National Council of Women[58] (pp.25-26) emphasises the need for all young people to be able to discuss their sexuality openly as part of the process of evolving their 'conscience' on sexual ethics, while Dallas draws attention to the need for sex education to confront 'the irrational aspects as well as the factual and conceptual matters'[14] (p.13).

Rogers' view[63] (p.5) is that a compromise is possible—'the straight presentation of facts pertaining to sexuality wherever they arise "naturally" in the curriculum (biology, health education, social studies, domestic science) plus the coverage of sexuality within a broadly covered scheme of moral education (i.e. one that does not place emphasis either on particular areas like sex or on particular ways of construing morality)'.

Contraception

Few commentators outside the education system have yet appreciated that the basic physiology of contraception has in fact been included in many public examination biology syllabuses for some years now[61]. Nevertheless, Watson[71] observed that schools often placed the subject lower on the list than parents, when asked to rate topics in order of importance. Gill et al[33] also reported in 1971 that mothers selected issues such as birth control and gave them high priority, alongside sexual morality etc.

The DES[20] (p.117) urges that pupils should discuss the 'morality and purposes of contraception' as well as the methods themselves, 'including the important factor of the growth of regard for the quality of life and of responsibility for others'. The paragraph concludes by stating that the 'most effective way of dealing with the techniques of contraception is to make certain that all boys and girls understand and have confidence in the professional services available to them as they grow up'. Reid[61] takes this argument a step further when he draws attention to an American school which combined counselling advice with 'an acceptable source of contraceptive supplies'.

The National Council of Women[58] (pp.21-22) urges that more consideration should be given to the importance of health during the preconception period, to the health risks of the pill, especially the link with cervical cancer, and to the whole area of personal relationships now that increasing numbers of barrier methods of contraception are so freely available to young people.

Sexually transmitted infections
According to Dallas[14] (p.86) the objectives of 'VD education' are twofold—the provision of basic facts and the production of a social climate in which young people can attend a clinic without shame if they need to. However, the DES's reticence to devote other than a few lines[20] (p.118) to the subject would appear to be reflected in schools, where less than half the pupils in one study were satisfied with the information on sexually transmitted infections[60]. Many schools ensure that the 'horrors of VD' are given a mention, but many young people complain that little information on treatment is given, the health hazards to themselves and their future children are glossed over and there is virtually no information on the more 'modern' diseases of herpes and AIDS[58] (p.19).

Marriage and education for parenthood
Nearly twenty years ago, mothers gave high priority to this emphasis on 'marriage and the family' in school sex education courses[33]. In today's changing pattern of family life, some people feel that such emphasis has little place and can cause distress to many single-parent families[58] (p.27). They prefer to support loving commitment to stable and happy relationships[26] and say sensitive, experienced teachers should be able to adapt to these changing circumstances[58] (p.27).

In the mid 1970s, there was still considerable dissatisfaction with aspects of preparation for parenthood[60], but more recent emphasis by organisations such as the HEC[39] has led to investigations into the way the subject is dealt with in schools, and recommendations for further improvements[1].

A detailed study has been carried out for the DES by the University of Aston: *Preparation for Parenthood in the Secondary School Curriculum,* Department of Educational Enquiry, University of Aston in Birmingham, 1983.

PRESENTATION AND RESOURCES

As Williams[75] points out, school health education is about more than content and information and is as much concerned with learning experiences, so that teaching and learning methods are as important as what is actually taught. In this he is supported, as regards sex education specifically, by the National Council of Women[58] (p.16), whose report argues that when material is carefully selected, it is not the resource itself but the way in which the teacher approaches it which matters most.

Dallas[14] (p.16) reminded us that the 'unemotional answering of children's questions' is often recommended, but feels this can imply a lack of sensitivity. 'This is an emotional subject and, in answering questions, regard should be taken for the emotions of the child.' She sees the 'invasion of personal privacy' as the 'most crucial aspect of sensitivity in sex education' and sympathises with teachers who feel embarrassed by pupils' attempts to get them to speak of their own personal experiences, while feeling that they ought to answer questions honestly. However, she warns, this shows a 'lack of awareness of the teacher's position in the continuum of human behaviour'[14] (p.17). Some years later, the DES concurred[20] (p.117). 'It is vitally important that the privacy and reticence of boys and girls are respected by teachers, and that teachers should never in any circumstances lift the veil from their own private lives.'

Techniques
Teaching methods are many and varied, ranging from formal lectures to project work, informal chats, question and answer sessions and the use of audiovisual materials. The main 'methodologies' are covered by Went[73] (pp.36-45) and in the Schools Council Working Paper[65] (pp.37-48). Barry[3] points out that experience of teaching sex education is so limited that nothing is really known as to the superior effectiveness of any method or in respect of any age group.

The value of regular discussion groups, rather than occasional formal lectures, is strongly promoted by Bury[8] (p.65) but she stresses that such groups should be small, so that they can be more personally relevant to the young people as they examine how the information given applies to them as individuals, and also to assist in dealing with pupils of differing maturity. Some of Leathar and Bostock's sample thought that talking to large groups 'created mutual embarrassment and inhibited open discussion, both individually and among the group as a whole'[53] (p.15). The Schools Council[65] (pp.39-42) offers guidance on organising discussion groups, the role of the teacher, and how to establish good teacher-pupil relationships.

Other techniques mentioned in the same report[65] (pp.45-46) include role play and drama, while Reid[61] recommends that further experiment should be undertaken on the technique of 'cross-age tutors', where older teenagers act as group leaders to discuss problems with small groups of younger pupils.

One recurrent theme throughout the literature is that of the vocabulary to use and this theme came up time and again in Isobel Allen's present study. Lee's experiences have given her a 'clear example of how language confines and defines'. She feels that many pupils are 'prisoners of their words, which were as injurious as blunt instruments in dulling their ability to experience what their words could not describe. . .for if tenderness is imprisoned by language, so brutality is encouraged by it'[54] (p.147). The need to establish an 'acceptable' vocabulary, the 'shock power' of many colloquialisms and means of reducing 'sniggering' and embarrassment are all dealt with by Dallas[14] (p.22) and Went[73] (p.38). The National Council of Women[58] (p.15) supports the view that precise scientific words and phrases should always be used.

Schools broadcasting

Both the BBC and commercial television companies produce programmes for use in schools, some of which are described and evaluated in Rogers[63] (pp.197-250) and Hemming[42]. The acceptance by the broadcasting authorities of responsibility for sex education was welcomed as a 'major step forward' by Rogers[63] (p.192), who commented that almost every school in the country could now have access to 'thoroughly professional' material produced from very large resources, presented in a way which is familiar to today's children and able to exploit non-verbal forms of communication, which may be particularly important when working with younger, or less able, children.

Books, pamphlets and audiovisual aids

The most up-to-date listings of materials presently available can be found in Went[73] (passim) and in the report from the National Council of Women[58] (pp.41-43). In addition, the Health Education Council produces many lists on appropriate topics.

Following on from their meeting on family planning and sex education of young people, the WHO Regional Office for Europe commented that a greater variety of educational target-group material should be produced, since little written or audiovisual material is aimed specifically at adolescents[76] (p.22). In 1975, the IPPF European Region[46] (p.42) had found that in Britain 'the supply of books and all kinds of audiovisual and textual materials was poor'.

Nowadays, audiovisual aids are felt to be of special significance, not only in the teaching of facts, but for the work on attitudes[65] (p.47), but Dallas reminds us of the importance of books, especially in the sex education of middle class children, who might be 'seriously at risk' from erroneous texts[14] (pp.94-95). The undue bias of some titles from 'Christian' sources is also referred to with concern[58] (p.18).

THE EFFECTS OF SEX EDUCATION

The value of carrying out research into the effects of sex education in schools is firmly supported by Rogers[63] (p.191), although Dallas[14] (p.94) laments that evaluation is often limited to ascertaining that the courses are 'not upsetting' pupils, teachers, parents or school governors, and urges more work to be undertaken.

In his important review, Reid[61] concludes that the 'reported effects of school or college sex education courses are remarkably benign'. Before him Schofield[64] observed sadly that 'all researches into the effect of sex education in schools conclude that it makes very little impact at all'.

Knowledge versus behaviour

After reviewing the available literature for his Ph.D thesis in 1979, Barry[3] detected considerable ambivalence about whether the outcome of health/sex education should be considered to be short-term or long-term, cognitive or affective. An anonymous editorial in the BMJ in 1976 was not so uncertain: 'Brief talks at schools to boys and girls on sex education and contraception are likely to be less successful than long-term programmes offering initial and continuing guidance on all aspects of sexual activity'.

Reid[61] concluded that 'appropriate courses can produce impressive short-term gains in knowledge', though they may only have 'a modest long-term effect'. He goes on to say that, in general, 'they seem to have a liberalising effect on attitudes to sexuality', but 'without any accompanying effect on personal behaviour'.

The Schools Council[65] (p.49) underlines the fact that 'success in health education depends more on the formation and development of attitudes than on the provision of facts', and Rogers[63] (pp.191 and 195) also deals with these distinctions, concluding that research indicates that school sex education does not seem to be related to later sexual behaviour.

Increased sexual activity and pregnancy

Many people argue that sex education has resulted in an increase in sexual activity amongst young people, though most researchers have found little evidence either way[58] (p.14). Went[73] (p.9) claims that 'there is no evidence so far that sex education either increases the amount of sexual activity, or is damaging in any way to the children receiving it'. On the contrary, she feels that 'without sex education irresponsible sexual behaviour takes place and that ignorance can be both humiliating and harmful'.

The complex factors involved in teenage pregnancy have been well summarised by both Ashton[2] and De'Ath[17], when considering both American and British evidence. The problem of the lack of British research results is nowhere more apparent than in this area. American studies (Appendix A) are far more numerous and are frequently quoted by British authors to support or refute their theories when British evidence is lacking.

One of the most recent conclusions on this issue, from Colin Francome[32], suggests that the 'evidence from Britain does not support the concern expressed in some quarters that birth control education for teenagers leads to more pregnancies'.

British background papers on schoolgirl pregnancies are those by Bennett[4], De'Ath[17], Joint Working Party[48] and Wellings[72]. Recent British research on teenage pregnancy includes that of Bury[8], Francome[32], Joint Working Party[48], Reid[61], Teenage mothers[68] and Wilce[74]. Simms and Smith have very recently brought together the findings from their long-term study of teenage mothers and fathers: Madeleine Simms and Christopher Smith, *Teenage Mothers and their Partners,* DHSS Research Report, No. 15, London 1986.

ATTITUDES TO SEX EDUCATION

Although very few researchers have actually investigated the attitudes of young people, their parents and/or the media towards sex education in schools, nevertheless some interesting insights can be gleaned from the available literature.

Young people

In 1984, the WHO[76] (p.21) recommended that there should be 'further research into adolescents' own perceptions of their needs in sex education and better dissemination of research findings'. The need to include the opinions and concerns of young people when planning sex education courses is one of the main conclusions from Clarke's study of teenage views in a Midlands school[11]. This is one of the few studies to address the problem of young people's own views on sex education in schools. Others include Goldmans[35] (pp.389-390), Leathar and Bostock[53] (pp.15-16) and Pearson and Lambert [60].

Cossey and Chambers[12] (pp.16-18) provide a useful summary of these and other recent important studies (for example, Farrell[28]), and Hagerdorn[37] mentions the work currently being undertaken by Trefor Williams into discovering what pupils, teachers and parents really want from health education.

From all this work, Went[73] (p.10) detects the consensus view that 'children in general do feel school is a good place to learn about sex', and that they accept it 'willingly and sensibly'.

The Goldmans' mass of evidence from several countries[35] (p.321) supports this view. Pearson and Lambert[60] detected 'dissatisfaction with the extent of their knowledge' in many of their adolescent study group. Later, Leathar and Bostock[53] (p.15) encouraged their young people to talk about the nature and extent of the sex education they had received at school and found the consensus picture 'discouraging'. There were large gaps, enormous variations in timing and content, embarrassment, lack of direction and repeated complaints of 'too little being taught too late'.

Parents

In spite of the vocal opposition from some quarters, there would appear to be increasing evidence that parents want sex education to be provided in schools[8] (p.54). Gill et al[33] found that four-fifths of the mothers in their study 'strongly favoured' it; Rogers[63] (p.123) reports a study which highlights the 'high acceptability' of formalised sex education to parents; Farrell[28] (pp.147 and 154) found that over 50 per cent of parents believed lessons at school were the best way for young people to learn about sex, while 96 per cent thought that, in general, sex education should be taught in secondary schools; Watson[71] comments that the parents he has approached have been 'warmly supportive'.

Yet fear of unfavourable parental reaction still prevents many teachers in this country, and especially headteachers, from seeking to implement or extend sex education programmes[8] (p.55).

Even when parents are willing to undertake sex education themselves, they are often too ignorant[71]especially fathers[35] (p.321)—or embarrassed[47].

Went[73] (pp.12-14 and p.31) provides an interesting summary of the difficulties faced by parents and some of the concerns they raise.

The media

After mothers and school teachers, the Goldmans[35] (p.321) reported that the media came a 'strong third' in the table of most popular sources of information about sex. In the view of the National Council of Women[58] (p.6) media reinforcement of the traditional perceptions of sex roles may have contributed significantly to the increase in sexual activity of the last twenty years, while in 1976 a BMJ editorial lamented that responsibility in sexual matters could hardly be expected in young people who live in a 'society which openly condones and even abets sexual permissiveness'.

In commenting that the press can play a valued part in the public debate 'from the plain ludicrous to the highly informative and critical', Dallas[14] (p.65) draws particular attention to women's magazines, which often do an excellent job in their well-researched articles, but show less realism in their stories, so that young girls 'take this fantasy world for reality'.

Both parents and teachers should examine their own attitudes so as not to subject children in their care to unconscious pressures to conform to sexual stereotypes[58] (p.6), and this idea of sex education aiming to counterbalance media portrayal finds support in the WHO report[76] (p.22). 'The ways in which sexuality and sexual relations are portrayed in the popular media and advertisements should be considered in all sex education programmes, stressing the importance of equality between the sexes and the emotional aspects of sexual relationships.'

The manipulative nature of dealings with the media is mentioned by some writers. In their analysis of press reports and readers' letters, Gill et al[33] discovered considerable differences of opinion which were claimed as majority views by those in both camps, thus tending to polarise opinion on contentious issues. Similarly, Rogers[63] (p.193) found that the mass media can manage to convey a 'general sense of disquiet' over sex education programmes, even though research shows a high level of parental approval on the issue.

The extent to which 'half-truths, statistical inaccuracies and emotive language'[72] can all be used to advantage by the media is well illustrated in the recent coverage of the Gillick case.

The 'Gillick ruling'

Before the House of Lords ruled against her, Mrs Gillick made it known that 'her next move will be to tackle sex education'[59]. The implications of the Appeal Court judgement in her favour were apparent to many, including Ashton[2] who commented on the 'run down of sex education in schools in some parts of the country' and drew attention to the 'intimidation of caring health workers'. For example, early in 1985, the Health Visitors Association issued a memo advising members that sex education classes in schools to young people under 16 should not take place until and unless the consent of the parent was obtained[40].

In the absence of the relevant data from the OPCS, the effects of the Gillick case on the incidence of unwanted teenage pregnancy are largely anecdotal[4] (p.5). However, some statistics (based on BPAS and Brook) are offered by Last[50] and Neustatter[59], while Woodroffe and McClinton[77] wrote up the Brook evidence in a letter to the BMJ in November 1985, reporting a 'sad upturn in conceptions to 15-year-olds'.

REFERENCES

(1)   Adams, L. and Tidyman, M. 'An investigation into education for parenthood in schools', *Health Educ. J.* 1983, 42(1), pp.24-28.
(2)   Ashton, J. 'Personal view', *BMJ*, 11 May 1985, *290*, p.1429.
(3)   Barry, S.M.K. *Sex education in its curricular context: the evaluation of a sex education programme in Borehamwood schools with a view to assessing its contribution to the development of 'social maturity'*, Ph.D. thesis, Brunel University, 1979.
(4)   Bennett, J. 'Schoolgirl mothers: protecting the young', *Listener*, 24 October 1985, pp.11-12.
(5)   BMJ Legal Correspondent, Teenage confidence and consent, *BMJ*, 12 January 1985, *290*, pp.144-145.
(6)   BPAS, Summaries of the *Gillick* case in various issues of BPAS Newsletter, 1980-1985.
(7)   Brook Advisory Centres, *Under sixteens*, Education and Publications Unit, 1983.
(8)   Bury, J. *Teenage Pregnancy in Britain*, Birth Control Trust, 1984, (pp.54-56: Sex education).

References

(9)   Chanter, A. *Sex education in the primary school*, Macmillan, 1966.
(10)   Children's Legal Centre, *Young people's rights and the Gillick case*, The Centre, 1985.
(11)   Clarke, L. 'Teenage views of sex education', *Health Educ. J. 1982, 41*(2), pp.47-51.
(12)   Cossey, D. and Chambers, J. *Men, sex and contraception*, Birth Control Trust/FPA, 1984, (pp.16-24: Sex education and boys).
(13)   Daines, J.W. *Contraceptive education: an investigation of attitudes and views*, J. Inst. Health Educ. 1970, *8*(2), pp.34-36.
(14)   Dallas, D.M. *Sex education in school and society*, N.F.E.R. 1972.
(15)   Dalzell-Ward, A.J. 'Education in personal relationships', *Health Educ. J.* 1965, *23*(1), pp.21-27.
(16)   David, K. and Cowley, J. *Pastoral care in schools and colleges*, Arnold, 1980.
(17)   De'Ath, E. *Teenage parents: a review of research*, National Children's Bureau, 1984.
(18)   DES, *Aspects of secondary education in England*, HMSO, 1979, (pp.206-240: Personal and social development).
(19)   DES, *Curriculum 11-16: a review of progress*, HMSO, 1981, (p.34: Education for personal development).
(20)   DES, *Health education in schools*, HMSO, 1977, (pp.109-119; sex education).
(21)   DHSS, *Family planning and abortion services for young people*, Health Circular HC(84) 34, 1984.
(22)   Dixon H. 'Sex education in schools: what can be done?' *Pastoral Care*, Nov. 1984, *2*(3), pp.205-207.
(23)   *Dunn restates policy on sex education*, TES, 20 Sept. 1985.
(24)   Dyer, C. 'Contraceptives and the under 16s: House of Lords ruling', *BMJ*, 26 October 1985, *291*, pp.1208-09.
(25)   Eaton, L. 'Bound to become parents?', *Soc. Work Today*, 17 June 1985, pp.13-14.
(26)   Eden, P. 'Contraception, misconception or contraception', *Health Educ. J.* 1985, *44*(2), pp.98-10.
(27)   Editorial. 'Legislation and teenage sex', *BMJ*, 17 December 1983, *287*, p.1826.
(28)   Farrell, C. *My mother said . . . the way young people learned about sex and birth control*, Routledge & Kegan Paul, 1978, (pp.122-146: Sex education in school; pp.147-159: Home and School).
(29)   Ferrer, H.P. and Hancock, F. 'Breaking down the barriers: an experiment in sex education', *Health Educ. J.*, March 1966, *25*(81), pp.22-27.
(30)   Fogelman, K. *Britain's sixteen-year-olds*, National Children's Bureau, 1976.
(31)   FPA, *Grapevine: a review of the FPA's North London based community project for young people*, 1971-81, FPA, 1982.
(32)   Francome, C. 'Unwanted pregnancies amongst teenagers', *J. Biosoc. Sci.* 1983, *15*(2), pp.139-143.
(33)   Gill, D.G. *et al.* 'Sex education, press and parental perceptions', *Health Educ. J.* 1971, *30*, 2-10.
(34)   Gingell, A. *Confusing messages*, TES, 24 April 1981, p.15.
(35)   Goldman, R. and Goldman, J. *Children's sexual thinking: a comparative study of children aged 5 to 15 years in Australia, North America, Britain and Sweden*, Routledge & Kegan Paul, 1982, (pp.53-55: The practical background to the study—sex education; pp.294-323: Children's perceptions of sex education; pp.389-90: How children perceive sex education; pp.391-393: The major findings of the study).
(36)   Greaves, J.N. 'Sex education in colleges and departments of education', *Health Educ. J.* 1965, *24*(4), pp.171-177.
(37)   Hagerdorn, J. *Sex education and your child*, Parents, May 1985, pp.77-79.
(38)   Hayton, P. 'The rationale for sex education in the school curriculum', *Health Educ. J.* 1985, *44*(2), pp.100-102.
(39)   Health Education Council, *Education and preparation for parenthood programme*, HEC Programme for 1984-5, pp.10-15.
(40)   Health Visitors Association, *Gillick judgement: HVA deeply concerned*, Press Release, 6 March 1985.
(41)   Heather, B. *Sharing: a handbook for those involved in training in personal relationships and sexuality*, FPA, 1984.
(42)   Hemming, J. *et al. Sex education of school children*, Royal Society of Health, 1971.
(43)   Hierons, G. *Sex education: working with children aged 5-11 years*, In Approaches to sex education. Report of the Seminar for health education officers, University of York, 1972, HEC, 1972, pp.20-23.
(44)   Holden, A. *Teachers as counsellors*, Constable, 1969.

Education in Sex and Personal Relationships

(45) IPPF, 'Meeting the needs of young people: policy statement', *IPPF Med. Bull.* April 1984, 18(2), pp.1-4.
(46) IPPF, Europe Region, *A survey on the status of sex education in European member countries*, IPPF, 1975.
(47) 'It's not who's telling the children about sex—it's what they're saying', *Woman*, 20 November 1982.
(48) Joint Working Party on Pregnant Schoolgirls and Schoolgirl Mothers, *Pregnant at school*, National Council for One Parent Families, 1979. (pp.13-16: Responsibility for prevention).
(49) Lambert, L. and Pearson, R. 'Sex education in schools', *J. Inst. Health Educ.* 1977, 15(4), pp.4-11.
(50) Last, J. *Fewer under-16s seek Pill advice*, TES, 21 June 1985.
(51) Law Report, 'DHSS contraceptive notice is unlawful', *The Times*, 21 December 1984, p.9.
(52) Law Report, *The Times*, 18 October, 1985.
(53) Leathar, D.S. and Bostock, Y. *Attitudes towards contraception among young people*, Scottish Health Education Group, 1981, (pp.15-16: School sex education).
(54) Lee, C. *The ostrich position: sex, schooling and mystification*, Writers and Readers, 1983.
(55) Lee, S. 'Parents and daughters', *New Society*, 21 June 1985, pp.448-450.
(56) Lewin, B. *Sex and family planning: how we teach the young*, WHO Regional Office for Europe, 1984.
(57) Modern Medicine, *Report on doctors' opinion poll on sex education*, Medical Surveys Ltd. 1970.
(58) National Council of Women of Great Britain, *Sex education - whose responsibility?* The Council, 1984.
(59) Neustatter, A. 'Gillick: the anxiety and opposition grow', *The Times*, 19 June 1985.
(60) Pearson, R. and Lambert, L. 'Sex education, preparation for parenthood and the adolescent', *Commun. Health*, 1977 9(2), pp.84-90.
(61) Reid, D. 'School sex education and the causes of unintended teenage pregnancies: a review', *Health Educ. J.* 1982, 41(1), pp.4-10.
(62) Ripley, G. 'Human relationships and social responsibility: health education within a school social studies course', *Int. J. Health Educ.* 1975, 18(3), pp.198-201.
(63) Rogers, R.S. (ed.), *Sex education: rationale and reaction*, Cambridge University Press, 1974.
(64) Schofield, M. *Is sex education any good?* LR Industries Contraceptive Information Service Digest, April 1977, 4, pp.1-3.
(64a) Schofield, M. The sexual behaviour of young people, Longmans, 1965, (pp.102-105: Sex education at school; pp.125-128: Attitudes to sex education; pp.248-250: Sex education).
(65) Schools Council, *Health education in secondary schools*, Evans/Methuen, 1976.
(66) Smith, D.J. 'The FPA: perspectives on sex education', *J. Curric. Stud.* July-September 1982, 14(3), pp.287-88).
(67) Statutory Instruments 1981 No.630, *Information relating to individual schools to be published by an Education Authority or by or on behalf of the governors of an aided or special agreement school*, The Education (School Information) Regulations, DES, 1981.
(68) 'Teenage mothers', *New Society*, 17 May 1984, p.291.
(69) Tuchler, H.G. 'Sex education', *Health Educ. J.* 1947, 5(2), pp.69-70.
(70) Tuchler, H.G. 'Sex education and the additional year', *Health Educ. J.* 1949, 7(3).
(71) Watson, G. 'The paradoxes of sex education', *TES,* 22 April 1983, p.50.
(72) Wellings, K. 'Preventing schoolgirl pregnancies', *Maternity Action,* March/April 1984, 14,6.
(73) Went, D. *Sex education: some guidelines for teachers,* Bell & Hyman, 1985.
(74) Wilce, H. 'Plight of the teenage mothers', *TES,* 23 September 1983.
(75) Williams, T. *Health education in the initial training of teachers*, Stage 1: National survey of schools in England and Wales—preliminary report. HEC, 1981.
(76) WHO, Regional Office for Europe, *Family planning and sex education of young people*, WHO 1984.
(77) Woodroffe, C. and McClinton, S. 'Contraceptives and the under 16s', *BMJ*, 2 November 1985.

AMERICAN REFERENCES

Barret, R.L. and Robinson, B.E. *Teenage fathers: neglected too long*, Soc. Work, November 1982, *27*(6), 484-88.

Brandt, C.L. *et al, Pregnant adolescents: some psychosocial factors*, Psychosomatics, December 1978, *19*(12), 790-93.

Brann, E.A. *et al, Strategies for the prevention of pregnancy in adolescents*, Adv. Plann. Parent., 1979, *14*(2), 68-76.

Byrne, D. and Fisher, W.A. *Adolescents, sex and contraception*, Lawrence Erlbaum Associates, 1983.

Clark, S.D. *et al, Sex, contraception and parenthood: experiences and attitudes among urban black young men*, Fam. Plann. Perspect., March/April 1984, *16*(2), 77-82.

Cvetkovich, G. *et al, On the psychology of adolescents' use of contraceptives*, J. Sex Res., August 1975, *11*(3), 256-70.

Dunn, P. *Reduction of teenage pregnancy as a rationale for sex education*, J. Sch. Health, December 1982, 611-13.

Evans, R.I. *et al, Social modelling films to deter smoking in adolescents: results of a three-year field investigation*, J. Appl. Psychol. 1981, *66*(4), 399-414.

Gordon, S. *The case for a moral sex education in the schools*, J. Sch. Health, April 1981, 214-18.

Hoch, L.L. *Attitude change as a result of sex education*, J. Res. Sci. Teach., 1971, *8*(4), 363-67.

Kantner, J.F. and Zelnik, M. *Sexual experience of young unmarried women in the United States*, Fam. Plann. Perspect. October 1972, *4*(4), 9-18.

Kantner, J.F. and Zelnik, M. *Contraception and pregnancy: experience of young unmarried women in the United States*, Fam. Plann. Perspect. Winter 1973, *5*(1), 21-35.

Kapp, L. *et al, Teaching human sexuality in Junior High School: an interdisciplinary approach*, J. Sch. Health. February 1980, 80-83.

Kilmann, P.R. *et al, Sex education: a review of its effects*, Arch. Sex. Behav. 1981, *10*(2), 177-205.

Kirby, D. *The effects of school sex education programs: a review of the literature*, J. Sch. Health, December 1980, 559-63.

Koenig, M.A. and Zelnik, M. *The risk of premarital first pregnancy among Metropolitan-area teenagers, 1976 and 1979*, Fam. Plann. Perspect. September/October 1982, *14*(5), 239-47.

Lewis, R.A. *Parents and peers: socialization agents in the coital behaviour of young adults*, J. Sex Res. May 1963, *9*(2), 156-70.

McAlister, A. *et al, Pilot study of smoking, alcohol and drug abuse prevention*, Amer. J. Pub. Health, July 1980, *70*(7), 719-21.

Morris, N.M. *The biological advantages and social disadvantages of teenage pregnancy*, Amer. J. Pub. Health, August 1981, *71*(8), 796.

Orr, M.T. *Sex education and contraceptive education in US public high schools*, Fam. Plann. Perspect. November/December 1982, *14*(6), 304-13.

Parcel, G.S. and Luttman, D. *Evaluation in sex education: evaluation research for sex education applied to program planning*, J. Sch. Health, April, 1981, 278-81.

Rotkin, I.D. *A comparison review of key epidemiological studies in cervical cancer related to current searches for transmissible agents*, Canc. Res. June 1973, *33*, 1353-67.

Scales, P. *How we guarantee the ineffectiveness of sex education*, SIECUS report, March 1978, *6*(4), 1-3.

Schinke, S.P. and Gilchrist, L.D. *Adolescent pregnancy: an interpersonal skill training approach to prevention*, Soc. Work in Health Care, Winter 1977, *3*(2), 159-67.

Schinke, S.P. *et al, Preventing unwanted adolescent pregnancy: a cognitive-behavioural approach*, Amer. J. Orthopsychiat. January 1979, *49*(1), 81-88.

Schinke, S.P. *et al, Role of communication in the prevention of teenage pregnancy*, Health and Soc. Work, 1980, *5*(3), 54-59.

Shah, F. *et al, Unprotected intercourse among unwed teenagers*, Fam. Plann. Perspect. January/February 1975, *7*(1), 39-44.

Sonenstein, F.L. and Pittman, K.J. *The availability of sex education in large city school districts*, Fam. Plann. Perspect. January/February 1984, *16*(1), 19-25.

Spanier, G.B. *Sexualization and premarital sexual behaviour*, Fam. Coord. January 1975, *24*(1), 33-41.

Thornburg, H.D. *Adolescent sources of information on sex*, J. Sch. Health, April 1981, 274-77.

Tolles, R. *Mothers so young*, Ford Foundation Letter, 1 June 1982, 3-4.

Zabin, L.S. *et al, The risk of adolescent pregnancy in the first months of intercourse*, Fam.

Plann. Perspect. July/August 1979, *11*(4), 215-22.

Zelnik, M. and Kantner, J.F. *Reasons for non-use of contraception by sexually active women aged 15-19*, Fam. Plann. Perspect. September/October, 1979, *11*(5), 289-96.

Zelnik, M. and Kantner, J.F. *Sexual and contraceptive experience of young unmarried women in the United States, 1976 and 1971*, Fam. Plann. Perspect. March/April 1977, *9*(2), 55-71.

Zelnik, M. and Kantner, J.F. *Sexual activity, contraceptive use and pregnancy among Metro-politan-area teenagers, 1971-79*, Fam. Plann. Perspect. September/October 1980, *12*(5), 230-37.

Zelnik, M. *et al, Probabilities of intercourse and conception among US teenage women, 1971 and 1976*, Fam. Plann. Perspect. May/June 1979, *11*(3), 177-83.

Zelnik, M. and Kim, Y.J. *Sex education and its association with teenage sexual activity, pregnancy and contraceptive use*, Fam. Plann. Perspect. May/June 1982, *14*(3), 117-26.

Zelnik, M. and Shah, F.K. *First intercourse among young Americans*, Fam. Plann. Perspect. March/April 1983, *15*(2), 64-70.